The World of Words

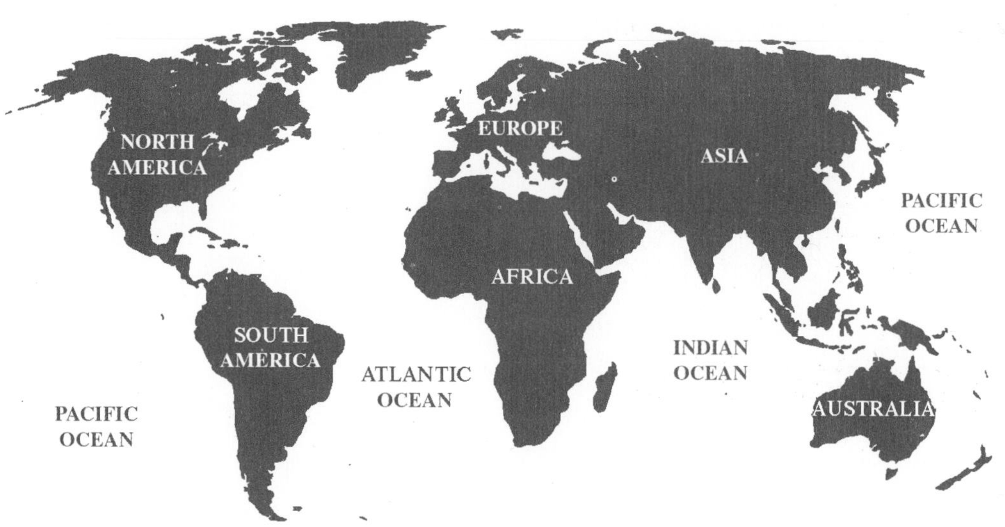

The World *of* Words

Vocabulary for College Success

EIGHTH EDITION

Margaret Ann Richek
Northeastern Illinois University

Australia • Brazil • Japan • Korea • Mexico • Singapore • Spain • United Kingdom • United States

The World of Words: Vocabulary for College Success, Eighth Edition
Margaret Ann Richek

Publisher: Lyn Uhl

Director, Developmental English and College Success: Annie Todd

Development Editor: Denise Taylor

Associate Editor: Janine Tangney

Editorial Assistant: Melanie Opacki

Media Editor: Emily Ryan

Marketing Manager: Kirsten Stoller

Marketing Coordinator: Ryan Ahern

Marketing Communications Manager: Martha Pfeiffer

Content Project Manager: Rosemary Winfield

Art Director: Jill Ort

Print Buyer: Betsy Donaghey

Permissions Manager: Margaret Gaston-Chamberlain

Production Service: S4Carlisle Publishing Services

Photo Manager: John Hill

Cover Designer: Robert Doren

Cover Image: Ichiro/Getty Images

Compositor: S4Carlisle Publishing Services

Library of Congress Control Number: 2009934719

ISBN-13: 978-0-495-80255-6

ISBN-10: 0-495-80255-7

Wadsworth
20 Channel Center Street
Boston, MA 02210
USA

Cengage Learning is a leading provider of customized learning solutions with office locations around the globe, including Singapore, the United Kingdom, Australia, Mexico, Brazil and Japan. Locate your local office at **international.cengage.com/region.**

Cengage Learning products are represented in Canada by Nelson Education, Ltd.

For your course and learning solutions, visit **www.cengage.com.**

Purchase any of our products at your local college store or at our preferred online store **www.CengageBrain.com**

Printed in the United States of America
1 2 3 4 5 6 7 14 13 12 11 10

Dedicated to the memories of my father, Seymour Richek, and my stepfather, Milton Markman; and to my husband, Perry Goldberg.

CONTENTS

PREFACE

The World of Words, Eighth Edition, will help students master strategies for becoming independent learners of vocabulary, learn specific words that will be useful in their academic and professional work, and develop a lifelong interest in words. Through a series of carefully paced lessons, students learn several hundred words that appear in the "Words to Learn" sections. In addition, they master three vocabulary development strategies that facilitate independent learning of word meanings: using the dictionary, context clues, and ancient Greek and Latin word elements.

The new edition of *The World of Words* continues to link vocabulary to students' general knowledge, covering such topics as food, styles, automobiles, and sports. I find that students enjoy these features and begin to appreciate that vocabulary learning is relevant to their lives and careers. While reinforcing these links, the text also supplies information that will help students to acquire a firmer knowledge base for college academic work. Thus, as the book progresses, students read more about science, art, and classic literature.

The word lists and the ancient Greek and Latin word elements have been carefully selected on the basis of their appropriate level and usefulness in students' academic work. Word elements are presented so that students can easily recognize them in modern English words. Avoiding complex discussions of infinitive, participle, and stem forms, the text nevertheless provides the spellings of the most common word elements in English.

Feedback from students and instructors has enabled me to adapt this book to the needs of today's diverse student population. Instructors will find *The World of Words*, Eighth Edition, suitable for students of many cultural and linguistic backgrounds, including those for whom English is not a native language.

Organization

Part 1 (Chapters 1 through 4) concentrates on dictionary skills and context clues; Part 2 (Chapters 5 through 12) stresses word elements (Greek and Latin prefixes, roots, and suffixes). To make vocabulary study cohesive, each chapter has a theme, such as Words About People, the Body and Health, and Words in the News.

Every chapter of *The World of Words* contains these features:

A **Did You Know?** feature gives word facts to spark students' interest.

Each **Learning Strategy** teaches methods to help students learn new words independently.

The **Words to Learn** section presents

- twenty-four *vocabulary words* with pronunciations, definitions, and examples in sentences;
- *related words* that allow students to see how one base word can be adapted to form other parts of speech;
- *usage notes* that help students use new vocabulary words correctly;
- *boxed features* with word facts, etymologies, and trivia quizzes that provide context for the vocabulary and help students internalize the definitions; and
- *art pieces*, including photos of students, that enliven the book and illustrate word meanings.

Exercises follow each set of Words to Learn. These widely varied, carefully scaffolded exercises include Matching Definitions, Words in Context, Related Words, and an application exercise.

The **Chapter Exercises**, found at the end of each chapter, expand the use of all the Words to Learn and the Learning Strategy. Chapter Exercises include Companion Words, Writing with Your Words, and Practicing Strategies. Enriching factual and cultural information is used extensively in all exercises.

A **Making Connections** feature helps students practice vocabulary words in an extended-writing format.

The **Passage** for each chapter uses many of the chapter words in context and gives students practice reading short essays. Each passage is followed by an exercise that checks word meanings, as well as three discussion questions.

Insight into Idioms presents the meanings of several widely used English expressions related to the chapter theme. An exercise is now included in this section.

New to This Edition

Extensive feedback from students and instructors has enabled me to refine the book's most useful features, as well as add the following new features to the Eighth Edition:

- A **new, additional exercise** at the end of each chapter combines an understanding of idioms with review of chapter words.
- An **audio section**, where students can hear each of the Words to Learn pronounced, is located at the Student Companion Website at **www.cengage.com/devenglish/richek8e**.
- **Photos of actual students** dramatizing the Words to Learn add to the relevance and sense of fun in the book.

- **Added features in vocabulary presentation** includes more irregular plurals, past tenses, participles, and common opposites for vocabulary words.
- **Revised and updated content** reflects contemporary developments. Changes include substantially revised example sentences, refreshed exercises, and several new passages.

Support for Students

- **A Student Companion Website** offers additional support for students. For each chapter, the online center features interactive practice quizzes, including a pretest on the words, four exercises for reviewing words, and one on idioms. Also provided is an audio section, in which chapter words and sentences are pronounced, and flashcards for words and word elements. In addition, for each chapter, the Student Companion Website features live links to websites that have been alluded to in the text, as well as a section providing interesting facts and insights into chapter words and topics. Finally, general resources in reading and writing are available for student support. The Student Companion Website can be found at **www.cengage.com/ devenglish/richek8e**. References to this center, and to other websites are easily identified within the book by a distinctive icon.

Support for Instructors

- An **Instructor's Annotated Edition** provides answers to exercises.
- In addition, the Cengage Learning **Instructor Companion Website** for this book contains notes and teaching suggestions for each chapter, mastery tests and review tests with answer keys, an answer key for exercises in the book, and supplementary and review exercises with answer keys. These resources make instruction easy to manage, as well as supplying additional facts and associations to enrich learning and spark student interest. The instructor's website is accessed at **www.cengage.com/devenglish/richek8e,** where instructors can register for the password-protected site.

Acknowledgments

I wish to thank the many people who have contributed ideas, inspiration, and support. These include the editorial staff of Cengage Learning. Development editor Denise Taylor provided invaluable assistance in shaping the manuscript. Janine Tangney provided excellent editorial assistance. Tiffany Timmerman of S4Carlisle provided outstanding editorial and design aid.

Thanks are also due to my family and friends for their support and ideas. These include Perry Goldberg, Jean Richek, Stephen Richek, Megan Readler, Marco Parra, Austin Okocha, Amy Sadykhov, Fikret Sadykhov, Ayba Sadykhov, Mamed Sadykhov, and Nasheli Vargas. Special acknowledgment is reserved for Sophia Ruiz, Rocio Ruiz, Semir Mohammed, Ashanti Roberts, William Mojica, and Viem Nguyen, whose student writings appear as exercises in the review sections.

The students who posed for photographs also deserve many thanks. These students from Joliet Junior College are Aloush Abdulrahman, Aileen Barnhart, Robert Battle, George Demaree, Kyung-Ran Feigel, Megan Follis, Brian Harris, Rashad Jackson, Adam Johnson, Carlee Koerner, Marcus Lee, Martez Moore, Karrie Ponko, Gertrudis Rodrigues, Ashley Russell, Amber Smith, Alexandra Violette, Myron Washington, and Dionte Yarborough. Their teacher, Susanne Picchi deserves special mention.

Finally, I wish to thank the reviewers whose valuable help enabled me to formulate revisions to this edition: Linda Mulready, Bristol Community College; Betty Payne, Montgomery College; Michael Larson, North Hennepin Community College; Jessica Focer, Community College of Beaver County; Thomas Butler, Paradise Valley Community College; Helen Carr, San Antonio College; Rebecca Suarez, University of Texas; Dan Purtscher, Pikes Peak Community College; John Kopec, Boston University; and Susanne Picchi, Joliet Junior College.

PART 1

Dictionary Skills and Context Clues

Did you know that the size of your vocabulary predicts how well you will do in school? This book will help you to improve your word knowledge so that you achieve better in all subjects—from accounting to zoology. Your comprehension of reading assignments and lectures will improve when you understand more word meanings. A larger vocabulary will also help you make a good impression both in a job interview and when you are working. People judge others by the way they communicate, and vocabulary is key to communication.

This book will help you use words more precisely and vividly. Instead of simply using the word *friendly*, you will be able to distinguish between *cordial*, *gregarious*, and *empathic* people. Instead of saying that someone gave money to a charity, you may call that person a *philanthropist* or a *benefactor*.

Working through this book will increase your vocabulary in two ways. First, you will learn the words presented in each chapter. Second, you will master learning strategies that enable you to learn words on your own. Chapters 1 through 4 will teach you the strategies of using the dictionary and of understanding context clues. In Chapters 5 through 12, you will learn how to use word elements such as prefixes, roots, and suffixes to unlock word meanings. Each chapter contains several sections:

Did You Know? highlights interesting facts about English words.

Learning Strategy provides methods that will help you learn words independently.

Words to Learn presents twenty-four words that appear frequently in college texts and on the Internet, as well as in books, magazines, and newspapers. Every *Words to Learn* section is divided into two parts, containing twelve words each.

The *Exercises* give you practice with the words and strategies. One set of exercises follows the first part of the *Words to Learn* section, another set follows the second part, and a final set appears at the end of the chapter. The last set of exercises will help you to incorporate your new words in speaking and writing. It includes opportunities to use the words in writing, as well as a reading selection that contains several chapter words.

The *Insight into Idioms* section discusses several phrases that have special meanings. These are incorporated into a short exercise that gives you another chance to practice the chapter's new words.

The Student Companion Website for this book is at **www.cengage.com/devenglish/richek8e.** This companion website for *The World of Words* offers self-checking quizzes as well as an audio feature, additional exercises, resources, and website links. The quizzes help you evaluate your knowledge of chapter words. The audio feature allows you to hear the actual pronunciation of words and sentences. The exercises, resources, and links deepen your vocabulary learning—and help you to improve your grades.

Parts of Speech

Parts of speech are essential to the definition and use of words. Knowing a word's part of speech enables you to use it effectively. In addition, if you understand how words can be changed to form different parts of speech, you can expand your vocabulary by using one base word in many forms.

Nouns, Adjectives, Verbs, and Adverbs

The words presented in this book are nouns, adjectives, verbs, and adverbs.

A **noun** is a person, place, thing, or idea.

Latisha is an excellent *student*. (people)

Santa Barbara has beautiful *beaches*. (places)

Ice covered the *highway*. (things)

Liberty and *justice* are precious. (ideas)

An **adjective** describes, or modifies, a noun.

The *busy* mother cleaned the kitchen. (*Busy* modifies *mother*.)

The towel was *wet*. (*Wet* modifies *towel*.)

At times, a noun is used as an adjective to modify another noun. Nouns used as adjectives in this way are called attributive nouns.

The *student* worker was underpaid.

A **verb** expresses an action or indicates a state of being.

I *study* vocabulary. (action)

The class *is* challenging. (state of being)

An **adverb** modifies a verb, an adjective, or another adverb. Many adverbs end in *-ly*.

The pregnant woman ran *slowly*. (*Slowly* modifies *ran*, a verb.)

We admired the *finely* painted mural. (*Finely* modifies *painted*, an adjective.)

The rumor spread *more rapidly* than we had expected. (*More*, an adverb, modifies *rapidly*, another adverb. *Rapidly*, in turn, modifies *spread*, a verb.)

A Closer Look at Verbs

Verbs can be divided into two categories: transitive and intransitive. A **transitive verb** has an action that is directed toward someone or something. A transitive verb needs a direct object to make a sentence complete. In contrast, an **intransitive verb** does not need a direct object.

Transitive verb: Bong-Chol *bought* a computer. (*Computer* is the direct object.)

Intransitive verb: The garbage *smelled*. (No direct object is needed.)

Some verbs can be used both transitively and intransitively. For example, *smelled* is a transitive verb in "The bears *smelled* the garbage."

Verbs can express past, future, or present action. Past-tense verbs are usually formed by adding the ending *-ed*.

Armando *rented* an apartment last year.

However, some past-tense verb forms are not regular. For example, the past-tense form of the verb *is* is actually *was*; the past tense of *ride* is *rode*.

The future tense of a verb is often expressed by using the helping verb *will*. This is often shortened to *'ll*.

I *will shop* tomorrow. *I'll* shop tomorrow.

When we use the present tense, we add an *s* to a third-person singular verb. Examples of subjects that need third-person singular verbs are *she*, *Joe*, and *the door*.

The musician *plays* the piano and the violin.

The city of Tucson *grows* rapidly each year.

Sometimes a third-person singular subject can be more than one person. For example, "The team *expects* to win today." In this case, the *team* is a collection of individuals. Verbs that have the subject *I, you, we, they*, or words that stand for *they* are **not** third-person singular.

We often express actions that started in the past and are still taking place by using a form of the helping verb *to be* and adding *-ing* to the end of the main verb. This is called the present progressive tense, and the *-ing* form is called a **present participle.**

I *am waiting* for a reply to my text message.

The sun *is shining*.

The *-ing* form can also be used to form nouns. The nouns that are formed are called **gerunds**.

Smoking is forbidden in the club, but there is lots of *dancing*.

The *-ing* and *-ed* forms of verbs can also form adjectives. These adjectives are called **participles**. Note the following meanings.

The *insulting* man upset others with his comments. (In this sentence, the man insults other people. A **present participle** is used.)

The *insulted* man felt terrible. (In this sentence, other people insult the man. A **past participle** is used.)

Pronouns, Conjunctions, Interjections, and Prepositions

In addition to nouns, adjectives, verbs, and adverbs, parts of speech include pronouns, conjunctions, interjections, and prepositions.

A **pronoun** replaces a noun.

Jennifer locked the door when *she* left.

They will pick *it* up at school.

A **conjunction** connects words, phrases, or clauses.

Andrew ate bean sprouts *and* tofu.

Will Mercedes go out with friends, *or* will she stay at home?

An **interjection** is a short, emotional word or phrase that may appear by itself or in a sentence.

Great! *Ugh, that's awful!*

A **preposition** joins a noun or pronoun with another word in a sentence. Prepositions appear at the beginning of prepositional phrases, which usually function as adjectives and adverbs.

I have a fear *of* needles.

In this sentence, the preposition *of* joins the noun *needles* to another noun in the sentence, *fear*. *Of* is the first word in the prepositional phrase *of needles*. The entire prepositional phrase functions as an adjective because it modifies the noun *fear*.

This sentence shows a prepositional phrase used as an adverb:

Carmen ran *across* the street.

Here, the preposition *across* connects the noun *street* to the verb *ran*. The prepositional phrase *across the street* functions as an adverb that modifies the verb *ran*.

Words and phrases commonly used as prepositions include *about*, *above*, *according to*, *across*, *after*, *against*, *before*, *behind*, *below*, *beside*, *by*, *during*, *for*, *from*, *in*, *inside*, *into*, *like*, *of*, *off*, *on*, *out*, *over*, *through*, *to*, *toward*, *under*, *until*, *up*, and *with*.

It is often difficult to know which preposition to use in a sentence. Mastery of these small words comes only with practice. To help you, this book has exercise sections called "Companion Words."

Word Endings and Parts of Speech

One word can often be changed to form several related words. These related words have similar meanings, but they usually function as different parts of speech. For example, the word *nation* (a noun) can form *national* (an adjective), *nationally* (an adverb), *nationalize* (a verb), and *nationality* (another noun).

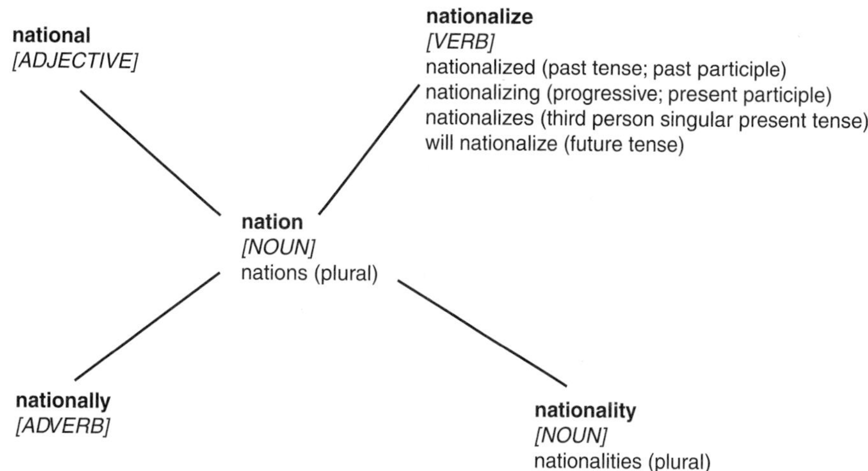

Related words are formed by adding *suffixes*—word parts attached to the ends of words—to change the part of speech. The following table shows a list of common suffixes and examples of words they form.

Suffix	*Base word*	*Suffixed word*
	Suffixes that form nouns	
-ance, -ancy	insure, truant	insurance, truancy
-ence	differ	difference
-er	teach	teacher
-ion, -tion	confuse, compete	confusion, competition
-ism	real	realism
-ity	reliable	reliability
-ment	require	requirement
-ness	happy	happiness
-ure	fail	failure

Suffixes that form adjectives

-able, -ible	wash, reverse	washable, reversible
-al	season	seasonal
-ful	watch	watchful
-ic	angel	angelic
-ous, -ious	fame, space	famous, spacious
-ive	react	reactive
-y	stick	sticky

Suffixes that form verbs

-ate	valid	validate
-ify	simple	simplify
-ize	idol	idolize

Suffix that forms adverbs

-ly	rapid	rapidly

Some suffixes change the syllable of the word that we stress in speech. A dark accent mark (**′**) shows which syllable of a word receives the main stress. A light accent mark (′) shows that another syllable is also stressed, but not as strongly as the syllable with the darker accent mark. These examples show pronunciation changes in words when suffixes are added. The accent marks are placed *after* the stressed syllables.

When *-ic* or *-tic* is added to a word, the stress moves to the syllable before the suffix. The stress remains on the syllable before the *-ic* or *-tic*, even if another suffix is added.

cha**′** os	cha′ ot**′** ic	cha′ ot**′** i cal ly
dip**′** lo mat	dip′ lo mat**′** ic	dip′ lo mat**′** i cal ly

When *-ion* or *-tion* is added to a word, the main stress falls on the syllable before the suffix. Sometimes an *a* is added before the *-ion* or *-tion*.

pro hib**′** it	pro′ hi bi**′** tion
con demn**′**	con′ dem na**′** tion (Note the added *a*.)

When *-ity* is added to a word, the main stress falls on the syllable before the suffix.

gul**′** li ble	gul′ li bil**′** i ty
am**′** i ca ble	am′ i ca bil**′** i ty

When you learn a new word, you will often be able to form a number of related words simply by adding suffixes. In *The World of Words,* these related words are listed with many of the words you will be studying.

As you work through this book, refer to the table of suffixes and the explanation of pronunciation changes in this introduction when you meet words ending in *-ic*, *-ion (-tion)*, and *-ity*.

Visit the Student Companion Website at **www.cengage.com/devenglish/richek8e** to access a large list of suffixes with examples, grouped by part of speech.

CHAPTER

Words About People

Are you social, or do you like to be alone? Are you generous, or do you like to save your money? Do you think through problems, or act on your feelings? The Earth is home to over six billion people, and each of us is different. So it's no wonder that we need so many words to describe people! The vocabulary in this chapter will expand your ability to speak and write about yourself and others.

Chapter Strategy: Using the Dictionary

Chapter Words:

Part 1

adroit	cosmopolitan	hypocritical
aficionado	disdain	intrepid
altruistic	fraternal	melancholy
capricious	gullible	venerable

Part 2

affluent	cordial	frugal
alien	dogmatic	gauche
astute	exuberant	novice
candid	frivolous	stoic

Visit the Student Companion Website for this book at **www.cengage.com/devenglish/richek8e** to find many additional resources:

- The pronunciation of each word, in the audio portion
- A self-checking quiz to evaluate your knowledge of words before you study
- Exercises for additional practice
- More information about the words and topics addressed in this book

Did You Know?

What's in a Name?

Did you know that many first names have meanings? Parents often research names before they select one for a baby. Here are the names most commonly chosen in the United States in 2008. Each is listed with its meaning.

For boys

1. Jacob—replacer
2. Michael—godlike
3. Ethan—firm
4. Joshua—God saves us
5. Daniel—God is judge
6. Alexander—defender of people
7. Anthony—priceless
8. William—determined protector
9. Christopher—carrier of Christ
10. Matthew—God's gift

For girls

1. Emma—nurse
2. Isabella—devoted to God
3. Emily—hard-working, striving
4. Madison—an English last name
5. Ava—noble, kind
6. Olivia—symbol of peace
7. Sophia—wisdom
8. Abigail—my father is joy
9. Elizabeth—God's promise
10. Chloe—young green plant; blooming

You may have noticed that many of these names have roots in religion. They also come from ancient languages. Several, including Jacob, Michael, Joshua, Abigail, and Elizabeth, are from Hebrew. Olivia comes from Latin, the language of the ancient Romans. Both languages were spoken thousands of years ago, and Hebrew is still spoken.

Note also that popular girls' names seem to change more frequently than boys' names. Only one of the ten most popular names for girls in 2008 was on the list for 1990. In contrast, five of the ten most popular boys' names for 1990 appear on the 2008 list.

At times, one name is used for both genders. Michael has held first or second place as a name for boys each year since 1990. But, during the early 1990s, it was also one of the 1,000 most popular girls' names. Dana appears for both boys and girls, although it is more popular as a boy's name. The name Terry, meaning "power of the tribe," serves even more purposes: it is used as a boy's name, a girl's name, and a last name.

New names are constantly coming into use. *Nevaeh,* which is "heaven" spelled backwards, was first registered in 1999. By 2005 it was within the top 100 names for girls. In 2008, it was ranked as number 34.

You can find links to statistics on name popularity all the way back to the 1880s at **www.cengage.com/devenglish/richek8e**.

A host of fascinating stories and associations lies behind many names. George, which meant "farmer" in ancient Greek, has been used as a name for thousands of years. In Spanish it appears as *Jorge*, and in Polish as *Jerzy*. In the 1880s, *George* was the fourth most popular name for boys. Since then it has declined in usage, and was ranked only 153rd in 2008. Still, you have probably heard of many famous Georges, including George W. Bush, George Clooney, and fictional *Curious George*. Other notable Georges are found throughout history.

1. *Saint George*, the patron saint of England, probably lived around the year 300. According to legend, an evil dragon threatened to destroy a town with his poisonous breath unless he was given a princess. George rescued the town, and the princess, by slaying the dragon. In return for his services, George asked the townspeople to convert to Christianity. Saint George is said to have baptized 15,000 people.
2. England has had six kings named *George*. George I, who ruled from 1714 to 1727, came from Germany and spoke no English. George III was considered insane and lost the American colonies that formed the United States. The leader of that rebellion, later the first U.S. president, was George Washington.
3. *Georgia*, a state in the United States, was named for the English king George II. It was founded as a colony where poor people who had been thrown in prison for their debts could start a new life.
4. *Georgia* is also a small country near Russia. It is known for farmland and yogurt. People claim that Georgians have lived to the age of 120!
5. Did you think all Georges were male? *George Sand* was the pen name of Amandine Lucie Aurore Dudevant, a nineteenth-century French novelist. She took a man's name so that the public would accept her work. She also adopted the free lifestyle generally reserved for men; she is famous for her many love affairs.
6. George is (almost) always a boy's name. But related names for girls include Georgina, Georgeanna, Georgette, Georgia, and Geena.

Learning Strategy

Using the Dictionary

The learning strategies presented in this book aid you in independently figuring out the meanings of words. About 500 words are presented in the Words to Learn sections of this book. However, by using techniques from the Learning Strategy sections, you can expand your vocabulary to include thousands of other words.

This chapter's learning strategy concentrates on the effective use of the dictionary. The dictionary is the best source for finding the precise meaning of a word.

There are many types of printed dictionaries. They vary in size from an abridged (or pocket) dictionary, to a college-level dictionary, to an unabridged dictionary. The world's most complete dictionary is the *Oxford English Dictionary*. It weighs a full 137.72 pounds!

Dictionaries are also written for different audiences. The *Longman Handy Learner's Dictionary of American English* and *The American Heritage English as a Second Language Dictionary* help people who do not speak English as a first language. Dictionaries also exist for slang, sports, medicine, and even insults!

In today's world, though, many of us look up words online or use electronic databases. This has created a whole new world of dictionary use. Printed dictionaries are limited by space, but electronic dictionary sources contain a wealth of information. Many online sources include several dictionaries together, and also have an audio component that pronounces the word.

The websites **www.onelook.com and www.dictionary.com** give definitions of words from several different published dictionaries. You can access these through the Student Companion Website for this book at **www.cengage.com/devenglish/richek8e**.

Dictionary entries contain lots of coded information and abbreviations that need to be "unlocked." A skillful user can find not only the meaning of a word but also its pronunciation, its history, and words related to it.

Here is an entry for *astute* from an online source. Each part will be discussed.

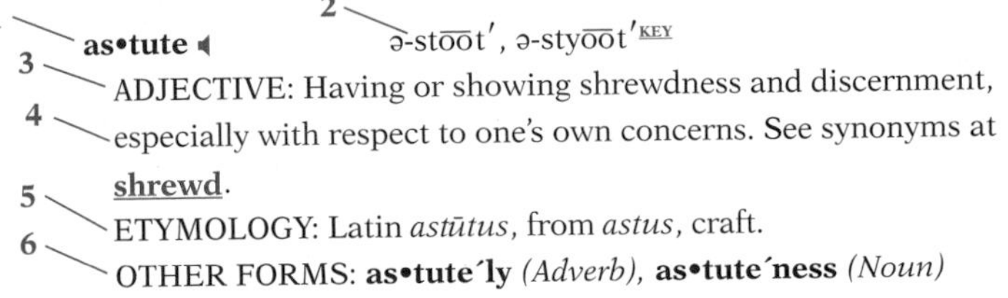

A standard dictionary entry contains the following parts:

1. **The word.** The entry word is shown and divided into syllables. If a small, raised number appears after the word, it means there is more than one entry for that word. For example, *hawk*^{2} indicates that there are (at least) two entries for the word *hawk*.

2. **Pronunciation.** Note that there are two ways to pronounce *astute*. When two are listed, the first one is preferred, but the second one is acceptable. On the website, you can actually hear the word pronounced by clicking on the symbol ◀.

Still, it is useful to know how to interpret pronunciation symbols such as ə. A pronunciation key gives a common word that contains a sound. For example, the symbol ə (the first sound in *astute*) should be pronounced like the sound of *a* in the word "*a*bout." Pronunciation keys appear on each page spread of a printed dictionary and within the links of an electronic dictionary. The inside front cover of this book also has one. The symbols used by dictionaries can vary. This book uses the *American Heritage* symbols. Note also that the website of *The World of Words* (**www.cengage.com/devenglish/richek8e**) contains an audio portion that pronounces each word presented in this book for you.

An accent mark (′) follows the syllable that should be stressed when you pronounce a word. In *astute*, only the second syllable is stressed. If two syllables have accent marks, the syllable with the darker accent mark receives more stress. (Most dictionaries put accent marks *after* the accented syllable, but some put the accent *before* the syllable.)

3. **The part of speech.** Sometimes, parts of speech are abbreviated.

n. —noun	*tr. v.* —transitive verb	*adv.* —adverb
adj. —adjective	*intr. v.* —intransitive verb	

4. **The definition(s).** If a word has more than one definition, you must choose the one that best fits the sentence you are reading. Choosing the best definition often requires some thought. Be sure to read all of the definitions before you select one. Then try to fit it into the sentence.

   Dictionary definitions usually state only the precise, or *denotative*, meanings of words. But words also have implied, or *connotative*, meanings, which are the images, ideas, and emotions that they suggest. For example, the words *skinny* and *slender* have the same denotative meaning, "thin," but they differ in connotative meaning. *Skinny* has negative connotations; *slender* has positive connotations. Most connotative information is learned simply by observing the ways people use words in writing and speaking.

   Finally, the word *shrewd* is a synonym for *astute.* More synonyms can be found at the entry for *shrewd*, which is shown (in blue) as an online link. In online dictionaries, synonyms are often presented in links, so that the reader can get to them easily for more information.

5. **The etymology.** In this section, the history of a word is traced to its origin. The word *astute* comes from Latin. It appeared as *astūtus* in Latin and is taken from the Latin word *astus*, meaning "craft." (A *crafty* person is clever and tricky.) When a word is traced through more than one language, the most recent forms are usually listed first and the oldest form is listed last. Languages commonly found in etymologies are listed below.

Middle English (ME), spoken in England from 1100 to 1500 CE (AD 1100 to 1500)
Old English (OE), spoken in England before 1100 CE
French (Fr.), spoken in France today
Old French (OFr.), spoken in France from 800 to 1200 CE
Latin (Lat.), spoken by the Romans in Italy about 2,000 years ago (near year 0 CE). Late Latin (LLat), was spoken at a later time. VLat indicates Vulgar Latin, spoken by the people, rather than written in formal Latin.
Ancient Greek (Gk.), spoken in Greece about 2,500 years ago (500 BCE, or BC)
In printed dictionaries, etymologies are often put in square brackets [ ].

6. **Related words** or **other forms.** These are usually words changed into different parts of speech by using *suffixes* (word endings). For instance, under the main entry *astute* (an adjective), an adverb (*astutely*), and a noun (*astuteness*) are also listed. (See the introduction to Part 1 of this book.)

The dictionary entry for *astute* is relatively simple; however, some entries are more complex. Here is an entry from a print source. This shows that the word *rule* has many definitions, which are separated according to parts of speech. Note the use of abbreviations.

> **rule** (ro͞ol.) *n.* **1a.** Governing power or its possession or use; authority. **b.** The duration of such power. **2a.** An authoritative prescribed direction for conduct. **b.** The body of regulations prescribed by the founder of a religious order for governing the conduct of its members. **3.** A usual, customary, or generalized course of action or behavior. **4.** A generalized statement that describes what is true in most or all cases. **5.** *Mathematics* A standard method or procedure for solving a class of problems. **6.** *Law* **a.** A court order limited in application to a specific case. **b.** A subordinate regulation governing a particular matter. **7.** See **ruler** 2. **8.** *Printing* A thin metal strip of various widths and designs, used to print borders or lines, as between columns. ❖ *v.* **ruled, rul•ing, rules** *—tr.* **1.** To exercise control, dominion, or direction over; govern. **2.** To dominate by powerful influence. **3.** To decide or declare authoritatively or judicially; decree. See Syns at **decide. 4a.** To mark with straight parallel lines. **b.** To mark (a straight line), as with a ruler. *—intr.* **1.** To be in total control or command; exercise supreme authority. **2.** To formulate and issue a decree or decision. **3.** To prevail at a particular level or rate. **4.** *Slang* To be excellent or superior: *That new movie rules!* *—**phrasal verb:*** **rule out** **1.** To prevent; preclude. **2.** To remove from consideration; exclude. *—**idiom:*** **as a rule**. In general; for the most part. [ME *reule* < OFr. < VLat. **regula* < Lat. *rēgula,* rod, principle. **—rul′a•ble** *adj.*

This entry shows that *rule* can be used as either a noun (line 1) or a verb (line 12). Notice, too, that it can be used as either a transitive (*—tr.*) verb (line 13) or an intransitive verb (*—intr.*) (line 17). *Rule* has different forms when it is used as a verb, and these are shown after the symbol ❖. The forms are (1) *ruled,* (2) *ruling,* and (3) *rules* (line 13), and they show

(1) the past participle, (2) the present participle, and (3) the third-person singular verb form.

In print dictionaries, if an entry is for a verb of more than one syllable, these forms are listed without the first syllable. For example, the forms for the verb *answer* are listed in the dictionary as *-swered*, *-swering*, *-swers*, with *an-* simply left out. Entries for nouns list the spelling of irregular plural forms. Entries for adjectives like *pretty* list spellings for comparative forms, such as *prettier* and *prettiest*.

As you look at the definitions within each part-of-speech category of *rule*, you will notice three other features of the dictionary entry. First, two or more closely related definitions may be listed under one number. This is true for several definitions of *rule*. Definitions 1, 2, and 6 of *rule* as a noun each have parts a and b (lines 1–5 and 8–10). Definition 4 of *rule* as a transitive verb also has two parts (lines 16–17).

Next you may notice that a word in italics (such as *Mathematics*, *Law*, or *Printing*) is included in some definitions. This word, which is called a *label*, indicates that a definition is used in a special manner. For example, the fifth definition of *rule* (line 7) as a noun is used mainly in math. Definition 6 is used in law, and 8 is used in printing.

Other labels give information about the style or use of a definition. For instance, the labels *Obs.* (for *obsolete*) and *Archaic* indicate that this meaning of a word is no longer used. The label *Informal* shows that this use of the word is acceptable only in informal speech. *Nonstandard* indicates a usage that is not commonly accepted.

The fourth definition of *rule* as an intransitive verb is used as *slang* (lines 20–21). Note that a sentence illustrates the definition: "That new movie *rules!*" In some cases, sentences written by well-known authors are quoted in dictionary entries. In other cases, a phrase is used to illustrate a meaning.

Toward the end of the entry for *rule* some phrases using the word are shown. A phrasal verb is a phrase that functions as a verb. In the entry for *rule*, the phrasal verb *rule out* is defined (line 21). An idiom is a common phrase. In this entry, the idiom *as a rule* is included (lines 22–23).

The last part of the entry shows the etymology of *rule*. It was first used in Latin, then in Vulgar Latin, then made its way to Old French, and finally entered Middle English. The English we speak is a descendant of Middle English.

A dictionary can also help you find other words that have the same meaning, or *synonyms*. The entry for *rule* shows that synonyms for the transitive verb, definition number 3, are listed at the entry for *decide*.

For practice, read a dictionary entry from an online source for *feign* and then answer the questions.

Main Entry **feign**
Pronunciation: \'fān\
Function: *verb*
Etymology: Middle English, from Anglo-French *feign-*, stem of *feindre*, from Latin *fingere* to shape, feign — more at DOUGH Date: 13th century
intransitive verb: PRETEND, DISSEMBLE
transitive verb 1 a: to give a false appearance of: induce as a false impression <*feign* death> b: to assert as if true: PRETEND
2 *archaic* a: INVENT, IMAGINE b: to give fictional representation to
3 *obsolete*: DISGUISE, CONCEAL
synonyms see ASSUME
— **feign.er** *noun*

1. In which language did *feign* originate? ____________
2. Give the numbers and parts of speech of definitions that are no longer in use. ____________
3. What common word uses the pronunciation like the *ei* in *feign?* _____

Answers are on page 399.

Words to Learn

All of the *Words to Learn* are pronounced on the audio portion of the website at **www.cengage.com/devenglish/richek8e.**

Part 1

1. **adroit** (adjective) ə-droit′

quickly skillful or clever

The **adroit** guard dribbled the basketball down the court.

The chess player was **adroit** in avoiding the traps his opponent set for him.

The **adroit** publicity agent arranged several important TV interviews for her client.

NOTE: The word *adroit* can refer to quick skill of body or mind.

► *Related Word*
adroitness (noun) The *adroitness* of her knitting amazed us.

2. **aficionado** (noun) ə-fĭsh′ē-ə-nä′dō

an enthusiastic fan, admirer, or follower

Aficionados of spicy food can subscribe to *Chili Pepper* magazine.

Sports **aficionados** may dress in the colors of their teams.

Words from Spanish

The word *aficionado* was borrowed from Spanish, where it often referred to fans of bullfighting. Its origin is in the Spanish verb *aficionar*, to inspire affection. Thousands of English words have Spanish origins, including *alligator, comrade, guerrilla, plaza, stampede*, and even *mosquito*. Some Spanish vocabulary originally came from languages native to Central and South America, Mexico, and the Caribbean. When the Spaniards, starting with Columbus in 1492, invaded these lands, they found many new things to describe and simply added these Native American words to Spanish. Then, we borrowed the words from Spanish into English. Examples are *tomato* and *chocolate* from Nahuatl (spoken by the Aztecs), as well as *potato* and *barbeque* from Taino (spoken in the Caribbean).

3. **altruistic** (adjective) ăl′tro͞o-ĭs′tĭk

dedicated to the good of others; unselfish

The **altruistic** man donated a kidney to save the life of a sick child.

In an **altruistic** gesture, businessman Bill Gates donated millions of dollars for research to end world hunger.

► *Related Word*

altruism (noun) (ăl′tro͞o-ĭz′əm) The minister's *altruism* inspired him to run a shelter for abused children.

4. **capricious** (adjective) kə-prĭsh′əs

unpredictable; changeable; not based on reason or judgment; impulsive

The **capricious** teenager would greet her friend warmly one day and ignore him the next.

Students could never predict whether the **capricious** assistant principal would punish them for skipping class.

► *Related Words*

capriciousness (noun) The *capriciousness* of a hurricane's path prevents weather forecasters from predicting exactly where it will hit.

caprice (noun) (kə-prēs′) Following a sudden *caprice*, she jumped into the pool with her clothes on.

5. **cosmopolitan** (adjective) kŏz′mə-pŏl′ĭ-tn

a. from several parts of the world; international

Los Angeles has a **cosmopolitan** population.

b. having a view of the world that is free from local bias

If we want to start to sell our product around the world, we need a marketing manager with a **cosmopolitan** outlook.

6. **disdain** (verb, noun) dĭs-dān′

a. to scorn; to treat as unworthy (verb)

The rich businesswoman **disdained** the homeless beggar.

The politician **disdained** to respond to the insult.

b. scorn (noun)

The opera critic treated hip-hop with **disdain.**

Teenagers often show **disdain** for their parents' advice.

▶ *Related Word*
disdainful (adjective) The neat college student was **disdainful** of her roommate's sloppy habits.

▶ *Common Phrases*
disdain for; disdainful of

7. **fraternal** (adjective) frə-tûr′nəl

a. referring to brothers

My loyal older brother taught me much about **fraternal** love.

b. like a brother; very friendly

Clarence had **fraternal** feelings for the other guys on the school football team.

▶ *Related Words*
fraternize (verb) (frăt′ər-nīz′) The supervisor did not **fraternize** with his employees. (*Fraternize* means "to socialize.")

Many Types of Brothers

The word *fraternity* comes from *frater*, the Latin word for "brother." College *fraternities* are meant to foster brotherly relationships. Other *fraternal* organizations, such as the *Fraternal* Order of Police, foster friendships and associations within a community or profession.

NOTE: *Fraternal* twins are twins who do not share identical genes. In contrast, *identical* twins have exactly the same genes.

8. **gullible** (adjective) gŭl′ə-bəl

easily deceived; easily cheated

The **gullible** eight-year-old believed the story that the abandoned house was haunted.

The **gullible** man lost all the money he sent overseas when he got involved in an e-mail scam.

▶ *Related Word*

gullibility (noun) (gŭl′ə-bĭl′ə-tē) Advertisers rely on the *gullibility* of people who believe false claims for pills or get-rich-quick schemes.

9. **hypocritical** (adjective) hĭp′ə-krĭt′ĭ-kəl

giving a false appearance of virtue; not sincere

The **hypocritical** governer spoke about the need to save energy, but drove around in a huge, gas-guzzling SUV.

▶ *Related Words*

hypocrisy (noun) (hĭ-pŏk′rĭ-sē) We were amazed by the *hypocrisy* of the drummer who complained that his neighbors made too much noise.

hypocrite (noun, person) (hĭp′ə-krĭt′) The boss was a *hypocrite* who took month-long vacations but complained when employees wanted just one day off.

NOTE: The word *hypocrite* comes from an ancient Greek word meaning "actor."

10. **intrepid** (adjective) ĭn-trĕp′ĭd

fearless; brave

The **intrepid** soldier volunteered to check the field for landmines.

11. **melancholy** (noun, adjective) mĕl′ən-kŏl′ē

a. deep sadness; depression; gloom (noun)

Lucia sank into a state of **melancholy** after she and her boyfriend broke up.

b. gloomy; sadly thoughtful (adjective)

After seeing the tragic war movie, I was in a **melancholy** mood.

Lucia sank into a state of *melancholy* after she and her boyfriend broke up.

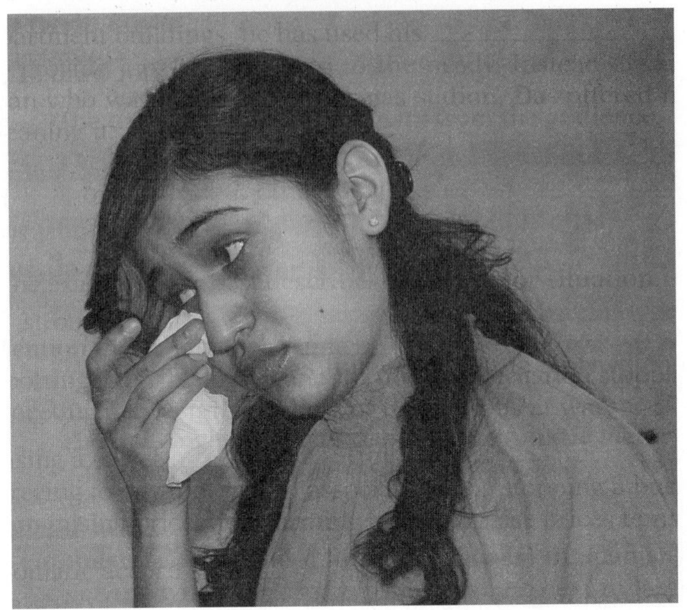

Courtesy author

12. **venerable** (adjective) vĕn′ər-ə-bəl

worthy of great respect because of dignity or age

The new instructor sought advice from the **venerable** professor.

Venerable Notre Dame Cathedral has stood in Paris since 1189.

NOTES: (1) *Venerable* often refers to people or things of great age. (2) Do not confuse *venerable* with *vulnerable*. (*Vulnerable* means "easily injured or hurt.")

▶ *Related Words*

venerate (verb) (vĕn′ə-rāt′) People *venerated* Mahatma Ghandi (1969–1948), who helped bring independence to India.

veneration (noun) In courtrooms, people show *veneration* of judges by standing when they enter.

Exercises

Part 1

Who's Who?

Match the word and definition. Use each choice only once.

1. An intrepid person ______ .
2. A melancholy person ______.
3. A cosmopolitan person ______ .
4. A venerable person ______ .
5. A hypocritical person ______ .
6. A gullible person ______ .
7. A capricious person ______ .
8. A fraternal relationship ______ .
9. An aficionado ______ .
10. An altruistic person ______ .

a. is scornful
b. is brave
c. is unpredictable
d. is unselfish
e. is with a brother
f. is easily fooled
g. has a broad worldview
h. is skillful
i. is sad
j. is worthy of respect
k. gives a false appearance of virtue
l. is a fan

Words in Context

Complete each sentence with the best word. Use each choice only once.

a. adroit	e. cosmopolitan	i. hypocritical
b. aficionado	f. disdain	j. intrepid
c. altruistic	g. fraternal	k. melancholy
d. capricious	h. gullible	l. venerable

1. Living in several different countries often makes a person more ________________.
2. The ________________ explorer traveled alone through the dangerous jungle.
3. Since we respect our ________________ grandfather, we often seek his advice.
4. The wine expert showed her ________________ for the stuff in the cheap bottle by spitting it out before she could swallow it.

5. The ____________________ billionaire Li Ka-Shing has given money to help victims of floods and earthquakes in his home town of Chaozhou, China.

6. The ____________________ waiter balanced two huge platters as he walked to the table.

7. The ____________________ manager lectured employees about honesty, but stole money from the company.

8. Children's tastes in food are ____________________ and change from day to day.

9. Problems with my college courses and my job put me in a(n)

____________________ mood.

10. The ____________________ woman believed the dishonest mechanic when he told her that the oil change would cost $10,000.

■ *Using Related Words*

Complete each sentence with the correct form. Use each choice only once.

THOMAS JEFFERSON (1743–1826): THIRD U.S. PRESIDENT

1. venerate, venerable

People of the United States ____________________ the "Founding

Fathers." Among the most ____________________ is Thomas Jefferson, chief author of the Declaration of Independence, third president of the United States, founder of the University of Virginia, talented architect, and speaker of seven languages. He was a brilliant man and a great patriot.

2. hypocrite, hypocritical

Despite his deep-seated belief in freedom, Jefferson was a

____________________ in some ways. In the Declaration of Independence, he wrote that people have a right to liberty, yet the

____________________ Jefferson kept slaves.

3. disdainful, disdaining

Jefferson also had a somewhat ________________ opinion of the need to live within a budget. He commonly imported expensive items from Europe, ________________ the notion that he could not afford them.

4. adroitness, adroitly

As president, Jefferson worked to establish his new country—the United States. He ________________ used wars between England and France to increase U.S. power. He also showed his ________________ when he made the Louisiana Purchase. By paying only $15 million, he doubled the land of the United States!

5. fraternized, fraternal

For years he ________________ with another founding father, John Adams. Later, though, they fought. As they grew old, they once again established a ________________ relationship, and died as friends.

■ *Find the Example*

Choose the example that best describes the action or situation.

1. Venerable, fraternal individuals _______
   a. elderly sisters b. senior citizen brothers
   c. young men in a college club

2. A disdainful and hypocritical act _______
   a. insulting others who show dishonesty b. praising the faults of others c. criticizing others who have the same faults as you

3. What an altruistic, but gullible, person might do _______
   a. refuse to give money b. give money to a phony charity
   c. give money to a charity he didn't believe in

4. When intrepid and adroit action is needed _______
   a. a snake attack b. a doctor's examination
   c. undergoing a painful medical test

5. A cosmopolitan aficionado _______
   a. snobbish brother b. generous, easily fooled donor
   c. worldwide museum-goer

Words to Learn

Part 2

13. **affluent** (adjective) ăf′lo͞o-ənt, ă-flo͞o′ənt

rich; prosperous

College graduates have a good chance of becoming **affluent**.

I want to teach in poor, city areas, rather than in **affluent** suburbs.

▶ *Related Word*

affluence (noun) The hard-working immigrant rose from poverty to *affluence*.

14. **alien** (adjective, noun) ā′lē-ən

a. strange; foreign (adjective)

Cruelty was **alien** to her kind nature.

The custom of sweeping graves is **alien** to most Americans, but is widespread in China.

b. a foreigner; a person who is not a citizen (noun)

Aliens may serve in the U.S. armed forces but may not vote.

c. a being from outer space (noun); coming from outer space (adjective)

In the movie, The **aliens** from Mars invaded earth. (noun)

Scientists study **alien** rocks from the moon. (adjective)

NOTE: All three meanings of *alien* hint at unknown, or strange.

▶ *Related Words*

alienate (verb) Your rudeness will *alienate* your friends. (*Alienate* means "to make hostile or unfriendly.")

alienation (noun) A fight about a friend led to Jamal's *alienation* from his family. (*Alienation* means "psychological isolation.")

An Alien Shake of the Head

In the country of Bulgaria, shaking one's head from side to side means "yes," and shaking the head up and down means "no." In Turkey, Greece, and parts of Italy, "no" is indicated by tossing one's head back. These are *alien* and confusing customs to people of most other countries, where nodding the head up and down indicates "yes" and shaking it from side to side means "no."

15. **astute** (adjective) ə-sto͞ot′

having excellent judgment; shrewd

The **astute** reporter could sense that despite their friendly words, the two politicians were enemies.

Astute public speakers know that jokes help to hold the attention of an audience.

▶ *Related Word*

astuteness (noun) The employee showed his *astuteness* by supporting his boss's point of view at a public meeting.

Is Astute *a Positive Word?*

Astute is generally a positive word, but it also can contain a negative element. *Astute* people often show slyness or trickiness. They usually know how to get what they want, even if it means some hypocrisy. For example, a worker might compliment his boss—and end up with a promotion. At other times, *astute* simply means clever and intelligent. Oprah Winfrey has a warm and charming public presence, and yet her *astuteness* has made her a billionaire. Barack Obama *astutely* judged that young voters would respond to technology—texting, blogs, and websites—and gained countless votes by conducting a new type of political campaign.

16. **candid** (adjective) kăn′dĭd

a. truthful; frank; honest in giving opinions

In the interview, the star was **candid** about her struggles with drug addiction.

b. not rehearsed or posed

The **candid** photograph caught me with my mouth open and my eyes shut.

▶ *Related Word*

candor (noun) When your girlfriend asks you if you like her dress, it is best to answer with compliments, not *candor*.

17. **cordial** (adjective) kôr′jəl

warm and sincere; friendly

The store manager urged cashiers to be **cordial** to customers.

▶ *Related Word*

cordiality (noun) The *cordiality* of my fiancée's father made me feel like I was already a member of the family.

Words from the Heart

The word *cordial* is taken from the Latin root *cord*, meaning "heart." Other words that stem from this root are *cardiac*, a medical word used to refer to the heart, and *courage*, or "having the heart" (bravery) to do something. The original sense of *cordial* was a food or drink that stimulates the heart. This can still be seen in the noun *cordial*, which refers to a sweet, alcoholic drink that usually gives people a feeling of warmth.

18. **dogmatic** (adjective) dôg-măt′ĭk

arrogant in belief; opinionated

Dogmatic people often state personal opinion as absolute truth.

Workers found it hard to give suggestions to their **dogmatic** boss.

▶ *Related Words*

dogmatism (noun)

The surgeon's *dogmatism* about following a set procedure for the operation prevented him from taking advantage of some modern techniques.

dogma (noun) (dôg′mə) The religious leader insisted that all believers follow the *dogma* of the church. (A *dogma* is a system of beliefs.)

19. **exuberant** (adjective) ĭg-zo͞o′bər-ənt

very enthusiastic; joyfully energetic

Exuberant at seeing his mother after ten years apart, Tran grabbed her and lifted her into the air.

Rosemary was **exuberant** when she found out she had won the lottery.

▶ *Related Word*

exuberance (noun) The cheerleaders' *exuberance* inspired the crowd to clap and shout.

Courtesy author

Rosemary was *exuberant* when she found out she had won the lottery.

20. **frivolous** (adjective) frĭv′ə-ləs

    a. unimportant; not worthy of serious attention

    The judge dismissed the million-dollar lawsuit over a bad haircut, calling it **frivolous.**

    b. lacking in seriousness; silly

    Some argue that video games are **frivolous**; others feel that they improve coordination and strategic thinking skills.

    ▶ *Related Word*

    frivolity (noun) Is a fancy wedding important to your family members, or do they think it is simply a *frivolity*?

21. **frugal** (adjective) fro͞o′gəl

    thrifty; economical; attempting to save money; not giving freely

    People who live through economic hard times often remain **frugal** for the rest of their lives.

    Unfortunately, my boyfriend is **frugal** with compliments.

    ▶ *Related Word*

    frugality (noun) Agnieszka showed her *frugality* by washing and reusing the plastic cups, rather than throwing them away.

22. **gauche** (adjective) gōsh

awkward; lacking in social graces and manners

At her wedding, the **gauche** bride complained about her gifts.

The **gauche** man wiped his mouth on his sleeve.

Right Is Right

In many languages, words that refer to the right side are positive, and words that refer to the left side are negative. Two words in this chapter have roots in the concepts of "right" or "left." In French, *à droit* means "to the right," and in both French and English, *adroit* is a positive word meaning "skillful." *Gauche*, French for "left," means "socially awkward" or "clumsy" in English.

23. **novice** (noun) nŏv′ĭs

beginner; person in a new situation

The expert chef patiently taught the **novice** how to make sauces.

NOTES: (1) *Novice* can be used as an adjective: *Novice* skaters often fall on the ice. (2) A *novice* can be a person who has entered a religious order but has not taken final vows.

24. **stoic** (adjective, noun) stō′ĭk

a. not showing the effects of pain or pleasure (adjective)

The **stoic** child bore the painful medical procedures without complaining.
Skilled card players maintain **stoic** expressions and do not reveal how good—or bad—their hands are.

b. a person not showing the effects of pain or pleasure (noun)

The **stoic** never talked about her disability.

▶ *Related Word*
stoicism (noun) (stō′ə-sĭ′zəm) Workers accepted the low pay and harsh working conditions with *stoicism*.

NOTE: In modern English usage, *stoic* is usually associated with pain or misfortune, so it often means "uncomplaining," or calmly accepting what is bad or painful.

A Philosophical Porch

A *Stoic* was a follower of an ancient Greek school of philosophical thought that originated in 308 BCE (before common era). The philosopher Zeno taught that because gods had made the world, it was perfect. Therefore, human beings must accept their fates without expressing sorrow or joy. The word *stoic* is taken from the covered porch (*stoa* in Greek) where Zeno taught.

Exercises

Part 2

Who's Who

Match the word and definition. Use each choice only once.

1. A frivolous person is_______.
2. A cordial person is_______ .
3. An affluent person is_______ .
4. An exuberant person is_______ .
5. A stoic person is_______ .
6. An alien is _______ .
7. An astute person is _______.
8. A candid person is _______.
9. A gauche person is_______ .
10. A dogmatic person is_______ .

a. honest
b. a foreigner
c. a beginner
d. silly
e. friendly
f. not likely to complain
g. someone with excellent judgment
h. awkward, lacking social graces
i. enthusiastic
j. wealthy
k. opinionated
l. thrifty, economical

Words in Context

Complete each sentence with the best word. Use each choice only once.

a. affluent	e. cordial	i. frugal
b. alien	f. dogmatic	j. gauche
c. astute	g. exuberant	k. novice
d. candid	h. frivolous	l. stoic

1. The __________________ audience members leapt from their seats and danced on the stage.
2. I am a(n) __________________ at tennis, and have never even held a racquet before.
3. She was __________________ and bought all her clothes at second-hand shops.

4. Some people feel that buying beautiful, expensive jewelry is a(n) ____________________ way to spend money, but others feel it is a good investment.

5. She always greeted her neighbors in a(n) ____________________ manner and asked about their families.

6. Basic training in the armed forces teaches soldiers to be ____________________ and not complain about difficult conditions.

7. The physician was ____________________ with the patient about the seriousness of her illness.

8. Your ____________________ statements leave no room for disagreement.

9. Sitting on the floor while eating is a(n) ____________________ custom to most Americans.

10. The ____________________ man started to talk loudly in the middle of the funeral service.

■ *Using Related Words*

Complete each sentence with the correct form. Use each choice only once.

ABRAHAM LINCOLN (1809–1865): SIXTEENTH U.S. PRESIDENT

1. affluent, affluence

   Although many U.S. presidents come from ____________________ families, Abraham Lincoln's family was poor. After his mother died when he was a small child, his family moved several times, making difficult journeys through wilderness. Lincoln attended school for only a few years, but through self-education, he was able to become a lawyer. In this profession, he rose to ____________________.

2. frugal, frugality

   Nevertheless, Lincoln remained quite ____________________. His simple life style was a habit from his childhood. His wife, however, did not enjoy ________________. She was criticized for her expensive parties and fine clothes.

3. cordiality, cordial

In the small towns of Illinois, Lincoln developed a reputation for ________________. As a lawyer, he spent many hours entertaining others by telling stories. His ________________ manner made him many friends.

4. astute, astuteness

This proved to be an ________________ courtroom strategy, for lawyers often underestimated him. Behind his friendly manner, though, lay much ________________ and sophistication in legal matters.

5. candor, candid

As president of the United States during the Civil War, Lincoln had to make many difficult decisions. At times, he was less than ________________ with his advisers. But Lincoln needed much support, and complete ________________ would have made many people unhappy. So, he entertained people with stories and put off decisions. Lincoln led the Union to victory in the Civil War, but shortly afterward, he was assassinated.

■ *Find the Example*

Choose the example that best describes the action or situation.

1. It is astute to be candid when you want to say ______
   a. something nice. b. something truthful.
   c. something hurtful.
2. A person who is exuberant about something frivolous would say: ______
   a. I sort of enjoyed that massage. b. Wow! What a great outfit!
   c. Outstanding! That will bring peace to the world!
3. A novice to frugality ______
   a. complaining guest b. new, enthusiastic fan
   c. first-time discount shopper
4. Exuberant aliens ______
   a. embarrassing next door neighbors b. friendly people from France
   c. happily excited Martians

5. What an affluent, gauche person might say _______
   a. I would be happy to pay for dinner. b. Can you lend me a dollar to buy food? c. I have more money than all of you together!

Chapter Exercises

■ *Practicing Strategies: Using the Dictionary*

Read the dictionary entries and answer the questions. These examples are taken both from online and print sources.

flor•id	flôr′ĭd, flŏr′- KEY
ADJECTIVE:	**1.** Flushed with rosy color; ruddy. **2.** Very ornate; flowery: *a florid prose style.* **3.** Archaic Healthy. **4.** Obsolete Abounding in or covered with flowers.
ETYMOLOGY:	French *floride*, from Latin *flōridus*, from *flōs*, *flōr-*, flower.
OTHER FORMS:	**flo•rid′i•ty** (flə-rĭd′ĭ-tē, flô-) KEY or **flor′id•ness** —NOUN **flor′id•ly** —ADVERB

1. Write the numbers of two meanings of *florid* that are no longer used.

   ____

2. Which syllable of *florid* is stressed in pronunciation?

   ____

3. What nouns are related to *florid*? _______________

4. From which language did *florid* enter English? _______________

Main Entry: **be•he•moth**
Pronunciation: \bĭ-ˈhē-məth, ˈbē-ə-məth\
Function: *noun*
Usage: *often attributive*
Etymology: Middle English, from Late Latin, from Hebrew *bĕhēmōth*
Date: 14th century
1. *often capitalized*: a mighty animal described in Job 40:15–24 as an example of the power of God
2. something of monstrous size, power, or appearance <a *behemoth* truck>

5. In total, how many ways can the first *e* in *behemoth* be pronounced?

   ____

6. In which language did *behemoth* originate? _______________

max•i•mum (măk′sə-məm) *n., pl.* **-mums** or **-ma** (-mə) **1a.** The greatest possible quantity or degree. **b.** The greatest quantity or degree reached or recorded; the upper limit of variation. **c.** The time or period during which the highest point or degree is attained. **2.** An upper limit permitted by law or other authority. **3.** *Astronomy* **a.** The moment when a variable star is most brilliant. **b.** The magnitude of the star at such a moment. **4.** *Mathematics* **a.** The greatest value assumed by a function over a given interval. **b.** The largest number in a set ❖. *adj.* **1.** Having or being the maximum reached or attainable: *maximum temperature.* **2.** Of, relating to, or making up a maximum: *the maximum number in a series.* [Lat. < neut. of *maximus*, greatest. See **meg-** in App.]

7. Which part of speech and definition number best fits this sentence: The police stopped me for driving over the *maximum*.

 ____

8. What are the two full plural spellings of *maximum*?

 ____

9. What two parts of speech can *maximum* be? ____________________

10. Give the part of the speech and number of the definition of *maximum* most often used in astronomy. ____________________

■ *Practicing Strategies: Using a Dictionary Pronunciation Key*

To practice using a pronunciation key, look up the symbols for each word in the key on the inside front cover of this book. Try saying the words out loud. Then check yourself on the audio website for this chapter at **www.cengage.com/devenglish/richek8e.**

1. accolade	ăk′ə-lād
2. pseudonym	so͞o′də-nĭm′
3. cuisine	kwĭ-zēn′
4. epitome	ĭ-pĭt′ə-mē
5. cliché	klē-shā′

■ *Practicing Strategies: Using the Dictionary Independently*

Use a print or online dictionary to answer the following questions.

1. What is a *babirusa*? ____________________

2. In what language was the word *nostril* first recorded?

 ____

3. How many syllables does the preferred pronunciation of the word *mischievous* have? ____________________

4. How does a *contrite* person feel? ____________________

5. What is a *tupelo*? ____________________

■ *Companion Words*

Complete each sentence with the best word. You may use choices more than once. Choices: for, of, with, about, to, in, from

1. The student was candid _________ the fact that he hadn't studied.
2. The math genius was disdainful _________ our problems in calculus.
3. Shouting is alien _________ my quiet nature.
4. The capriciousness _________ my friend's moods suggested mental illness.
5. Don't fraternize _________ friends if you want to finish your work!
6. I am frugal _________ my money.
7. The gullibility _________ our unsophisticated neighbor amazed us.
8. The prisoner's alienation _________ society caused him unhappiness.
9. My husband is an aficionado _________ rare stamps.
10. Your insulting comments reveal your disdain _________our feelings.

■ *Writing with Your Words*

To practice effective writing, complete each sentence with an interesting phrase that indicates the meaning of the italicized word.

1. The *altruistic* woman ____

____.

2. If I were very *affluent*, ____
____.

3. My *dogmatic* father ____
____.

4. The *capricious* employer ____
____.

5. I knew he was a *hypocrite* when ____
____.

6. A *novice* at dating might ____
____.

7. The *stoic* ____
____.

8. My *frugal* aunt ____
____.

9. When I feel *melancholy*, ____
____.

10. The *aficionado* of deep-dish pizza ____
____.

■ *Making Connections*

To connect new vocabulary to your life, respond to these assignments.

1. Describe a situation in which you felt gauche.
2. If you wanted to do something frivolous, what would you do?
3. Have you found that, in general, immigrants are more cosmopolitan than people born in this country? Explain.

Passage

Once a troubled youth, Jimmy John Liautaud now runs a chain of over 900 sandwich shops.

Courtesy of Jimmy John's Franchise LLC

The Sandwich King

Jimmy John's high school years were spent largely in the discipline office, but through hard work and a sense of fun he became a business success.

Almost no one would have predicted a life of **affluence** for this guy. He graduated next to last in his high school class. He didn't have an easy time socially, either. Awkward and overweight, **(1)** he felt he was the object of **disdain** from his classmates, who were often from more **affluent** families. To add to his problems, **(2)** he often embarrassed himself by saying things that were too **candid.** He got in so much trouble for smoking, fighting, and skipping class that the school staff considered kicking him out. Yet today, more than twenty years later, Jimmy John Liautaud runs a chain of over 900 sandwich shops that proudly bears his name: Jimmy John's.

How did he do it? The answer is lots of hard work, and some help from friends and family. His father was an **intrepid** business owner and inventor who was willing to risk going broke to test a good idea. His mother too had made it through difficult times. Originally from Lithuania, she had escaped from Communism, lived in camps, and finally immigrated to an **alien** land, the United States. The family expected children to be hardworking and self-supporting.

Jimmy John also received some important help in high school. Dean of Discipline Jim Lyons recognized that **(3)** inside the **gauche** teenager there was a gentle giant. The dean asked Jimmy John what things interested him. There were two answers: a good-looking female classmate and food. Lyons told his student to concentrate on the food!

So Jimmy John decided to open up a sandwich shop, partially funded by a loan from his father. For research, he ate in all the sandwich places he could find within a five-state area. The sandwich **aficionado** soon became an expert judge. His family evaluated his proposed creations, voting down his favorite—liver sausage and mayonnaise.

(4) The **novice** businessman had just completed high school when he opened a shop in a garage near Eastern Illinois University. Since he sold only two sandwiches the first day, **(5)** he was **astute** enough to try a marketing plan: distributing free sandwiches. Giving away food proved to be a hit. People started streaming into the shop to buy lunch.

Soon Jimmy John hired two helpers—and assigned them all the difficult jobs. Sensing his **hypocrisy,** both employees quit. Jimmy John learned a valuable lesson: the boss must work hard. He is now **affluent,** but **(6)** he **stoically** continues to put in long hours.

Starting in one store, Jimmy John developed a chain. He now has shops in large cities throughout the Midwest and Southeast.

There are many reasons for the success of the chain. The food and service are dependable and fast. There is no room for **capriciousness** in Jimmy John's stores. His motto is "Make a Deal, Keep a Deal." All ingredients are fresh. In fact, **(7)** the **adroitly** made sandwiches are often delivered within seconds. The menu also accommodates different needs. People who are concerned about their weight may order the "unwich," ingredients wrapped in lettuce without the bread. The management of the shops is very systematic. Employees get a detailed "to do" list, which includes such tasks as turning out the lights at closing time.

But, like Jimmy John, the shops have their **frivolous** side. Signs posted on the wall give advice about life. One reads, "If you think your teacher is tough, wait till you get a boss." Guides to behavior are also posted. The DOs include "Say please and thank you," "Disable dorky ring tones on your cell phone," and "Remember to smile." The DON'Ts contain: "Don't play with your food" and "Don't take stuff too seriously."

(8) Jimmy John also believes in **cordiality.** Staff members tell customers to, "Come back soon." All employees, including office executives, wear T-shirts saying "Your mother wants you to eat at Jimmy John's." This gives a **fraternal** feeling to all parts of the business.

Jimmy John also believes in listening to his employees. His early struggles taught him that **(9)** a **dogmatic** boss is a bad boss. So he requires all managers to hold weekly sessions that discuss employee complaints and suggestions. Good pay helps to keep employees loyal, but so does Jimmy John's concern for them. He named a sandwich for a manager who was killed in an accident. Look for the "Billy Club" on the menu.

Success has enabled Jimmy John to be **altruistic.** In 2008, he donated a million dollars to his former school for a new building. He insisted that **(10)** the building must bear the name of the **venerable** dean of discipline who helped him: Jim Lyons. Today the Liautaud-Lyons upper grade center stands on the campus of Elgin Academy, the high school where Jimmy John struggled. It was built by the sandwich king, John Liautaud, who combined hard work with fun to build a food empire.

■ *Exercises*

Each numbered sentence corresponds to a sentence in the passage. Fill in the letter of the choice that makes the sentence mean the same thing as its corresponding sentence in the passage.

1. He felt he was the object of ______ from classmates.
   a. pity b. scorn c. envy d. saving money
2. He often embarrassed himself by saying things that were too ______.
   a. new b. generous c. truthful d. foreign
3. Inside the ______ teenager, there was a gentle giant.
   a. truthful b. awkward c. not doing what he said d. business-like
4. The ______ businessman had just completed high school.
   a. brave b. believing c. clumsy d. new
5. He was ______ enough to try a marketing plan.
   a. desperate b. rich c. frightened d. shrewd
6. Jimmy John ______ continues to put in long hours.
   a. strangely b. sadly c. without complaint d. without believing
7. The ______ made sandwiches are often delivered within seconds.
   a. scarefully b. skillfully c. freshly d. shrewdly
8. Jimmy John also believes in ______.
   a. hard work b. beginners c. friendliness d. customers
9. A(n) ______ boss is a bad boss.
   a. opinionated b. clumsy c. selfish d. insincere
10. The building must bear the name of the ______ dean of discipline.
    a. newly rich b. very kind c. respected d. very understanding

■ *Discussion Questions*

1. List three reasons why Jimmy John's chain has been successful.
2. Give two ways in which Jimmy John shows that he values employees.
3. How did Jimmy John's early struggles contribute to his success?

INSIGHT INTO IDIOMS

Expressions for Color

Have you ever *felt blue?* Do you *have a green thumb?* Would you rather be *in the black* or *in the red?* All of these questions contain idioms. Idioms are commonly used phrases that have special meanings. These meanings differ from the meanings of the individual words. For example, the words *green thumb* seem to mean a finger that is the color green. But the idiom *to have a green thumb* is not about a strange medical condition. Rather, it's a way of saying someone is skilled at growing plants. A good gardener is often said to *have a green thumb.*

The last page of each chapter in this book presents the meaning of some English idioms. Since the Chapter 1 passage is about a colorful (lively and interesting) businessman, the idioms that follow are about colors.

a. *Feeling blue* means feeling depressed or sad.

b. *Yellow-bellied* means cowardly.

c. People who look at the world *through rose-colored glasses* see things as much better than they really are.

d. A person with a *green thumb* has a talent for gardening.

e. *Green-eyed monster* is an idiom that indicates jealousy.

f. A firm that is *in the red* is losing money.

g. A firm that is *in the black* is profitable.

Practice chapter words one more time by filling in the letter of the correct idiom into the blank before each sentence:

______ 1. The _________ sergeant was a *hypocrite* who ordered his soldiers into battle, and then hid inside.

______ 2. It was a *melancholy* day for her, and she was _________.

______ 3. When your friends are more *affluent* than you are, you may become a victim of the _________.

______ 4. People who think of only *frivolous* things often look at the world _________.

______ 5. After the *adroit* _________ manager took charge, the business went from being to being _________.

Links to lists of English idioms and their meanings can be found at the Student Companion Website for this book: **www.cengage.com/devenglish/richek8e**.

CHAPTER 

Words in the News

News travels fast in today's world. The Internet brings us the latest developments in politics, sports, and finance within seconds of when they happen. Videos shot on site using mobile phones show firsthand accounts of triumphs and disasters from faraway places. With so much information available so fast, it is important to understand words that relate to the news.

Chapter Strategy: Context Clues of Substitution

Chapter Words:

Part 1

accord	cartel	entrepreneur
appease	catastrophe	intervene
attrition	corroborate	ominous
bureaucracy	diplomacy	renegade

Part 2

apprehend	hegemony	radical
chaos	pacify	liberal
defer	supplant	conservative
epitome	thrive	reactionary

Visit the Student Companion Website at **www.cengage.com/devenglish/richek8e** to test your knowledge of these words before you study, hear each word pronounced, find additional practice exercises, and access more information on words and topics.

Did You Know?

How Many Ways Can a Team Win or Lose?

There is a constant stream of news from the action-filled world of sports. Sports writers, the people who compose this news, are masters of the English language. However, they have a challenging task. Day after day, they report thousands of basketball, baseball, soccer, and hockey results. In each contest, one team (or person) wins and another loses. Yet the reports that sports writers compose are original and enthusiastic.

How do they do it?

One important trick is the use of clever synonyms (words that mean the same thing) for the words *win* and *lose*.

Let's look at two of the many ways to say *win*, with examples taken from newspaper sports pages. The synonyms appear in italics.

Patriots *top* Panthers.

Brazil *clinches* World Cup.

And here are synonyms for *lose*.

Cubs *drop* heartbreaker.

Hawks *are doormats* again.

These headlines show big wins.

Aussies *overpower* Sri Lanka.

Iowa State *rips* number 4 Kansas.

On the other hand, the connotations of these words show that the winners barely got by.

Bengals *slip past* Rams.

Johnson *edges* Liukin for Olympic gold.

This headline shows that the game changed in the middle.

Bears *struggle,* then *cruise* past Packers.

Names can be used with great imagination. The headlines that follow are metaphors, whose meanings are suggested by team names.

Cowboys *lasso* Steelers. (Cowboys commonly *lasso* animals.)

Stars *outshine* Redwings.

Buffalo Bills *shipwreck* Vikings. (The original Vikings were invaders who traveled by boat.)

Pirates *slice up* Cubs. (The Pirates take their swords and "slice up" the Cubs.)

Hurricanes *blow away* Bruins.

At other times, sports writers use rhyme.

Bears *sack the Pack.*

Hoosiers *fake, shake, break* Illini.

A headline can tell much about a game. What happened below?

1. Bruins' rally on ice from 2 down stuns Rangers 4–3.
2. Penn surprises Ohio in overtime.
3. Bulls butcher Bucks, end road slump.

Answers are on page 399.

Learning Strategy

Context Clues of Substitution

Using *context clues* is a powerful strategy that can help you figure out the meanings of unknown words. *Context* refers to the words, sentences, or even paragraphs that surround a word. When you use context clues, you use the words that you know in a selection to make an intelligent guess about the meaning of an unknown word.

Perhaps the thought of guessing seems strange to you. After all, it is better to know the answer on a test than just to guess. However, intelligent guessing is very important in reading. English has so many words that no one can know them all. Good readers often use context clues when they meet unfamiliar vocabulary.

Context clues have two important advantages:

1. You do not have to interrupt your reading to go to the dictionary.
2. You can rely on your own common sense. Common sense is a very effective learning tool.

In fact, you probably use context clues already, although you may not realize it. For example, context clues are the only way to choose the correct meaning for words that have more than one meaning, such as *hot*. You must use context clues to figure out what the word *hot* means in the following sentences.

a. The fire is *hot*.

b. Yolanda has a *hot* temper.

c. This chili pepper is really *hot*.

In which sentence does *hot* mean

1. quick, emotional? ________
2. having a high temperature? ________
3. spicy? ________

Answers are on page 399.

Let's turn to a more difficult word. What are the meanings of the word *concession* in these sentences?

a. He bought some food at the hot-dog *concession*.
b. Because the country wanted peace, leaders made a *concession* of land to the enemy.

In which sentence does *concession* mean

1. something that is surrendered or given up? ________
2. a business that sells things? ________

Answers are on page 399.

Context clues and the dictionary are natural partners in helping you determine the meaning of unknown words. Context clues usually suggest an approximate meaning for a word and allow you to continue reading without interruption. After you have finished reading, you can look up the word in a dictionary.

You may be wondering exactly how to determine the meaning of unknown words that you find in your reading. Many people find the following steps helpful:

1. As you are reading, try to pinpoint words you do not know. This advice sounds almost silly, but it isn't. Many people lose the opportunity to learn vocabulary simply because they let unknown words slip by. Don't let this happen to you. Try to capture difficult words!
2. Use context clues to make an intelligent guess about an unknown word's meaning. The strategies you will learn in Chapters 2, 3, and 4 will help you do this. Remember that context clues often give you approximate—not exact—meanings.
3. Mark the word and check it in a dictionary. This step will tell you how close your guess was and will give you a more exact definition.

How does a person learn to make "intelligent guesses"? This book presents three methods: substitution in context (this chapter), context clues of definition (Chapter 3), and context clues of opposition (Chapter 4).

Substitution in context is perhaps the most useful way to determine a word's meaning. To use this strategy, simply substitute a word or phrase that makes sense in place of an unknown word. The word you substitute will usually be an approximate definition for the unknown word. Here are some examples.

> The *pusillanimous* bully ran away when his victim fought back. (Since people who lack courage run away, *pusillanimous* means *cowardly*.)
>
> Smoking has *deleterious* effects on health. (We know that smoking is *harmful* to health, so the word *harmful* may substitute for *deleterious*.)

Of course, context clues of substitution are not always effective. Some sentences simply do not provide enough clues. For example, in the sentence "Jane saw the *conger*," there are a great number of substitutions for *conger*. (A *conger* is a type of eel.) However, since many sentences do provide good context clues, substitution in context will help you much of the time.

In the next two examples, try using context clues of substitution to make intelligent guesses about the meanings of the italicized words. To do this, take out the unknown word and substitute a word or phrase that makes sense in the sentence.

1. Your smiling *countenance* suggests that you are happy.
2. The *polyglot* spoke Polish, Russian, German, Japanese, and English.

Answers are on page 399.

Each of the following sentences contains a word that is presented in the Words to Learn section. Use a context clue of substitution to make an intelligent guess about its meaning.

1. The two countries reached an *accord* that enabled them to stop fighting.

   Accord means To agree_______________.
2. Should a teacher *intervene* when children fight on the playground?

   Intervene means To interfere_______________.

Answers are on page 399.

Words to Learn

Part 1

1. **accord** (noun, verb) ə-kôrd′

   a. agreement; harmony (noun)

An **accord** between the workers and management settled the strike.

The skater's family was in **accord** with his decision to withdraw from the competition.

Of his own **accord** Mark decided to quit the football team. ("Of his own accord" means making his own decision.)

b. to give or grant (verb)

Iranian lawyer Shirin Ebadi was **accorded** the 2003 Nobel Peace Prize for her fight to protect human rights.

▶ *Related Word*

accordance (noun) In **accordance** with school policy, students caught using illegal drugs will be expelled.

▶ *Common Phrases*

in accord with; reach an accord (reach an agreement); of one's own accord (willingly); in accordance with (in agreement with)

Terrell and Andre shook hands after they reach an *accord*.

Courtesy author

2. **appease** (verb) ə-pēz′

a. to satisfy or calm

To **appease** his nosy friends, Carlos told them about his date.

b. to achieve peace or satisfy by giving in to demands

Giving table scraps to dogs may temporarily **appease** them, but most will soon be begging for more.

NOTE: When we *appease* someone, we often sacrifice what is right or good for temporary calm or relief.

▶ *Related Word*

appeasement (noun) A policy of *appeasement* often encourages people to be even more aggressive.

3. **attrition** (noun) ə-trĭsh′ən

slowly wearing down; wearing away

Stone turns to sand by a process of **attrition**.

Attrition tends to be high in very difficult college courses.

Employee **attrition** is low when jobs are hard to get.

4. **bureaucracy** (noun) byo͝o-rŏk′rə-sē (plural: **bureaucracies**)

administration by employees who follow fixed rules and complex procedures

The newly elected mayor promised to reform the inefficient city **bureaucracy**.

▶ *Related Words*

bureaucratic (adjective) Because of *bureaucratic* problems in the registration office, my transcript was lost.

bureaucrat (noun) For twenty years, the *bureaucrat* made four copies of every letter she received.

NOTE: *Bureaucracy* is usually a negative word, involving officials more concerned with following rules than with getting things done. In government, *bureaucrats* are appointed, not elected.

Red Tape and Bureaucracy

Bureaucracy is often associated with the term *red tape*, as in "There is too much *bureaucratic red tape*." In the 1700s, red tape was used to bind piles of English government documents. Since government offices were inefficient and *bureaucratic*, the term *red tape* came to refer to excessive and silly official routines.

5. **cartel** (noun) kär-tĕl′

a combination of independent suppliers or manufacturers formed to control prices

The Organization of Petroleum Exporting Countries (OPEC) is a powerful oil **cartel** made up of twelve nations.

When a **cartel** is effective, sellers control prices—and buyers pay more.

6. **catastrophe** (noun) kə-tăs′trə-fē

a great disaster

A 2008 earthquake in southwest China was a **catastrophe** that killed over 70,000 people.

The computer worm was a **catastrophe** that shut down systems worldwide.

▶ *Related Word*

catastrophic (adjective) (kăt′ə-strŏf′-ĭk) Cheating can have **catastrophic** effects on a student's career.

7. **corroborate** (verb) kə-rŏb′ə-rāt′

to confirm; to make more certain

Five eyewitnesses **corroborated** the police report.

The White House press secretary **corroborated** rumors that the president was visiting troops in Afghanistan.

▶ *Related Words*

corroboration (noun) Not even one report of an alien spaceship landing on Earth has received scientific *corroboration.*

corroborative (adjective) We need *corroborative* evidence for this statement.

The Loch Ness Monster: Looking for Corroboration

More than 1,500 years ago, someone walking by Loch Ness (*loch* means "lake") in Scotland claimed to have seen a strange creature coming out of the water. It looked like a combination of a snake and a dinosaur. Since then, there have been thousands of reports of the Loch Ness monster. In 2003, the British Broadcasting Company sent researchers to determine whether the legend was true. Despite the use of satellite navigation and 600 sonar beams, they could not *corroborate* the existence of the monster. So it doesn't exist, or does it . . . ?

8. **diplomacy** (noun) dĭ-plō′mə-sē

a. official international relations

Successful **diplomacy** led to the release of the hostages.

b. tact; skill in dealing with people without causing anger or embarrassment

It can be difficult to combine honesty and **diplomacy**.

▶ *Related Words*

diplomatic (adjective) In preparation for war, the two countries broke off *diplomatic* relations.

The teacher tried to be *diplomatic* when she explained the failing grade to the student.

diplomat (noun) *Diplomats* often speak several languages.

NOTE: (1) *Diplomacy* often refers to negotiating treaties and alliances between groups of nations or nation-like groups (such as rebels or leaders of provinces). (2) *Diplomats* are officials who represent their country in a foreign nation. They are often housed in an embassy or consulate.

9. **entrepreneur** (noun) ŏn′trə-prə-nûr′

a person who organizes, runs, and assumes the risk of a business

Young **entrepreneur** Markus Frind turned his programming hobby into a multimillion-dollar online dating service.

▶ *Related Word*

entrepreneurial (adjective) The *entrepreneurial* employee quit his job to start a new business.

10. **intervene** (verb) ĭn′tər-vēn′

a. to interfere; to act in a matter involving others

The bouncers **intervened** to stop a fight between two guys at the dance club.

The government of Kenya **intervened** in the illegal hunting of elephants.

b. to come between in time

The weeks that **intervene** between Thanksgiving and Christmas are the height of the shopping season.

▶ *Related Word*

intervention (noun) We hope that United Nations *intervention* will stop the massacres in the Sudan.

11. **ominous** (adjective) ŏm′ə-nəs

warning of bad things; threatening evil

Rising unemployment is an **ominous** sign for the economy.

As I walked through the house, I heard the **ominous** growl of an angry dog.

12. **renegade** (noun, adjective) rĕn′ĭ-gād′

   a. traitor; disloyal person; outlaw; person who rejects conventional behavior (noun)

      The leader of the country was a **renegade** who refused to follow international guidelines on nuclear weapons.

      According to legend, Robin Hood, born a nobleman, became a **renegade** who stole from the rich and gave to the poor.

   b. rebellious; changing one's loyalty (adjective)

      The **renegade** U.S. senator refused to follow her party's leader.

Exercises

Part 1

■ *Matching Words and Definitions*

Match the word and definition. Use each choice only once.

1. ominous ______
2. bureaucracy ______
3. renegade ______
4. appease ______
5. intervene ______
6. diplomacy ______
7. cartel ______
8. accord ______
9. catastrophe ______
10. attrition ______

a. agreement
b. to confirm; make more certain
c. interfere
d. threatening evil
e. person who starts a business
f. disaster
g. administration by employees who follow fixed rules
h. official international relations
i. rebel; disloyal person
j. to give in to demands
k. a group that agrees to control prices
l. wearing away

Words in Context

Complete each sentence with the best word. Use each choice only once.

a. accord	e. cartel	i. entrepreneur
b. appease	f. catastrophe	j. intervene
c. attrition	g. corroborate	k. ominous
d. bureaucracy	h. diplomacy	l. renegade

1. A(n) ________________ often must fund a business using her own money.
2. The ________________ deserted to the enemy.
3. The ________________ dark clouds warned of a thunderstorm.
4. To ________________ the fact I found on a personal blog, I checked it in the newspaper.
5. Instead of continuing to fight, the two divorcing people reached a(n) ________________ on child custody.
6. Workers in a(n) ________________ often take days to process a simple form.
7. As more and more books are ordered through the Internet, bookstores have suffered ________________, and have closed.
8. Seven large companies that supplied sugar tried to form a(n) ________________ to control prices.
9. Because of her great ________________, Nadia was able to criticize others without hurting their feelings.
10. I asked my professor to ________________ with the financial aid officials and make sure I would get my money quickly.

Using Related Words

Complete each sentence with the correct form. Use each choice only once.

1. corroborate, corroboration, corroborative

Eyewitness reports of crimes are often not reliable. Even when several witnesses ________________ each other, they may convict the wrong person. Kirk Bloodsworth, a U.S. Marine who had fought for his country, was convicted of rape and murder. Several eyewitnesses gave ____________________. But, in fact, he was innocent of the crime! Working in the prison library, Kirk found out about the use of DNA evidence in England. In Kirk's case, DNA provided ____________________ evidence that he was not the criminal. He was the first person to use DNA in a U.S. trial.

2. appeasing, appeasement, appease

In a famous historical example of ____________________, European countries granted Hitler much of Czechoslovakia's borderland in 1938. The country of Czechoslovakia was not even invited to the meeting that decided its fate. France, England, and other countries hoped that granting Hitler the land would ____________________ him, but as is often the case with such ____________________ efforts, he was not satisfied. In 1939, Hitler's continued aggression resulted in World War II.

3. catastrophe, catastrophes, catastrophic

Many scientists' predict a ____________________ due to global warming. In fact, some are predicting that by 2015, the Arctic will thaw in the summer, releasing ____________________ flooding. To avoid such ____________________, U.S. President Obama is considering using new technology, including shooting pollution particles into the upper atmosphere to block the sun's rays.

4. bureaucratic, bureaucracy

Texan Calvin Graham won medals for bravery in World War II, but navy officials expelled him and took away his medals when they discovered he was only twelve years old! Graham spent the last years of his life asking the military ____________________ to return his awards. But ____________________ agencies move slowly. The last medal, a Purple Heart, was returned only after his death.

5. entrepreneur, entrepreneurial

Reverend Man Singh Das is an ____________________ who makes money while doing good. Owner of a service station and apartment buildings, he has used his ______________ skills to provide jobs and housing to the needy. Instead of arresting a man who was trying to rob his gas station, Das offered him a job cleaning it.

■ *Find the Example*

Choose the example that best describes the action or situation.

1. Intervention in a catastrophe ______
   a. reporting a terrible hurricane b. an outside nation stopping a war c. a meeting between the leaders of two nations at war
2. Appeasing a cartel ______
   a. agreeing to pay more to an association b. stopping a business from raising prices c. forming a club to raise prices temporarily
3. A diplomatic accord ______
   a. the start of a war b. the president and Congress passing a law c. a peace agreement
4. An ominous sign for an entrepreneur ______
   a. a boss refusing to talk to her b. opening a new store c. a drop in sales
5. Corroborating attrition ______
   a. a news report that more people are being employed b. a second report, confirming a first one, that many people are retiring c. an article stating that employment is expected to drop

Words to Learn

Part 2

13. **apprehend** (verb) ăp′rĭ-hĕnd′

   a. to arrest or take a criminal into custody

   The officials **apprehended** the suspects as they attempted to flee.

   b. to understand mentally; to grasp

   Many people find it difficult to **apprehend** the principles of physics.

► *Related Words*

apprehension (noun) The *apprehension* of the gunman calmed the neighborhood. I had *apprehensions* about the test. (In the first sentence, *apprehension* means "arrest"; in the second sentence, it means "fear.")

apprehensive (adjective) Anna was *apprehensive* about speaking in front of the class. (*Apprehensive* means "fearful.")

14. **chaos** (noun) kā′ŏs′

a state of total disorder or confusion

Chaos broke out when shoppers heard they could get a free plasma TV.

The rush-hour blizzard left traffic in **chaos**.

► *Related Word*

chaotic (adjective) The nightclub became *chaotic* as people rushed to escape from the fire.

15. **defer** (verb) dĭ-fûr′

a. to delay

My college will allow me to **defer** tuition payment until my financial aid check arrives.

b. to show respect; to submit to the wishes of another

In many cultures, the young **defer** to the elderly.

I **deferred** to my father's wishes and attended college.

► *Common Phrase*

defer to

► *Related Words*

deference (noun) (dĕf′ər-əns) Out of *deference* to vegetarians, the hostess made some food that didn't contain meat or fish. (*Deference* means "polite respect for the needs and wishes of others.")

deferential (adjective) The student used a *deferential* tone when talking to his professor.

16. **epitome** (noun) ĭ-pĭt′ə-mē

a defining example; the best example; a symbol

An **epitome** of the American dream, Darnell, a poor boy from the inner city, started a business and became a millionaire.

Many consider Adolf Hitler to be the **epitome** of evil. (In this sentence, *epitome* is used in a negative sense.)

► *Common Phrase*

epitome of

▶ *Related Word*

epitomize (verb) Rising 630 feet into the air, the graceful Gateway Arch has come to *epitomize* the city of St. Louis.

NOTE: The final *e* of *epitome* is pronounced.

17. **hegemony** (noun) hĭ-jĕm′ə-′nē; hĕj′ə-mō′nē (plural: **hegemonies**)

dominance of one country, region, or group over others

In the 1700s, England established **hegemony** over colonies across the world.

18. **pacify** (verb) pas′ə-fī′

to calm; to establish peace

When the band didn't appear, the management issued refunds to **pacify** the angry crowd at the concert.

The mother **pacified** her crying infant by feeding him.

▶ *Related Word*

pacification (noun) We hope the temporary cease-fire leads to permanent *pacification*.

NOTES: (1) *Pacify* can also mean to establish peace by conquering, as in "The army *pacified* the rebels."
(2) The *y* of *pacify* changes to *i* in the third-person singular (He *pacifies*), past tense (I *pacified*), and noun form (*pacification*).

A Peaceful Ocean

In 1513, after crossing many miles of Central American jungle, the Spanish explorer Vasco Núñez de Balboa found himself facing a large body of calm water. He chose the Spanish word for *peaceful* as a name for his discovery. In English it is now called the *Pacific* Ocean.

19. **supplant** (verb) sə-plănt′

to replace

No other pet could **supplant** the girl's first puppy in her affections.

Computers have **supplanted** typewriters in modern offices.

20. **thrive** (verb) thrīv

to grow strong; to do well

Wild animals **thrive** in protected rain forests.

Children **thrive** on affection.

Political Left and Right

The next four words—*radical, liberal, conservative,* and *reactionary*—refer to political opinions that range from left to right.

Radical and liberal politicians are called *left-wing* because they sat on the left side (or wing) of the French National Assembly of 1789. *Radical* politicians want swift reforms that will benefit poor people, minorities, and others without political power. *Liberal* politicians favor the extension of rights and privileges through gradual reform. Between liberals and conservatives, in the middle, are *moderate* politicians.

Conservatives and *reactionaries* are called *right-wing* because they sat on the right side of the French National Assembly. *Conservative* politicians favor tradition and oppose change. They protect business interests, religion, and traditional family values. *Reactionary* politicians oppose change so strongly that they often want to return to what was done in the past. *Radical, liberal,* and *conservative* also have nonpolitical meanings.

21. **radical** (adjective, noun) răd′ĭ-kəl

    a. favoring great change; extreme (adjective)

    The **radical** activist chained himself to a tree until the city promised that the forest would not be cut down.

    In a **radical** change, the room's furniture went from old-fashioned to modern.

    Leshan's new business suit was a **radical** departure from the nose ring and T-shirt he usually wore.

    b. a person favoring great change (noun)

    Radicals seized control of the government and distributed all the farmland to poor workers.

    NOTE: The definition of *radical* depends on the political situation. In some countries, *radical* means favoring a return to strict religious obedience. In others, it means favoring an equal distribution of wealth. In all countries, however, *radicals* favor great change.

22. **liberal** (adjective, noun) lĭb′ər-əl; lĭb′rəl

    a. favoring gradual progress and reform (adjective)

    Many **liberal** politicians in the United States favor providing government health insurance for everyone.

    b. favoring liberty; tolerant (adjective)

    The company's **liberal** dress code allows us to wear jeans.

c. plentiful; generous in amount (adjective)

I helped myself to **liberal** amounts of shrimp at the buffet.

d. a person favoring gradual progress and reform (noun)

The **liberal** voted for increased legal aid for the poor.

▶ *Related Word*

liberalize (verb) When the government *liberalized* rules on immigration, people streamed into the country.

liberality (noun) Our generous holiday bonuses showed the boss's *liberality*. (*Liberality* means "generosity.")

23. **conservative** (adjective, noun) kən-sûr′və-tĭv

a. favoring traditional beliefs and actions; traditional (adjective)

The **conservative** Supreme Court justice argued that the display of the Ten Commandments is an appropriate tribute to U.S. religious and legal history.

Coming from a **conservative** background, George believed that mothers should stay home to raise children.

It's hard to have a **conservative** appearance if your face has tattoos.

b. cautious or moderate (adjective)

A **conservative** estimate was that there were 20,000 people at the rally; there may have been more.

c. a cautious, traditional person (noun)

The **conservative** investor felt that stocks were risky.

▶ *Related Word*

conserve (verb) People who live in the desert try to *conserve* water. (*Conserve* means "to save.")

24. **reactionary** (adjective, noun) rē-ăk′shə-nĕr′ē (plural: **reactionaries**)

a. opposing progress in an extreme way (adjective)

The **reactionary** educator wanted to use a textbook published in 1850 to teach reading.

b. a person opposing progress in an extreme way (noun)

Taliban **reactionaries** insisted that women walking on streets wear clothing that revealed only their eyes.

NOTE: *Reactionary* usually has a negative connotation.

Exercises

Part 2

■ *Matching Words and Definitions*

Match the word and definition. Use each choice only once.

1. conservative ______
2. thrive ______
3. defer ______
4. hegemony ______
5. chaos ______
6. supplant ______
7. reactionary ______
8. pacify ______
9. apprehend ______
10. epitome ______

a. favoring gradual progress and reform
b. dominance
c. to replace
d. to understand
e. favoring traditional beliefs
f. to delay
g. opposing progress in an extreme way
h. to calm
i. to grow strong
j. confusion
k. best example
l. favoring great change

■ *Words in Context*

Complete each sentence with the best word. Use each choice only once. You may have to capitalize some words.

a. apprehend	e. hegemony	i. radical
b. chaos	f. pacify	j. liberal
c. defer	g. supplant	k. conservative
d. epitome	h. thrive	l. reactionary

1. ______ erupted when someone in the crowd yelled "Fire!"

2. Marla's 150-pound weight loss caused a(n) ______ change in her appearance.

3. Two thousand years ago, the ______ of Rome extended over most of the known world.

4. The ______________ team owner wanted baseball to return to the rules of 1900.

5. Plants ______________ when they have rich soil and enough light.

6. To ______________ his angry wife, the man washed the dishes.

7. Our ______________ estimate is that we will save $200 ordering the refrigerator online, but we might actually save more.

8. The political event organizers recruited volunteers by promising ______________ supplies of pizza.

9. We fear that Internet news sites may soon ______________ printed newspapers.

10. Can we ______________ that conversation until the boss gets here?

■ *Using Related Words*

Complete each sentence with the correct form. Use each choice only once.

1. epitome, epitomize

   The figure of Uncle Sam, with his white spiky beard and red, white, and blue suit, has come to ______________ the United States. The symbol probably originated with Samuel Wilson, a meat inspector who put "U.S." on barrels that supplied the U.S. Army during the war of 1812. Soon, people started saying that *U.S.* stood for "Uncle Sam Wilson." The famous picture that has become the ______________ of U.S. army recruitment, however, was done by artist J.M. Flagg in 1916.

This poster of "Uncle Sam" has come to *epitomize* U.S. army recruitment.

James Montgomery Flagg/Swim Ink/CORBIS

2. liberal, liberalized, liberality

A peek into an 1896 book of etiquette (rules of behavior) shows how social customs have liberalized. According to *Youth's Educator for Home and Society*, by Anna Rice, gentlemen were supposed to wear suits or dinner jackets to dine. Dinners were known for their liberality, with each one consisting of six or seven courses. Romance was different too. Even a liberal-thinking person would not tolerate men and women making their own dates. If a gentleman wanted to get to know a lady, he could leave a calling card at her home. Then, the young woman's mother might choose to invite him to visit them.

3. defer, deference, deferring

   In 2009, Michelle Obama, wife of the U.S. president, accidently forgot to ____________ to protocol. Obama made headlines around the world by hugging Queen Elizabeth of Britain. Shocking! An important rule of ____________ is not to touch the queen—and Michelle broke it. But, perhaps ____________ to personal feeling and forgetting about protocol for a moment, Queen Elizabeth actually smiled, and seemed to hug her back.

4. apprehend, apprehended, apprehensive

   In many cities it is illegal to dine in a restaurant with your dog, and if you try, you may be ____________ by the police. But in New York, dogs can accompany owners to outdoor cafés. Although an occasional diner may become ____________ when a huge dog looks longingly at his hamburger, most dogs behave very well. In fact, at Fido's, a dog spa, canines are served biscuits while people eat. Fido's now hosts parties for owners who cannot ____________ how a dog's birthday can pass without a celebration.

■ *Reading the Headlines*

Here are some headlines that might appear in newspapers. Read each and answer the questions. (Remember that small words, such as *is, are, a,* and *the,* are often left out of headlines.)

RADICAL LEADER APPREHENDED BY POLICE

1. Did the leader want lots of change? ________
2. Was the leader let go? ________

REACTIONARY POLITICIANS FORCE LIBERALS TO DEFER BENEFIT

3. Did the people who got their way favor reform? ________
4. Will the benefit come soon? ________

CHAOS ERUPTS WHEN POLICE TRY TO PACIFY CROWD

5. Is there confusion? _______

6. Did the police try to calm the crowd? _______

HEGEMONY THRIVES

7. Are more people independent now? _______

8. Is the hegemony growing? _______

WOODS SUPPLANTS NICHOLSON AS EPITOME OF GOLF GREAT

9. Did Woods replace Nicholson? _______

10. Are these people an embarrassment to the sport of golf? _______

Chapter Exercises

■ *Practicing Strategies: Context Clues of Substitution*

In each sentence, one difficult word is italicized. Use context clues of substitution to make an intelligent guess about its meaning.

1. The *parsimonious* millionaire bought a cheap used car.

   Parsimonious means ________________________________.

2. After shopping for the party, the cabinets were *replete* with food.

   Replete means ________________________________.

3. The "smiley face" logo ☺ appears in so many places that it seems *ubiquitous*.

   Ubiquitous means ________________________________.

4. The rotten food gave off a *noisome* odor.

   Noisome means ________________________________.

5. The deep water was so *limpid* that we could see the fish swimming at the bottom.

   Limpid means ______________________________________.

6. Thanh was *livid* when she learned that her brother had taken her car without permission.

   Livid means ______________________________________.

7. Because we want to see justice done, we hope to *redress* these wrongs.

   Redress means ______________________________________.

8. With its motor turned off, the boat *undulated* in the waves.

   Undulated means ______________________________________.

The next two examples are famous quotes and may be challenging.

9. It is *folly* to punish your neighbor by fire when you live next door. (Publilius Syrus, Ancient Roman Author)

   Folly means ______________________________________.

10. The most difficult character in comedy is that of a fool, and he must be no *simpleton* who plays the part. (Miguel de Cervantes)

    Simpleton means ______________________________________.

■ *Practicing Strategies: New Uses of Familiar Words in Context*

Context clues can often help you determine the meaning of words used in unusual ways. Guess the meaning of the italicized word or phrase in each sentence.

1. After spending the day at the library, they *repaired* to the restaurant.

   Repaired means ______________________________________.

2. In her anger, she *stormed* out of the room.

   Stormed means ______________________________________.

3. The president was alone, *save for* a few friends.

   Save for means ______________________________.

4. Jose wanted to *air* his opinions by participating in a public debate.

   Air means ______________________________.

5. He couldn't vote because he was a few months *shy of* eighteen.

   Shy of means ______________________________.

■ *Companion Words*

Complete each sentence with the best word. You may use choices more than once. Choices: to, with, on, of, in, about, reached, own.

1. Of my ________ accord, I decided to go to college.
2. The child was apprehensive ________ sleeping in the dark.
3. Should a person intervene ________ a fight between two friends?
4. I show deference ________ senior citizens and give them my seat on the bus.
5. Puppies thrive ________ love and attention.
6. Should children always defer ________ the wishes of their parents?
7. Alexander the Great was the epitome ________ a great general.
8. The two fighting factions ________ an accord.

9–10. Sophia's actions were ________ accord ________ the rules of our club.

■ *Writing with Your Words*

To practice effective writing, complete each sentence with an interesting phrase that indicates the meaning of the italicized word.

1. One *ominous* trend in society is ______________________________

   ______________________________.

2. After the country established *hegemony* over its neighbors, ________

____.

3. To *pacify* the crying child, ________________________________

____.

4. The crowd became *chaotic* when ____________________________

____.

5. By a process of *attrition*, ________________________________

____.

6. When I gave my application to the *bureaucracy*, ______________

____.

7. It is important to be *diplomatic* when ______________________

____.

8. I *appeased* my friend by __________________________________

____.

9. I cannot *apprehend* how __________________________________

____.

10. I would favor a *radical* change in ________________________

____.

■ *Making Connections*

To connect new vocabulary to your life, write extended responses to these questions.

1. Do you consider yourself to be conservative or liberal on social issues? Defend your answer.
2. Who is an epitome of an entrepreneur? Why do you think so?
3. Describe a person whom you consider to be a renegade.

Passage

Sneakers: A Multibillion-Dollar Industry

Once used only for sports, sneakers are now everywhere. Urban teenagers, sports figures, and rap stars have changed the lowly athletic shoe to a world cultural symbol and luxury item.

Index Stock Imagery (RF)/PhotoLibrary

Sneakers have undergone dramatic changes over the years.

Back in 1964, Motown rocker Tommy Tucker's hit song "Put on Your High-heeled Sneakers" for "going out tonight" seemed ridiculous. But today high-heeled sneakers are a well-accepted dress-up shoe. In fact, nearly everybody wears some form of sneakers, whether they are at the gym or at a party. Within the business community, **(1)** there is general **accord** that sneaker sales are a powerful market force. People buy about $10 billion dollars worth every year, **(2)** although sales reports can be difficult to **corroborate**.

Sneakers were invented in 1899, when Humphrey O'Sullivan got a patent for a rubber heel that could be hardened through a new heating process. These new heels were more durable than leather ones. The first rubber-soled shoes were produced by Keds, a company that is still in business. They were called "sneakers" because the heels were so quiet that wearers could "sneak up" on other people.

After World War I, the German Dassler brothers started making the sneakers in their backyard. When Jesse Owens, the African-American runner, stunned the world by winning the 1936 Olympics, he was wearing Dasslers. The two Dassler brothers separated, and each became a successful **entrepreneur**. Rudolf started the Puma Company. Adolf became head of Adidas.

For years, sneakers were used only as sports shoes, but slowly, things began to change. **(3)** The 1950s were a **conservative** time with rigid fashions in clothes and shoes. **(4)** So people were thrilled when **renegade** James Dean appeared in the movie *Rebel without a Cause* wearing sneakers on the street. Suddenly, the shoe was in fashion, and by the 1970s, people were commonly using sneakers as everyday shoes.

Clever promotion turned sneakers into a multimillion-dollar business. In 1980 Philip H. Knight founded a company named Nike, after the Greek goddess of victory, and imported a shoe from Japan. He paid an Oregon artist $35 for the now-famous "swoosh" design. Then he hired Michael Jordan, the **epitome** of a great basketball player, to promote the shoe, and coined the phrase "Just do it." Overnight, Air Jordan™ shoes became a sensation.

Local neighborhood traditions also helped to popularize sneakers. Basketball was, and continues to be, an important sport in urban neighborhoods. And the new music of rap and hip-hop emerged from these very same neighborhoods. **(5)** Words and music were clever, **radical**, and at times violent. Neighborhood kids often imitated great basketball players by buying the shoes they wore. No longer just a shoe, sneakers became an important status symbol. **(6)** As rap and hip-hop **thrived**, their music and fashion spread to the rest of America. What the artists wore was hot! When a famous Paris fashion house started designing "Ghetto Fabulous" clothes, they became best-sellers. Soon everyone was listening to rap and hip-hop—and wearing sneakers.

Popular musicians celebrated sneakers in such songs as Nelly's "Air Force Ones." Run DMC's "My Adidas" thanked the company that introduced new sneakers named after their favorite Cadillacs: the Eldorado, Brougham, and Fleetwood. **(7)** Gradually, sneakers **supplanted** leather shoes as the most popular footwear in the United States.

Today, companies produce sneakers in every imaginable color, shape, and finish. Rappers have become designers. Figures like Kanye West and 50 Cent sell their ideas to such companies as Louis Vuitton and Reebok. Prices have skyrocketed as designers have issued "limited editions." The diamond-encrusted Solitare Kicks, for example, go for $50,000. Used sneakers that have been worn by famous athletes have become collector's items. One pair that belonged to basketball great Wilt Chamberlain sold for $55,000.

Teenaged "sneakerheads" collect pairs by the hundreds, spending countless hours in specialty stores. They beg their parents for ever more **liberal** allowances so they can buy the most desirable pairs. **(8)** Some **defer** wearing their new shoes, storing them in closets until they become rare and valuable.

But is all of this a good thing? **(9)** Some of the effects of sneaker popularity have been **catastrophic**. When "fly" sneakers became desirable, teens started stealing them from each other. There have even been incidents of people who were killed for their shoes. **(10)** School administrators have **intervened** by requiring dress codes limiting what students can wear. But in a truly **ominous** sign, the hit song "My Adidas" was sung by pallbearers, wearing matching white Adidas sneakers, for the funeral of Run DMC's murdered Jam Master Jay.

It has also been reported that several big sneaker companies employ workers in poor nations at low wages and under harsh working conditions. The Christian Aid society has worked to reach **accords** between producers and factories to ensure that workers are treated fairly.

Despite these problems, new sneakers continue to set fashion trends—and record-breaking prices. A style largely popularized by urban teenagers has become a multibillion-dollar business. Thanks to them, **conservative** middle-aged people throughout the United States wear sneakers to business lunches, to the opera, and to formal dinners. Some of us even "put on our high-heeled sneakers" when "we're going out tonight."

■ *Exercise*

Each numbered sentence corresponds to a sentence in the passage. Fill in the letter of the choice that makes the sentence mean the same thing as its corresponding sentence in the passage.

1. There is general _______ that sneakers sales are a powerful market force.
   a. reality b. suspicion c. knowledge d. agreement

2. Sales reports can be difficult to _______.
   a. determine b. get c. explain d. confirm

3. The 1950s were a time of _______.
   a. great change b. longing for the past c. traditional values
   d. gradual expansion of liberty

4. _______ James Dean thrilled people when he appeared in sneakers.
   a. Businessman b. Actor c. Change agent d. Rebel

5. Words and music were clever, _______, and at times violent.
   a. disastrous b. confused c. unchanged d. extreme

6. Rap and hip-hop _______ in urban neighborhoods.
   a. interfered b. were delayed c. grew d. sold

7. Gradually, sneakers _______ leather shoes as the most popular footwear.
   a. helped b. replaced c. grew with d. tied with

8. Some _______ wearing their new shoes.
   a. become examples b. are caught c. appear d. delay

9. Some of the effects of sneaker popularity have been ______.
   a. confirmed b. old fashioned c. terrible d. well understood

10. School administrators have ______.
    a. interfered b. agreed c. been replaced d. worn away

Discussion Questions

1. Which culture made sneakers fashionable? Explain your answer.
2. What are two ways this trend might have negative effects?
3. Do you think celebrities' involvement in promoting sneakers is good? Why or why not?

INSIGHT INTO IDIOMS

Communication

Idioms sometimes have unexpected origins. Today, we use the phrase *ham it up* to describe when an actor overacts, or exaggerates emotions so much that they are no longer believable. To *ham it up* can also mean to joke around. The idiom probably refers to the lard (or ham fat) that performers in the late 1800s rubbed on their faces to help them remove stage makeup. These actors were known for overacting and putting on comic shows, or *hamming it up.*

This chapter deals with Words in the News, and the idioms in this section are about communication.

a. *Ham it up* means to joke and overact.
b. *By word of mouth* means through personal contact.
c. When you *can't make heads or tails* of something, you can't understand it.
d. When you *bring something to light,* you expose or reveal it.
e. To *rub someone the wrong way* is to annoy someone.
f. To *raise eyebrows* is to shock someone.
g. When you *see eye to eye* with someone, you agree with that person.

Practice chapter words one more time by filling in the letter of the correct idiom into the blank before each sentence.

_____ 1. I want to reach an *accord* with him, and so I plan to tell him that I __________ with him, and share his views.

_____ 2. Your presentation is a *catastrophe*; we __________ of it.

_____ 3. The rumor spread __________, but I wanted to *corroborate* it by seeing it in a printed news source.

_____ 4. When the public realizes how high the cartel is setting-prices, it will __________ among consumers.

_____ 5. It is an *ominous* sign for a friendship if you __________.

Links to lists of English idioms and their meanings can be found at the Student Companion Website for this book: **www.cengage.com/devenglish/richek8e**.

CHAPTER 

Words for Feeling, Expression, and Action

Feelings, expressions, and actions are a constant part of life. We may feel *elated* by a happy event, *chagrined* by something embarrassing, or *harassed* by being overloaded at work and school. We may express ourselves *articulately* when we say something in an impressive way, or we may be *boisterous* at an exciting game. Finally, human actions include *emulating* a role model or *frenetically* trying to finish a task. This chapter increases your options for describing these activities.

Chapter Strategy: Context Clues of Definition

Chapter Words:

Part 1

bland	contemplate	enigma
boisterous	dynamic	ludicrous
clarify	elated	skeptical
concise	emulate	thwart

Part 2

appall	condemn	flamboyant
articulate	contend	frenetic
belligerent	elicit	harass
chagrin	emphatic	undermine

Visit the Student Companion Website at **www.cengage.com/devenglish/richek8e** to test your knowledge of these words before you study, hear each word pronounced, find additional practice exercises, and access more information on words and topics.

Did You Know?

How Do Cars Get Their Names?

The process of naming automobiles involves feeling, expression, and action. A car's name is important to its image. By choosing words that *express* speed, power, glamour, science, or even economy, manufacturers hope to give you positive *feelings* that translate into *action* when you make a purchase.

Long ago, Detroit auto pioneer Henry Leland named early cars after his heroes. *Cadillac* is taken from Antoine de La Mothe Cadillac, the French adventurer who founded Detroit in 1701. The *Lincoln* honored President Abraham Lincoln, the man Leland voted for in the 1860 election.

From that time on, car names have been selected with care. Car names have suggested nobility and royalty. Chrysler's *LeBaron* is a noble title; Dodge's *Coronet* is a crown; *El Dorado* was the name of a mythical South American ruler who was supposedly covered with gold.

The animal kingdom has also been a popular source of car names. Autos like *Jaguar, Stingray, Barracuda, Viper,* and *Cougar* suggest speed and power. Bird names usually bring to mind the freedom of flight. For example, five car models have been called *Eagle.* But the 1912 *Dodo* was a disaster. It was named for an extinct bird that could not fly. Like the real dodo, the car "never got off the ground."

More recently, numbers and abbreviations suggest advanced technology in names like the *Nissan 350Z* or the *Honda S2000*. Another trend is to use words that connote exciting travel. Names such as the Ford *Explorer, Expedition, Escape,* and *Excursion,* as well as the Toyota *LAND Cruiser* invoke the idea of a journey.

Today, with concerns for economy and the environment, many new cars are hybrids of electric and gasoline power. One name for a popular Toyota hybrid is taken from a language spoken two thousand years ago. The *Prius*, one of the first hybrids, means "to go before" in the ancient language of Latin. *Aveo,* produced by Chevrolet, means "I desire" in Latin. The name given to a recent Honda hybrid, the *Insight,* means a clear understanding of a complex situation.

Autos sold in Japan may carry English names that seem odd in the United States. There is the Honda *Life Dunk*, the Daihatsu *Naked*, and the Toyota *Deliboy*.

You studied two car-name words in Chapter 1: Honda's *Accord* and Dodge's *Intrepid*. In Chapter 8, you will study *bravado*, which was the source of Oldsmobile's *Bravada.* The *Bravada* and *Intrepid* are no longer being produced, but the *Accord* continues to be a bestseller.

Learning Strategy

Context Clues of Definition

The learning strategy in this chapter focuses on *context clues of definition*. Often, words that you don't know are actually defined for you as they are used in sentences. Context clues of definition appear frequently in textbooks. How do these clues work? Usually, a sentence provides a *synonym* (a word that means the same thing or nearly the same thing) for the unknown word. For example, look at the word *effervescent* as it is used in a sentence.

Coca-Cola® is an effervescent, or bubbly, beverage.

The word effervescent means . . . ? Bubbly. Thus, bubbly is a synonym for effervescent.

Such clues of definition are quite easy to use if you can recognize them. Here are some common types:

1. Words or phrases set off by commas, dashes, or parentheses:

   The man's altruistic, unselfish, motives led him to donate money to charity. (A defining phrase within commas is called an appositive.)
   The man's altruistic—*unselfish*—motives led him to donate money to charity.
   The man's altruistic (*unselfish*) motives led him to donate money to charity.

2. Direct definition:

   She thought his motives were altruistic, *which means unselfish*.
   She thought his motives were altruistic, *that is to say, unselfish*.

3. Indirect definition:

   He was an altruistic person *who often acted out of unselfish motives*.

4. The use of *or, and,* or *also*:

   The man's altruistic, *or unselfish*, motives pleased his family.
   (The use of commas with *or* is an extra hint signaling that a context clue of definition is being used.)
   The man's altruistic *and unselfish* motives pleased his family.
   (Sometimes, however, words joined by *and* and *or* do not mean the same thing. Examples are "The man was lazy and dishonest" and "People shouldn't be lazy or dishonest.")

5. Words signaling agreement, such as *therefore, likewise, in the same way, as well as,* and *similarly*:

   The man was altruistic; *therefore, he donated money to charity and did volunteer work with children*.

As you can see, the word *altruistic*, which you learned in Chapter 1, has been defined in each sentence. Many sentences use the synonym *unselfish*. Others provide a longer definition through examples, such as *donated money to charity and did volunteer work with children*.

Here are three more examples of context clues of definition. Can you make an intelligent guess about the meaning of each italicized word?

1. In 776 BCE, the first Olympic games were held on the plain of *Olympia*, a sacred place in Greece. (An appositive phrase is used.)
2. The margin of the leaf was *sinuated*, and indented curves ran along the edge. (An *and* clue is used.)
3. The ruler took *draconian* measures against the renegades, and their supporters were also punished severely. (*And* and *also* clues are used.)

Answers are on page 399.

Try using context clues to figure out the meanings of words you will learn in this chapter.

1. I was *chagrined*, really embarrassed, when my cousin revealed our family secrets on a national television talk show. (An appositive is used.)

   Chagrined means ______________________________.
2. I am *contemplating* buying a car, but I need to think more about it.

   Contemplating means ______________________________.
3. Now that you have shortened your speech, it is *concise* enough to fit into the time limit. (Indirect definition is used.)

   Concise means ______________________________.

Answers are on page 399.

Words to Learn

Part 1

1. **bland** (adjective) blănd

   a. calming; not spicy or sharp tasting

      The mayor's **bland** responses calmed the angry crowd.

      He hid his anger beneath a **bland** expression.

      Mashed potatoes are a truly **bland** food.

   b. dull

      Almita perked up her **bland** brown outfit with a colorful scarf and shiny silver jewelry.

▶ *Related Word*
blandness (noun) The *blandness* of the airport's gray walls was complemented by a colorful mural.

2. **boisterous** (adjective) boi′stər-əs

noisy; rowdy; rough

After their team won, the **boisterous** soccer fans spilled out into the street, cheering, dancing, and stopping traffic.

▶ *Related Word*
boisterousness (noun) Unfortunately, our upstairs neighbors were known for the *boisterousness* of their parties.

3. **clarify** (verb) klăr′ə-fī′

to make clear or sensible

The chart in the book **clarifies** the points the professor made in her lecture.

▶ *Related Words*
clarification (noun) We asked our accountant for *clarification* of the instructions on our tax form.
clarity (noun) The *clarity* of the night sky allows us to see hundreds of stars.

NOTE: The *y* of clarify changes to an *i* when forming the third-person singular (He *clarifies*), the past tense (You *clarified*), and the noun (*clarification*).

4. **concise** (adjective) kən-sīs′

short; clear but using few words

Most students prefer a **concise** definition of a word to a lengthy one.

A Concise *Speech That Became Famous*

Shorter can be better! Two speakers were chosen to pay tribute to the brave soldiers who were killed in the 1863 American Civil War battle of Gettysburg. Edward Everett, the principal speaker, gave a long and dramatic address that lasted over two hours. Then President Abraham Lincoln stood up and spoke 270 words. Lincoln's *concise* speech took two minutes to deliver. Which is remembered today? Everett's words have been forgotten. Lincoln's Gettysburg Address is now considered one of the masterpieces of the English language.

5. **contemplate** (verb) kŏn′təm-plāt′

to think about carefully and for a long time

Kate **contemplated** whether Rich was the right man for her.

Mario **contemplated** renting a more expensive apartment that was closer to the bus route.

► *Related Word*

contemplation (noun) Long walks alone provide time for *contemplation*.

6. **dynamic** (adjective) dī-năm′ĭk

a. energetic; forceful

The **dynamic** back-up dancers drew attention away from the lead singer.

The **dynamic** new pastor doubled church membership and raised funds for a new building.

b. fast moving; fast changing

Investors have lost fortunes within minutes on **dynamic** stock exchanges.

► *Related Words*

dynamics (noun) Sports psychologists often study team *dynamics*. Experts studied the *dynamics* of the hurricane. (*Dynamics* means "social or physical forces.")

dynamo (noun) The CEO was a *dynamo* who ran his company, wrote books, and maintained a demanding speaking schedule.

7. **elated** (adjective) ĭ-lā′tĭd

thrilled; very happy

Natasha was **elated** when she was promoted to manager.

8. **emulate** (verb) ĕm′yə-lāt′

to try to equal or excel through imitating; to imitate

Many teenagers try to **emulate** star athletes or singers.

Many companies will try to **emulate** the success of the on-line game, Farmville.

► *Related Word*

emulation (noun) The successful economy of Chile makes its policies worthy of *emulation*.

Emulating the Gecko

Remember how painful it can be to remove a sticky adhesive bandage? The gecko, a type of lizard, has an adhesive force in its toes that, in theory, would enable just one toe to support a 250-pound person! Yet, the gecko can let go of something instantly, without force or pain. In developing better adhesives, scientists are *emulating* the gecko, which uses a weak magnetic force called Van Der Waals. A gecko tape is now available that attaches and releases without leaving a sticky mess. Boots using this force may even enable robots in outer space, where other adhesives don't work, to climb up vertical walls.

9. **enigma** (noun) ĭ-nĭg′mə

   something unexplainable or puzzling

   The cause of the growing number of people with allergies remains an **enigma** to medical professionals.

   ▶ *Related Word*

   enigmatic (adjective) The *enigmatic* expression in the famous portrait *Mona Lisa* makes us wonder what she is thinking and feeling.

Gianni Dagli Orti/CORBIS

Mona Lisa's smile is *enigmatic*. Is she sad, happy, kind, cruel?

10. **ludicrous** (adjective) lo͞oʹdĭ-krəs

absurd, ridiculous, or outrageous

The fat, middle-aged singer looked **ludicrous** playing a young girl in the opera.

It is **ludicrous** to demand full price for used items sold at a flea market.

Ludicrous Ludacris

The popular hip-hop star Ludacris takes his name from the word *ludicrous*. As the name suggests, he exposes the ridiculous side of rap. His crazy hairdos and the clearly visible logos and slogans on his clothes help him to mock the "Ghetto Fabulous" lifestyle. His videos and songs such as "Rollout" and "Act a Fool" exaggerate the style of other rappers.

11. **skeptical** (adjective) skĕpʹtĭ-kəl

doubting; tending to disbelieve

We were **skeptical** of an ad claiming that the cleaner could remove any possible stain.

▶ *Common Phrases*
skeptical of; skeptical about

▶ *Related Words*
skeptic (noun) The *skeptic* doubted the effectiveness of the herbal medicine—until it cured her flu.
skepticism (noun) A scientist should show *skepticism* and demand proof of every theory.

12. **thwart** (verb) thwôrt

to prevent from happening

The kidnapping was **thwarted** by an alert security officer.

Lack of funds can **thwart** a student's wish to finish college.

Exercises

Part 1

■ *Definitions*

Match the word and definition. Use each choice only once.

1. An enigma is a(n) ______.
2. Something bland is ______.
3. To thwart is to ______.
4. To be elated is to be ______.
5. Something concise is ______.
6. Something ludicrous is ______.
7. To be boisterous is to be ______.
8. When we contemplate, we ______.
9. To emulate is to ______.
10. When we clarify, we ______.

a. think
b. puzzle
c. thrilled; very happy
d. make clear
e. imitate
f. energetic
g. noisy
h. ridiculous
i. doubtful
j. not spicy
k. short; to the point
l. prevent from happening

■ *Words in Context*

Fill each sentence with the best word. Use each choice only once.

a. bland	e. contemplate	i. enigma
b. boisterous	f. dynamic	j. ludicrous
c. clarify	g. elated	k. skeptical
d. concise	h. emulate	l. thwart

1. The ______________ woman held two jobs and volunteered, while raising three children.

2. The man was ______________ when the woman of his dreams said yes to his marriage proposal.

3. We should all ______________ the politeness of that wonderful waiter.

4. I'm afraid that rain will ______________ our plans for the softball game.

5. The new TV sitcom was so ______________ that I fell asleep watching it.

6. Before I make an important decision, I always ______________ for a few weeks.

7. The babysitter tried hard to keep the ______________ children under control, but they continued to shout and run around.

8. Your essay can only be a half-page long, so it will have to be ____________________.

9. The child believed the ____________________ story that the moon was made of green cheese.

10. I am ____________________ that anyone could carry a thousand-pound weight.

■ *Using Related Words*

Complete each sentence with the correct form. Use each choice only once.

1. dynamo, dynamics, dynamic

   How did VELCRO®, that fabric that has replaced many shoelaces and buttons, actually originate? George Mestral was an inventing ____________________ who received his first patent at the age of twelve. As an adult, he became interested in the annoying burrs that stuck to his dog's fur. How could burrs attach themselves with such ____________________ power? A microscope revealed the ____________________. The burrs were actually tiny hooks that fit into the very small loops in clothes. Using this hook and loop idea, Mestral invented VELCRO®, a material popular with anyone who dislikes the bother of tying a shoelace.

2. clarify, clarification

   In 2000, the U.S. presidential election was decided in the state of Florida, where votes were cast by punching holes in cards. Many cards were not punched through, resulting in "chads," or punched-out pieces that clung to the ballots. These could not be read accurately, so volunteers studied each card to try to determine what the voter had intended. Finally, the courts were asked to ____________________ whether or not a "hanging chad" should count as a vote. The ____________________ of this issue, which involved many court cases, resulted in the election of George W. Bush—and in better voting machines.

3. skeptics, skeptical, skepticism

   Would you believe that, pound for pound, ash from coal is more radioactive than nuclear waste? Do you react with

__________________ when you hear that looking at the sun actually makes some people sneeze uncontrollably? Are you __________________ of the fact that Earth actually has seven north poles? While __________________ may doubt the truth of these statements, articles claiming each one is true each one have been published by *The Scientific American*, a well respected journal.

4. emulate, emulation

   Eating disorders may arise when girls seek to __________________ extremely thin models. Since body types differ, a weight that is healthy for one girl may be too low for another. The __________________ of a skinny star or model can actually result in death from starvation. In the United States, an estimated ten million females and one million males suffer from eating disorders.

5. enigma, enigmatic

   The rare condition of "face blindness," or prosopagnosia, makes a person unable to recognize other people. Even when such a person meets family and old friends, their identity remains an __________________. Although some cases of this disorder are caused by injury, the cause of others remains __________________.

■ *Reading the Headlines*

Here are some headlines that might appear in newspapers. Read each and answer the questions. (Remember that small words such as *is*, *are*, *a*, and *the* are often left out of headlines.)

PUBLIC IS SKEPTICAL OF CANDIDATE'S LUDICROUS CLAIM

1. Does the public believe the claim? ________
2. Is the claim ridiculous? ________

BLAND MEETING BECOMES BOISTEROUS AFTER ELATED MAYOR ANNOUNCES THAT CITY WILL HOST OLYMPICS

3. Did the meeting start out calm? ________
4. Did the meeting end up calm? ________
5. Is the mayor happy? ________

MANY TEENS TRY TO EMULATE DYNAMIC RAP STAR

6. Do the teens want to be like the star? _________

7. Is the star energetic? _________

REQUESTS FOR CLARIFICATION THWART PRESIDENT'S ATTEMPT TO GIVE A CONCISE STATEMENT

8. Was the president clear? _________

9. Did the president want to make the statement short? _________

10. Was the president able to make the statement short? _________

Words to Learn

Part 2

13. **appall** (verb) ə-pôl′

horrify; fill with horror, dismay, or shock

The public was **appalled** by reports that fourteen children were living in a filthy, roach-infested apartment.

You will **appall** your date if you lick your fingers during dinner.

► *Related Word*

appalling (adjective) The food and service at the restaurant were so *appalling* that Dan demanded a refund.

► *Common Phrases*

appalled by

14. **articulate** (adjective) är-tĭk′yə-lĭt; (verb) är-tĭk′-yə-lāt′

a. skilled in using language; well expressed (adjective) är-tĭk′yə-lĭt

An **articulate** person often has a well-developed vocabulary.

Our union representative is an **articulate** spokesperson for workers' rights.

b. to express clearly and distinctly (verb) är-tĭk′-yə-lāt′

Feelings of love can be hard to **articulate**.

► *Related Word*

articulation (noun) To improve his *articulation*, the ancient Greek Demosthenes practiced speaking with marbles in his mouth.

15. **belligerent** (adjective, noun) bə-lĭj′ər-ənt

a. hostile; engaged in warfare (adjective)

Belligerent rebels attacked the troops.

The minor disagreement between fathers of the soccer players turned into a **belligerent** shouting match.

b. a hostile or aggressive person (noun)

The two **belligerents** drew their guns.

▶ *Related Word*
belligerence (noun) Because of the customer's *belligerence*, security guards escorted her out of the store.

Words of War

Belligerent comes from the Latin words *bellum*, "war," and *gerere*, "to carry on." *Bellum* is also the root of the word *rebellion*, a war waged against a ruling power, and of the word *rebel*, a person who defies authority. Two other words that come from bellum are *bellicose* (warlike) and *antebellum*, the period in the United States before the Civil War. (*Ante-* means "before.")

16. chagrin (noun) shə-grĭn′

embarrassment or unhappiness caused by failure; a feeling of shame

Much to my **chagrin,** the cookies I baked and served to my mother-in-law were burned on the bottom.

The world-famous skater was filled with **chagrin** when he failed to qualify for the local team.

▶ *Common Phrases*
filled with chagrin

NOTE: Chagrin is used with a personal pronoun, as in "to my chagrin . . . ," "to your chagrin . . ." "to her/his chagrin . . ." "to their chagrin . . ."

17. **condemn** (verb) kən-dĕm′

a. to criticize; to express strong disapproval of

The Senate **condemned** the racist comments of one of its members.

b. to give a punishment; to find guilty; to express disapproval

The judge **condemned** the criminal to life in prison.

Slaves were **condemned** to a harsh, joyless life.

The city inspectors **condemned** the decayed old building. (In this case, *condemn* means "decide to destroy.")

▶ *Common Phrase*
condemn to

▶ *Related Word*
condemnation (noun) (kŏn′dĕm-nā′shən) The university issued a *condemnation* of students who turned in essays they had bought online.

18. **contend** (verb) kən-tĕnd′

a. to compete; to struggle against something

Over five hundred colleges **contended** in the Recyclemania competition.

Firefighters have to **contend** with dangerous smoke and fumes.

b. to put forth a point of view; argue

Some scientists **contend** that Mars once had enough water to support life.

NOTE: The phrase *contend with* means "to cope with."

▶ *Related Words*
contender (noun) How many *contenders* are in the race?

contention (noun) It was the CIA director's *contention* that listening in on private conversations without a search warrant was necessary to national security. (*Contention* means "point of view.")

contentious (adjective) My *contentious* sister will argue just for the fun of it. (*Contentious* means "argumentative.")

Contenders and Their Sports

Can you match these **contenders** with their sports?

1. Ronaldinho	a. swimming
2. Walter Ray "Deadeye" Williams Jr.	b. soccer (football)
3. Nastia Liukin	c. bowling
4. Michael Phelps	d. baseball
5. Albert Pujols	e. wrestling
6. The Undertaker	f. gymnastics

Answers are on page 399.

19. **elicit** (verb) ĭ-lĭs′ĭt

to draw forth (a response)

The tragic movie **elicited** tears from the audience.

The lawyer was famous for his ability to **elicit** information from closed-mouth witnesses.

20. **emphatic** (adjective) ĕm-făt′ĭk

strong; definite

"Absolutely not!" was Juliet's **emphatic** reply when her boyfriend asked to use her toothbrush.

The Los Angeles Lakers scored an **emphatic** victory over the Chicago Bulls.

► *Related Words*

emphasis (noun) (Plural form: **emphases**) In Spanish, *emphasis* within a word is usually on the next-to-last syllable.

emphasize (verb) Using an exclamation point in writing allows us to *emphasize* text.

Courtesy author

"Don't you dare!" was mom's *emphatic* reply when her son asked if he could lend the family car to a friend.

21. **flamboyant** (adjective) flăm-boi′ənt

showy, flashy, dramatic

The **flamboyant** movie star arrived in a red, strapless gown with five-carat diamonds hanging from her ears.

The TV chef's **flamboyant** style included throwing knives into the air and shouting at the audience.

► *Related Word*

flamboyance (noun) The *flamboyance* of wrestlers is shown in their props, wild costumes, and boasting.

Flamboyant Flames

Like a *flamboyant* person, a flame is eye-catching. In fact, *flamboyant* comes from the same root as the word *flame*. Other words containing this root are *flammable* and *inflammable* (both meaning "catching on fire easily"), and that flame-colored bird, the *flamingo*.

22. **frenetic** (adjective) frə-nĕt′ĭk

wildly active or excited; frantic

I had to work at a **frenetic** pace to get the house clean before my parents arrived.

Amelia's **frenetic** waving and gesturing finally caught our attention.

23. **harass** (verb) hə-răs′; hăr′əs

to annoy or attack repeatedly

The young puppies **harassed** the old dog by continually trying to bite him.

► *Related Words*

harassed (adjective) With a full-time job and three children, Milagros constantly felt *harassed*. (Here *harassed* means "bothered and under stress.")

Many wrestlers are *flamboyant*.

Courtesy author

harassment (noun) When Mario wore the opposing team's colors on game day, he became the target of **harassment.**

harasser (noun) The **harasser** fled when an onlooker called the police.

NOTE: *Harass* comes from the Old French *Hare!*—a command telling a hunting dog to "Get it!"

24. **undermine** (verb) un′dər-min′

to weaken or injure slowly

Gossip, even if it is not true, can **undermine** someone's reputation.

Eating junk food and not exercising **undermined** Agustin's health.

He **undermined** his business by being rude to customers.

Exercises

Part 2

■ *Definitions*

Match the word and definition. Use each choice only once.

1. To condemn is to _______.
2. To contend is to _______.
3. Flamboyant means _______.
4. To undermine is to _______.
5. A belligerent person is _______.
6. Something emphatic is _______.
7. A frenetic person is _______.
8. When we elicit a response, we _______.
9. To feel chagrin is to feel _______.
10. Articulate people are _______.

a. express disapproval
b. skilled in using language
c. hostile
d. fill with shock
e. showy
f. wildly excited
g. compete
h. annoy repeatedly
i. strong or definite
j. draw it out
k. weaken
l. embarrassed

■ *Words in Context*

Complete each sentence with the best word. Use each choice only once.

a. appall	e. condemn	i. flamboyant
b. articulate	f. contend	j. frenetic
c. belligerent	g. elicit	k. harass
d. chagrin	h. emphatic	l. undermine

1. The ____________________ child often hit others.

2. To my ____________________, I fell on the stage while performing in the play.

3. The floor of the stock exchange was ____________________ with people shouting, gesturing, and running back and forth.

4. Try not to ______________________ your boss's authority by questioning his policies in front of customers.

5. A boring lecture might ______________________ yawns from students.

6. To make his statement more ______________________, he spoke in a louder voice.

7. I tried to ______________________ my feelings, but I was too shocked to say anything.

8. Those pictures of abused prisoners will ______________________ the public.

9. Photographers sometimes ______________________ celebrities by following them everywhere to get pictures of their private lives.

10. The engineers are expected to ______________________ the unsafe bridge.

■ *Using Related Words*

Complete each sentence with the correct form. Use each choice only once.

1. contended, contender, contention, contentious

The great African-American athlete Jesse Owens ______________________ in the Olympic Games of 1936. These games, held in Germany, were presided over by Nazi leader Adolf Hitler. It was Hitler's racist ______________________ that the "Aryan" race was superior to all others and that no black ______________________ could win. However, Owens earned four gold medals in running events. The ______________________ Nazi leader refused to attend the award ceremonies. Owens, who died in 1978, remains a symbol of black athletes' struggle for equality.

2. appalled, appalling

In a famous play entitled *Pygmalion*, George Bernard Shaw presents a language expert who is ______________________ by the speech of a working-class woman. She and the professor work hard to improve her ____________________ articulation. After several months of work, she convinces others that she is a great lady! This play, remade as the musical *My Fair Lady*, shows how important speech is to social position.

3. condemned, condemnations

In the 1930s, the Great Depression in the United States

____________________ many people to lives of poverty. In some cities, three-quarters of workers were unemployed. Some analysts felt

that democracy had failed, and even issued ____________________ of our form of government. But President Franklin Delano Roosevelt restored faith in government "by the people" through his New Deal policies. One New Deal program, the Works Projects Administration (WPA), funded artists to do creative work. Today, their murals can be found in public buildings throughout the United States. Have you ever seen one?

4. harassing, harassment

Road rage has become a widespread problem. Some drivers

respond to the slightest frustration by ____________________ the

drivers in front of them. When mild, this ____________________ takes the form of honking and tailgating. But things can get worse. At times, drivers and passengers have been rammed by the out-of-control drivers behind them! So when you see an angry driver, get out of the way!

5. flamboyant, flamboyance, flamboyantly

Why do rap, hip-hop, and rock stars dress so ____________________?

Well, expensive or unusual clothes help us to remember them. Their

____________________ also helps convince the public that they are successful: It takes a lot of money to afford heavy gold chains and

____________________ diamonds. Perhaps when they are relaxing out of sight of a camera, they wear jeans and t-shirts, just like the rest of us!

■ *Find the Example*

Choose the example that best describes the action or situation.

1. A belligerent, emphatic response _______
   a. You're the best! b. Are you picking a fight? c. I hate you!

2. An appalling condemnation _______
   a. giving a criminal a second chance b. locking up an innocent person c. giving a criminal jail time

3. Articulation of chagrin _______
   a. "I'm so ashamed!" b. hiding one's face c. "I'll do it again, if you like!"

4. A harassed contender _______
   a. racer being nagged by mother b. champion receiving an honor c. speaker being booed by crowd

5. How to undermine flamboyance in clothes _______
   a. forbid people to wear black and grey b. require uniforms c. have a Halloween party

Chapter Exercises

■ *Practicing Strategies: Context Clues of Substitution*

In each sentence, one difficult word is italicized. Use context clues of definition to make an intelligent guess about its meaning in this sentence.

1. Selling our house directly to the buyer *precluded* many of our costs, as well as eliminating the need for a real estate agent.

   Precluded means ____.

2. We could hear his *stentorian* voice from one hundred feet away.

   Stentorian means ____.

3. Many religious organizations provide assistance to the needy and *succor* to the seriously ill.

   Succor means ____.

4. President Calvin Coolidge was a *taciturn* person who seldom talked.

   Taciturn means ______________________________.

5. Wandering through the rain forest of Costa Rica, we looked for parrots, doves, woodpeckers, and *Scrub Euphonia.*

   Scrub Euphonia means ______________________________.

Items 6–10 are taken from newspaper sources.

6. If possible, use a variety of fresh mushrooms such as shiitake, *crimini,* and chanterelle.

   A crimini means ______________________________.

7. *Schadenfreude*—pleasure in others' misfortunes—has become the new barbarity on an island called Blog.

   Schadenfreude means ______________________________.

8. People with *dyslexia,* a learning disability, have difficulties with accurate and fluent word recognition and have poor spelling and decoding abilities.

   Dyslexia means ______________________________

   ______________________________.

9. A yeast known as *candida albicans* normally hangs out in the gut, but sometimes it grows wild.

   Candida albicans means ______________________________.

10. A flight cut short: One woman's *truncated* journey represents that of thousands who are regularly caught and sent home.

    Truncated means ______________________________.

■ *Practicing Strategies: Using the Dictionary*

The following entry is taken from a print source. Read it and answer the questions.

> **hawk**[1] (hôk) *n.* **1.** Any of various birds of prey of the order Falconiformes, esp. of the genera *Accipiter* and *Buteo,* having a short hooked bill and strong claws for seizing. **2.** Any of various similar birds of prey. **3.** A person who preys on others; a shark. **4a.** One who demonstrates an aggressive or combative attitude. **b.** A person who favors military action to carry out foreign policy. ❖ *intr. v.* **hawked, hawk•ing, hawks 1.** To hunt with trained hawks. **2.** To swoop and strike in the manner of a hawk. [ME *hauk* < OE *hafoc.*> See **kap-** in App.] — **hawk′ish adj.**

1. In which language did *hawk* originate? ____________________

2. What adjective is related to *hawk*? ____________________

3. The vowel in *hawk* is pronounced like the vowel in which common words? ____________________

4. Give the part of speech and definition number that best fits the use of *hawk* in this sentence: "The *hawk* wanted to invade the neighboring country immediately." ____________________

5. Give the part of speech and definition number that best fits this sentence: "The plane suddenly *hawked* from the sky and fired on the enemy." ____________________

■ *Companion Words*

Complete each sentence with the best word or words. You may use answer choices more than once, and you may have to capitalize some answers. Choices: to, of, by, for, filled with

1. He undermined his happiness __________ working too hard.
2. Many great artists were condemned __________ lives of poverty.
3. The forward's attempts to score were thwarted __________ an alert guard.

4–5. The spies asked the head of intelligence ________ clarification ________ their mission.

6. The professor was appalled ________ the spelling errors in the assignment.

7. Alarmed by the boisterousness ________ the crowd, we fled the scene.

8. I was skeptical ________ our candidate's ability to win the election.

9. ________ my chagrin, my date kissed me passionately in front of my mother.

10. The twelve-year-old was ________ chagrin when she was caught shoplifting.

■ *Writing with Your Words*

To practice effective writing, complete each sentence with an interesting phrase that indicates the meaning of the italicized word.

1. My favorite *emphatic* expression is ______________________________
____.

2. The man was *frenetic* because ______________________________
____.

3. The *bland* meal consisted of ______________________________
____.

4. The teenager tried to *emulate* the hip-hop artist by ______________
____.

5. The bully *harassed* people by ______________________________
____.

6. The child had the *ludicrous* idea that ______________________________

____.

7. You will *elicit* my anger if ______________________________

____.

8. My life's efforts will be *thwarted* if ______________________________

____.

9. To my *chagrin,* ______________________________

____.

10. It is an *enigma* to me how ______________________________

____.

■ *Making Connections*

To connect new vocabulary to your life, respond to these assignments.

1. Which two life decisions do you feel require the most *contemplation*? Defend your choices.
2. Do you consider yourself *articulate*? Why or why not?
3. Describe a time when you, or someone you know, felt *chagrined*.

Passage

Jackie Robinson, Baseball Hero

As incredible as it may seem today, at one time African Americans were forbidden to play baseball in the major leagues. The ban was first broken by Jackie Robinson, a star athlete from the "Negro Leagues" who went on to enrich major league baseball with his exciting and competitive style. This is Robinson's story, but as you read it, you should also think of Satchel Paige, "Smokey" Joe Williams, Rube and Willie Foster, Josh Gibson, Cool Papa Bell, "Bullet" Joe Rogan, and other African American greats who were long denied the chance to play major league baseball.

Almost sixty years ago, a quiet man made baseball history. In 1947 Jackie Robinson became the first African American to play major league

Jackie Robinson "broke the color line" in major league baseball.

baseball in the twentieth century. **(1)** He bravely faced **appalling** persecution and **(2)** helped **undermine** racial prejudice in the United States. Jackie Robinson "broke the color line." For years before Robinson's brave act, blacks could not play in the majors. Although they had their own leagues, the games were not well publicized. So, although many black players were as good as, or better than, white major league players, blacks were **condemned** to receive almost no national attention.

But in 1947, the Dodgers' management made a historic decision to sign an African-American player—Jackie Robinson. **(3)** The team issued a purposely **bland** announcement: "The Brooklyn Dodgers today purchased the contract of Jackie Roosevelt Robinson from the Montreal Royals." The baseball world reacted strongly. Some applauded the move to end discrimination. **(4) Skeptics**, though, predicted disaster. How could an African American succeed in white baseball? **(5)** Some critics **contended** that Robinson would never be able to live peacefully with white teammates or tolerate the insults of fans. Still others doubted Robinson's ability as a baseball player.

All the doubters were wrong.

The Dodgers' general manager, **(6)** Branch Rickey, had **contemplated** the problems before he acted. Rickey ensured Robinson's success in the major leagues by working with him on how to respond to **harassment**. "Hey," he would say, impersonating a hotel clerk. "You can't eat here." He imitated a prejudiced white ballplayer and charged into Robinson, saying, "Next time get out of my way, you bastard." Robinson was puzzled. Rickey explained, "I'm looking for a ballplayer with guts enough not to fight back.

Those **boisterous** crowds will insult you, **harass** you, do anything to make you start a fight. And if you fight back, they'll say, 'Blacks don't belong in baseball.' "

Of all the struggles Robinson was to have, the hardest one would be to keep calm in the face of insults. **(7)** Nobody would be able to **elicit** an outburst from Jackie Robinson. This fiercely proud man, who had refused to sit in the back of an army bus, found the ultimate courage—the courage to be quiet.

In the 1947 season, Robinson was to face trouble that would have defeated a lesser man. Roars of "Go home!" and "Kill him!" were heard from **belligerent** crowd members. Robinson was hit in the head by more "beanballing" pitchers than any other player in the major leagues. Sometimes it became too much for his friends. Robinson's teammate Pee Wee Reese once challenged some **harassers** by shouting at them to take on somebody who could fight back. But Robinson never **articulated** his grievances publicly.

Instead, Robinson gained revenge in another way. To the amazement of his critics, he succeeded brilliantly in the major leagues. **(8)** Although not a **flamboyant** man, it was apparent that he was a marvelous ballplayer. In his first year in the majors, he achieved a batting average of .297, the team high, and was named Rookie of the Year. In his ten years in baseball, his superior playing helped his team win the pennant six times. **(9)** He must have been **elated** when he was elected the first black member of the Baseball Hall of Fame.

Robinson is perhaps best remembered for his daring base stealing. Sleepy pitchers had to beware, for Robinson could steal a base at a moment's notice. As he ran from base to base, he confused infielders into making mistakes and losing control of the ball. **(10)** A fellow player gave a **concise** description of Robinson as "a hard out." He stole home base eleven times! Although many have tried to **emulate** him, this feat has never been equaled.

In his later years Robinson became ill with diabetes. Although he left baseball, he never stopped fighting for a just society. He championed civil rights and made investments to help build good housing in slums.

Jackie Robinson's name lives on in history. We all owe a debt to a brave man who bore the burdens of a prejudiced society. No one could **thwart** the ambitions of this great baseball player and civil rights pioneer.

■ *Exercises*

Each numbered sentence corresponds to a sentence in the passage. Fill in the letter of the choice that makes the sentence mean the same thing as its corresponding sentence in the passage.

1. He bravely faced ______ persecution.
   a. shocking b. public c. loud d. ridiculous

2. He helped to _______ racial prejudice in the United States.
   a. bring forth b. weaken c. demonstrate d. publicize

3. The team issued a purposely _______ announcement.
   a. calm b. thoughtful c. short d. exciting

4. _______ predicted disaster.
   a. Doubters b. Critics c. Competitors d. Speakers

5. Some critics _______ that Robinson would never live peacefully with white teammates.
   a. wrote b. hoped c. argued d. thought

6. Branch Rickey had _______ the problems.
   a. asked for b. answered questions about c. solved d. thought about

7. Nobody would be able to _______ an outburst from Jackie Robinson.
   a. bring forth b. stop c. imitate d. be surprised by

8. Robinson was not a _______ man.
   a. loud b. short c. shocked d. showy

9. He must have been _______ when he was elected to the Baseball Hall of Fame.
   a. doubtful b. honored c. shocked d. thrilled

10. A fellow player gave a(n) _______ description of Robinson as a "hard out."
   a. short b. energetic c. calming d. doubting

■ *Discussion Questions*

1. Did Robinson have the support of his team? Defend your answer.
2. Why was Robinson's refusal to lose his temper important?
3. In 1955 Rosa Parks refused to obey a law that required blacks to sit in the back of buses. How is Robinson's struggle similar to her act, and how is it different?

Jackie Robinson began his baseball career in the "Negro Leagues." For more information on these baseball teams, see links at the website **www.cengage.com/devenglish/richek8e**.

INSIGHT INTO IDIOMS

Feelings and Actions

If you try to look up an idiom in the dictionary but cannot find it, *don't sweat it.* (Don't worry.) Many print dictionaries do not define idioms. You will find, however, that it's easy to find the meanings of idioms on the Internet. The many online dictionaries of idioms include www.usingenglish.com/reference/idioms/. You can go to this site and just type in an idiom, such as "bury the hatchet" to get the definition. However, most websites don't give the source of idioms. *Bury the hatchet* has an origin rooted in history. Centuries ago, warring Native American tribes buried hatchets in the ground to symbolize that they had made peace.

This chapter's idioms are about expression, feelings, and actions.

a. *Don't sweat it* means don't worry.

b. To *bury the hatchet* means to make peace.

c. If something *can't hold a candle to* something else, it is inferior to that other thing.

d. To *hit the books* means to study.

e. To *drive someone up the wall* means to bother or annoy them greatly.

f. People who are *at loose ends* don't have a direction, and don't know what they will do.

g. To *hit the nail on the head* means to get something exactly right.

Practice chapter words one more time by filling in the letter of the correct idiom into the blank before each sentence.

_____ 1. It's hard to be around him because his *frenetic* activity can _________.

_____ 2. At the meeting, the two *belligerents* were able to _________; they actually became friends!

_____ 3. I'll admit that I'm _________ and can't even *contemplate* what life will be like after graduation.

_____ 4.–5. You say "_________, but I'm afraid that if I don't _________, I'll get an *appalling* grade on the exam."

Links to lists of English idioms and their meanings can be found at the Student Companion Website for this book: **www.cengage.com/devenglish/richek8e**.

CHAPTER 4

Other Useful English Words

This chapter presents a variety of words that college students have identified as important and useful. The author's classes collected them from textbooks, newspapers, magazines, websites, and the media. You, too, should find them valuable additions to your vocabulary.

Chapter Strategy: Context Clues of Opposition

Chapter Words:

Part 1

accolade	cryptic	mandatory
augment	fabricate	meticulous
chivalrous	indulge	obsolete
complacent	jeopardize	zealous

Part 2

adulation	discretion	pinnacle
chronological	euphemism	procrastinate
copious	mammoth	successive
cultivate	mitigating	withstand

Visit the Student Companion Website at **www.cengage.com/devenglish/richek8e** to test your knowledge of these words before you study, hear each word pronounced, find additional practice exercises, and access more information on words and topics.

Did You Know?

How Does English Get New Words?

Which language has the most words? Which one is most used for international communication? The answer to both questions is English!

Mandarin Chinese is the most widely spoken language in the world, but English is number two. Perhaps more important, English is the world's most widely used international language. Most international scientific journals are published in English. Foreign companies train many employees in English. In fact, it is estimated that up to a billion people worldwide are currently learning the language you are reading.

English influences other languages too. *Guddobai* and *hottodoggu* are now used in Japanese for "goodbye" and "hot dog." The position of English has caused some resentment. Wanting to keep their language "pure," the French even passed a law forbidding their government from using terms based on English words like *le weekend* and *le Big Western*.

New inventions, discoveries, and customs are constantly adding words to English. In 1928, the first *Oxford English Dictionary* had ten volumes; its size has since more than doubled. Editors continue to add new terms like *reality television*, *24/7* (all the time), and *geekfest* (unfashionable people having a technical discussion). Technology has given us words such as *software* and *texting*. Many new technological words are taken from parts of older words. *Retail* refers to buying at a store; *e-tail* means buying on the Internet; an *e-zine* is a magazine on the Internet. *Netiquette* combines *Internet* and *etiquette*; it refers to how one behaves when using the Internet.

Food also gives us new words. Those who object to genetically modified food call it *Frankenfood*, a combination of *Frankenstein* (from the famous horror story) and *food*. A *locovore* is a person who eats only food produced and grown locally. The *loco* is taken from "local" and the *vore* part is from "eater," as in *carnivore*—an animal that eats meat. The term *phood* hasn't made it into dictionaries yet, but is used in the food industry. Responding to a demand for healthy foods, many companies enriched their products with nutritional supplements. The resulting products are often called *phood*, combining the terms *pharmaceutical* and *food*.

Other new words are business related. Hours in the office are called *face time*. The Canadian government put a picture of a loon, a water bird found in Canadian lakes, on its dollar coin. People nicknamed the coin *loonie*. Then, when the government issued a two-dollar coin, it was promptly nicknamed the *toonie*! Business conditions can also draw attention to existing words. When the U.S. government aided businesses in the 2008 recession, *bailout* became the most looked-up word on the Merriam-Webster dictionary website.

Ancient Greek and Latin words are also used to create English words. A person who is interested in the quality of sound reproduction is an *audiophile*. The word is formed from the Latin verb *audire* (to hear) and the ancient Greek noun *philos* (love). People may suffer from *technophobia,* formed from *technology* and *phobia*, fear of advanced technology and computers. Both parts come from ancient Greek: *technologia* is a systematic technique and *phobia* means fear. In this book, you will study many words from Greek and Latin.

Finally, using old words in new ways is a time-honored tradition. The meanings of many words have changed over centuries of use. *Husband* once meant "master of the house." *Lady* meant "kneader of bread."

New Words

Can you match these new words and phrases with their definitions?

1. bottom feeder
2. hold the hail
3. wedsite
4. bloviate
5. boo

a. no ice
b. a person who thrives on the bad luck of others
c. to write or speak in an unnecessarily long and complex manner
d. girlfriend, boyfriend
e. an Internet means of posting pictures and news about a marriage ceremony.

Answers are found on page 399.

Interested in new words? You can access websites that list and define them through the Student Companion Website at **www.cengage.com/devenglish/richek8e**.

Learning Strategy

Context Clues of Opposition

Some sentences give the opposite definition or sense of a word you are trying to understand. A simple opposition clue is the word *not*. Here is an example:

The movie was *not* good, but terrible.

Good is, of course, the opposite of *terrible*. Context clues of opposition can also be used for more difficult words.

The word was not used correctly, but was a *malapropism*. (A *malapropism* is a word that is incorrectly used.)

Often a clue of opposition provides an *antonym*, or a word opposite in meaning. In the first example, *terrible* is an antonym of *good*. Clues of opposition are easy to use if you become familiar with them. Some of the common structures are as follows.

1. The use of *not* and *no*.

   Denise was *not happy*, but despondent.

2. Words signaling opposition. These include *but*, *nevertheless*, *despite*, *rather than*, *regardless of the fact*, *unless*, *if not*, and *although*.

   Denise was despondent *despite* the fact that her friend was *happy*.

3. Words with negative senses. Certain words have a negative meaning. These include *merely*, *mere*, *barely*, *only*, *rarely*, *never*, *hardly*, *nowhere*, and *nothing*.

   Denise was despondent and *rarely* felt happy.

4. Words containing negative prefixes, such as *anti-*, *un-*, *dis-*, *non-*, and *in-*. For example, when the prefix *un-* is added to *happy*, it forms *unhappy*, which means the opposite of *happy*.

   Denise was despondent and felt *unhappy*.

From these examples, it is clear that *despondent* means "sad" or "depressed." In the examples, the antonym of *despondent (happy)* is given as a context clue.

Three examples of context clues of opposition follow. Can you guess the meaning of the italicized words? Remember that context clues of opposition, like all context clues, may give only the general sense of a word.

1. That is not believable; in fact, it is *preposterous*. (A *not* clue is used.)
2. There was so much *enmity* between the two brothers that they refused to speak to each other. (A word with a negative sense is used.)
3. Although Joanna hoped that the new book would make calculus clearer, it only *obfuscated* the topic. (A word signaling opposition is used.)

Answers are on page 399.

Now try using context clues to determine the meaning of some words in this chapter.

1. The puppy was small, but it grew into a *mammoth* dog. (A word signaling opposition is used.)

   Mammoth means ____.

2. We were unable to understand the ancient *cryptic* message. (A negative prefix is used.)

   Cryptic means ____.

3. We don't want to *augment* the size of our group because we want it to stay small. (A *not* clue is used.)

   Augment means ______________________________________.

Answers are on page 399.

Words to Learn

Part 1

1. **accolade** (noun) ăk′ə-lād′

   a. great praise

      The dentist received **accolades** for starting a clinic that served the poor.

   b. an honor or award

      In 2008, the **accolade** of the Nobel Peace Prize was awarded to Martti Ahtisaari, former President of Finland, for working to end warfare in Namibia, Indonesia, Kosovo, Ireland, and Iraq.

   NOTE: *Accolade* used in the singular means an award or honor; in contrast, *accolades*, the plural, usually signifies general praise or applause.

Courtesy author

Emil received the *accolade* of Best Student of 2010.

Customs of Knighthood

The word *accolade* comes from a ceremony during the Middle Ages in which a warrior was made a knight. The ruler gave the knight an accolade (an embrace) and dubbed him (tapped him on the shoulder with a sword). Thus, the word *accolade* is related to the word *chivalrous*, the third word in this section. Knighthoods are still awarded: In 2009, U.S. Senator Ted Kennedy was made British knight, Sir Ted.

2. **augment** (verb) ôg-mĕnt′

   to increase

   The university's foreign language offerings were **augmented** by classes in Mandarin and Hindu.

   We built additional cabinets to **augment** our kitchen storage space.

   ▶ *Related Word*
   augmentation (noun) The Internet has resulted in considerable *augmentation* of readily available information.

3. **chivalrous** (adjective) shĭv′əl-rəs

   having qualities of honor, including courtesy, bravery, and loyalty

   In a **chivalrous** gesture, the man gave his seat on the bus to an elderly woman.

   The **chivalrous** knight refused to attack his enemy while his back was turned.

   ▶ *Related Word*
   chivalry (noun) In a famous act of *chivalry*, Sir Walter Raleigh laid his cloak across a puddle so that Queen Elizabeth I could cross without getting her feet wet.

   NOTE: Chivalry usually refers to the actions of men and often refers to courtesy and consideration for women.

Chivalry *in the Middle Ages*

Chivalry was the ideal code of conduct for European knights in the Middle Ages. A true knight was brave, loyal, and fair; he showed mercy to the defeated and loyalty to his overlord, or master. In the tradition of courtly love, a knight dedicated poems to his lady and fought tournaments in her name. However, this idealized passion involved only worship from afar. Today, *chivalrous* gestures are considered old-fashioned, but in the Middle Ages they represented an improvement in the treatment of women. Note that the word *chivalrous* comes from the Latin word for horse, *caballus*, for only the wealthy could afford to use horses in battles or tournaments.

4. **complacent** (adjective) kəm-plā′sənt

overly self-satisfied

People in the United States were **complacent** about airline security before the September 11 terrorist attacks.

After getting straight A's, Sakeena became **complacent** and stopped studying.

NOTE: *Complacent* is a somewhat negative word.

► *Related Word*

complacency (noun) The *complacency* of the company's management allowed its competitors, who did more advertising, to succeed.

5. **cryptic** (adjective) krĭp′tĭk

puzzling; mysterious in meaning

I was puzzled by the **cryptic** text messages sent to my cell phone.

Egyptian hieroglyphics remained **cryptic** until the discovery of the Rosetta Stone in 1799 enabled them to be translated.

6. **fabricate** (verb) făb′rĭ-kāt

a. to construct or manufacture

The artist **fabricated** a sculpture from steel and stone.

b. to invent in order to deceive; to lie

Don't **fabricate** an excuse; just tell the truth.

► *Related Word*

fabrication (noun) The suspect's story was a complete *fabrication*.

7. **indulge** (verb) ĭn-dŭlj′

to pamper; to yield to desires

Grandpa Perry **indulged** Fikki by buying extra games for his Wii.

This afternoon, I plan to **indulge** myself by taking a long bubble bath.

► *Common Phrases*

indulge in

indulge oneself (*Indulge* often uses a reflexive pronoun. Examples are "I indulge *myself*"; "They indulge *themselves*"; "He indulges *himself*.")

Courtesy author

Lucia loves to *indulge* herself by eating chocolate.

▶ *Related Word*
indulgence (noun) After a long day of work, dinner at a fancy restaurant was a great *indulgence*.

8. **jeopardize** (verb) jĕp′ər-dīz′

to risk loss or danger

Repeatedly reporting to work late can **jeopardize** a person's job.

A single computer virus can **jeopardize** an entire hard drive.

▶ *Related Word*
jeopardy (noun) Driving while drunk puts both your life and the lives of others in *jeopardy*.

9. **mandatory** (adjective) măn′də-tôr′ē

required; commanded

English 101 was **mandatory** for college graduation.

Military service is **mandatory** in some countries.

▶ *Related Words*
mandate (noun) (măn′dāt′) A state *mandate* requires that schools conduct "lock-down" drills that prepare them for terrorist attacks. (Here *mandate* means "command.")

The president interpreted the wide margin of his election victory as a *mandate* to reform health care. (Here *mandate* refers to the unspoken wishes of the people who have elected an official.)

mandate (verb) Massachusetts *mandates* that all citizens have health insurance.

10. **meticulous** (adjective) mĭ-tĭk′yə-ləs

extremely careful; concerned with details

Farm workers harvested the fruit with **meticulous** care.

My English professor is **meticulous** about correcting grammatical errors.

▶ *Related Word*
meticulousness (noun) The reporter's *meticulousness* in checking facts assured that there were no errors in the articles she wrote.

11. **obsolete** (adjective) ŏb′sə-lēt′

no longer in use; outmoded; old-fashioned

The process of photocopying has made carbon paper largely **obsolete.**

Obsolete words, like *welkin* and *grece,* make Shakespeare's plays difficult to understand.

▶ *Related Words*
obsolescent (adjective) (ŏb′sə-lĕs′ənt) VHS video technology is now *obsolescent*. (*Obsolescent* means "becoming obsolete.")

obsolescence (noun) Despite their *obsolescence,* some people still collect vinyl records. (*Obsolescence* means a "state of becoming obsolete.")

12. **zealous** (adjective) zĕl′əs

extremely dedicated or enthusiastic

The **zealous** office worker often stayed after hours to complete tasks.

▶ *Related Words*
zeal (noun) (zēl) The champion athletes showed competitive *zeal*.

zealot (noun) (zĕl′ət) Religious *zealots* arrested women who were not fully veiled.

Tragic Zealots with Zeal

The first *zealots* were Jews who fought against Roman rule. After Romans destroyed the second Jewish temple in 70 CE, the Zealots retreated to the mountaintop fortress of Masada. There, one thousand people held off a Roman force of fifteen thousand for over two years. Preferring death to defeat, the Zealots committed suicide when they realized they would have to surrender.

NOTE: *Zealous* can refer to enthusiasm that is excessive, and thus, often negative.

Exercises

Part 1

■ *Matching Words and Definitions*

Match the word and definition. Use each answer choice only once.

1. cryptic ______	a. no longer used
2. indulge ______	b. having qualities of honor
3. complacent ______	c. award
4. obsolete ______	d. yield to desires
5. fabricate ______	e. to risk loss or danger
6. zealous ______	f. mysterious in meaning
7. meticulous ______	g. dedicated or enthusiastic
8. chivalrous ______	h. very careful
9. mandatory ______	i. overly self-satisfied
10. accolade ______	j. to increase
	k. construct, invent
	l. required

■ *Words in Context*

Complete each sentence with the best word. Use each choice only once.

a. accolade	e. cryptic	i. mandatory
b. augment	f. fabricate	j. meticulous
c. chivalrous	g. indulge	k. obsolete
d. complacent	h. jeopardize	l. zealous

1. The ________________ volunteer worked sixty hours each week in the soup kitchen.

2. If the restaurant could ________________ the number of people it could seat, it would make more money.

3. The ________________ of the Purple Heart has been awarded to many soldiers who served in Iraq and Afghanistan.

4. The ________________ gardener pulled up even the smallest weeds.

5. I don't understand the ________________ abbreviations teenagers use when they send text messages.

6. Despite living in an area that often flooded, the ________________ man refused to prepare for water damage.

7. It is ________________ to have a driver's license if you want to operate a car.

8. The horse and chariot are now ________________ in warfare.

9. If you don't use a seat belt while driving, you will ________________ your safety.

10. Products from crude oil are used to ________________ plastic wrap.

■ *Using Related Words*

Complete each sentence with the correct form. Use each choice only once.

THE GREAT ELEANOR OF AQUITAINE

1. chivalry, chivalrous

The tradition of the ________________ knight owes much to Eleanor of Aquitaine, 1122–1204. As perhaps the most powerful woman of her century, she ran the court of Aquitaine (now part of France) and invited poets and performers to write about the

________________ of the Middle Ages.

2. augment, augmentation

   When Eleanor inherited the province of Aquitaine, it was actually larger than France. In those days, when there was little commerce, land was the only real source of power. So an ____________ of territory meant more authority. By marrying Eleanor, any king could considerably ____________ the land under his control. Eleanor was a sought-after bride, and her first marriage was to the French king Louis VII.

3. indulged, indulgences

   But in her youth, Eleanor ____________ in some wild behavior. In fact, King Louis VII divorced her for unfaithfulness. As the heir to enormous lands, she soon remarried. Unfortunately, her second marriage, to King Henry II of England, was also unhappy. This time, it was Henry's ____________ with other women that caused problems.

4. jeopardy, jeopardized, jeopardizing

   Life was stressful for Eleanor. Nobles of this time traveled frequently, moving among their many properties. Often robbers and storms ____________ their safety. Even when pregnant, Eleanor moved by horseback or in small, unsafe boats, ____________ her health. Her frequent arguments with Henry made her spend much of her time apart from him, ruling her court in Aquitaine. She even put herself in ____________ by supporting a revolt against him. In revenge Henry imprisoned her for sixteen years. She was freed only when their son Richard the Lion-Hearted assumed the throne. In her last years, she remained strong. When almost eighty, she crossed the English Channel by boat —a dangerous journey in those days. We honor her memory every time we tell a story of knights in shining armor and courtly love.

■ *Find the Example*

Choose the example that best describes the action or situation.

1. The thing a complacent student would be most likely to indulge in before an exam ______
   a. eating an ice cream cone while studying b. a nap c. a prayer

2. A cryptic communication that might jeopardize people _______
   a. unclear battle orders b. clear assignment direction
   c. working traffic signals

3. An obsolete, fabricated means of transportation _______
   a. horse b. automobile c. covered wagon

4. A way to augment the zeal of a salesperson _______
   a. give him a raise if the company sells more
   b. have the boss make more money c. give an automatic raise

5. A job in which it is most mandatory to be meticulous _______
   a. movie star b. surgeon c. king

Words to Learn

Part 2

13. **adulation** (noun) ăj′ə-lā′shən

extreme admiration or flattery

The bride looked at the groom with **adulation** as she said, "I do."

With her elegant style and caring manner, U.S. first lady Michelle Obama has received **adulation** from people around the world.

▶ *Related Words*

adulate (verb) Youngsters often *adulate* famous athletes.

adulatory (adjective) The actor's performance received *adulatory* comments from critics.

14. **chronological** (adjective) krŏn′ə-lŏj′ĭ-kəl

arranged in order of time, from first to last

Rachel's job application listed her work experience in **chronological** order.

▶ *Related Word*

chronology (noun) (krə-nŏl′ə-jē) A *chronology* of Civil War battles is listed in the front of the textbook.

15. **copious** (adjective) kō′pē-əs

plentiful; abundant

The student's **copious** lecture notes filled ten pages.

There is a **copious** supply of canned goods in the shelter.

NOTE: *Copious* cannot be used to refer to a single large thing. We cannot say "a copious piece of cake." We can, however, refer to "a copious amount of candy," "copious office supplies," or "a copious supply of water." These are all composed of many things, or continuous things, and may be described as *copious*.

▶ *Common Phrase*
copious amount

▶ *Related Word*
copiousness (noun) The *copiousness* of the corn harvest ensured that the tribe would survive the winter.

16. **cultivate** (verb) kŭl′tə-vāt′

to grow deliberately; to develop

Fruits and vegetables can be **cultivated** in greenhouses throughout cold winters.

Free time allows a person to **cultivate** interests and hobbies.

The lobbyist **cultivated** contacts with important senators.

The college student **cultivated** a relationship with his rich aunt, who he hoped might pay his tuition.

▶ *Related Words*
cultivated (adjective) My *cultivated* professor read widely and attended many plays and lectures. (*Cultivated* and *cultivation* can describe people who are cultured and have interests in history, art, classical music, literature, etc.)

cultivation (noun) *Cultivation* of crops is difficult in the desert. Stefano's musical *cultivation* impressed us.

17. **discretion** (noun) dĭ-skrĕsh′ən

a. good judgment; the ability to keep secrets and avoid embarrassment

Criticizing your supervisor in public shows your lack of **discretion**.

Because her job demanded **discretion**, the nanny refused to talk to reporters about the movie star who employed her.

b. power granted to make decisions

The owner granted the coach the **discretion** to choose team members.

▶ *Related Words*

discreet (adjective) The *discreet* emergency room nurse whispered, so that only the patient could hear her.

discretionary (adjective) The dean has a *discretionary* fund that she can spend as she pleases.

NOTES: (1) *Discreet* is related to the first meaning of *discretion* (good judgment); *discreet* can also mean "modest, not showy."
(2) *Discretionary* is related to the second meaning of *discretion* (power to make decisions).
(3) Don't confuse *discreet* and *discrete*; *discrete* means "separate."

18. **euphemism** (noun) yo͞o′fə-mĭz′əm

a more positive word or phrase substituted for a negative one

"The departed" is a **euphemism** for "the dead."

▶ *Related Word*

euphemistic (adjective) "Landfill" is a *euphemistic* expression for "garbage dump."

Identify the Euphemisms

Euphemisms are used frequently. A bank recently announced that it was "downsizing" by "lowering payroll costs through reducing head count." In other words, it was firing people. What do these euphemisms mean?

1. He has *lost his marbles*.
2. He has *bitten the dust*.
3. The child *appropriated* his friend's pencil.
4. This will be a slightly *uncomfortable* procedure.
5. She *stretched the truth* a bit.

Answers are on page 399.

You can access websites that list and define more euphemisms through the Student Companion Website at **www.cengage.com/devenglish/richek8e**.

19. **mammoth** (adjective) măm′əth

huge; very large

Providing affordable health care is **mammoth** task.

Millions of years ago, the **mammoth** arthropleura, an insect over six feet long, lived on forest floors.

NOTE: The word *mammoth* originates in the Russian name for a huge woolly elephant that is now extinct. Other animal names have become common words in English. A *chicken* is a coward. To *parrot* means to repeat. For more animal idioms, see the "Insight into Idioms" section on page 332 in Chapter 10.

20. **mitigating** (adjective) mĭt′ĭ-gāt′ĭng

making less severe or intense; moderating

An ocean breeze has a **mitigating** effect on tropical heat.

Declaring the thief's young age a **mitigating** circumstance, the judge reduced his jail term.

▶ *Common Phrase*
mitigating circumstance(s)

▶ *Related Words*
mitigate (verb) Grandpa *mitigated* his harsh words with a wink.

mitigation (noun) The city formulated a *mitigation* plan to minimize losses through earthquakes and mudslides.

21. **pinnacle** (noun) pĭn′ə-kəl

top; highest point

The **pinnacle** of Mount Everest is the highest point on Earth.

At the **pinnacle** of her career, the newscaster earned $15 million in one year.

22. **procrastinate** (verb) prō-krăs′tə-nāt′

to delay; to put off

Credit card users who **procrastinate** paying balances wind up with large late fees.

▶ *Related Words*
procrastinator (noun, person) The National *Procrastinators'* Club celebrates New Year's Day in October.

procrastination (noun) *Procrastination* is the strategy I use when it's my turn to wash the dishes.

Procrastination *and Problems*

Procrastination can be dangerous to your health. According to a study of 374 freshmen, students who don't study until the last minute report more colds, flus, and digestive problems than classmates who complete their work long before deadlines. Part of the reason for this may be that *procrastinators* experience lots of stress. Psychologists also believe that repeated procrastination is associated with low self-esteem and depression. Some *procrastinators* believe that if they work under that last-minute stress, their performance will improve. However, studies have shown that those who plan ahead do better.

23. **successive** (adjective) sək-sĕs′ĭv

following one after another without interruption

My family has lived on this farm for four **successive** generations.

► *Related Words*

successor (noun, person) The *successor* of the free-spending CEO instituted cost-cutting measures.

succession (noun) A *succession* of students lined up to receive their diplomas.

The prince's *succession* to the throne was greeted with joy. (*Succession* can mean the inheritance of a crown or title.)

24. **withstand** (verb) wĭth-stănd′ (past tense: **withstood**)

not to surrender; to bear (the force of)

Russia has **withstood** many attacks but has never been conquered.

The dieter could not **withstand** the temptation of the dessert buffet.

Shakespeare's plays have **withstood** the test of time.

Mike, Who Withstood *So Much*

When you meet smiling, friendly Mike, it is difficult to imagine the hardships he *withstood* in the Vietnam War. Drafted at eighteen into the U.S. Army, he lived in war zones, in the midst of mud and roaches. He had to kill, or be killed. He was captured by the enemy and tortured. Finally, he was able to escape, but only by killing his guard. For comfort from the terrible conditions he endured and to rid himself of the ghosts that haunted him, he turned to drugs. When he returned from the war, it took him thirteen years to overcome his addiction. Mike must also *withstand* the burden of his guilt. He has apologized to the Vietnamese people for his role in what he considers a tragedy for Vietnam—and for U.S. soldiers.

Exercises

Part 2

■ *Matching Words and Definitions*

Match the word and definition. Use each choice only once.

1. pinnacle ______
2. cultivate ______
3. successive ______
4. withstand ______
5. euphemism ______
6. mammoth ______
7. copious ______
8. procrastinate ______
9. mitigating ______
10. discretion ______

a. extreme admiration
b. good judgment
c. use of a positive word in place of a negative one
d. to grow
e. following without interruption
f. very large
g. top
h. plentiful
i. to delay
j. making less severe
k. not to surrender
l. in order of time

■ *Words in Context*

Complete each sentence with the best word. Use each choice only once.

a. adulation	e. discretion	i. pinnacle
b. chronology	f. euphemism	j. procrastinate
c. copious	g. mammoth	k. successive
d. cultivate	h. mitigating	l. withstand

1. The boy's ________________ stopped when he realized his baseball hero had taken steroids.

2. Being awarded the Olympic Gold Medal was the ________________ of the swimmer's career.

3. The office worker tried to ________________ the friendship of his supervisor.

4. Computers of the 1940s, which filled entire rooms, seem _______________ when compared to today's hand-held devices.
5. Unable to _______________ her father's criticism, the child cried and ran from the room.
6. The _______________ "tipsy" is sometimes used to mean "drunk."
7. If you _______________ about paying a parking ticket, you may end up with a late fee.
8. A time line is a(n) _______________ of important events, listed in order of their occurrence.
9. Practicing _______________, the therapist refused to discuss his client's case with others.
10. For five _______________ days, you have been late for class!

■ *Using Related Words*

Complete each sentence with the correct form. Use each choice only once.

THE LIFE OF ELVIS PRESLEY

1. adulated, adulation

   Elvis Presley, perhaps rock 'n' roll's most legendary performer, was _______________ by millions. So great was their _______________ that over thirty years after his death, his home, Graceland, in Memphis, Tennessee, remains a shrine.

2. chronology, chronological

   The _______________ of Elvis's life began in 1935 in Tupelo, Mississippi. He served in the army, married, had a daughter, and divorced. At the time of his sudden death at Graceland in 1977, he had sold over 500 million records, and had made thirty-five movies.

   This _______________ retelling of his life, however, cannot capture his enormous influence.

Elvis was *adulated* by millions of fans.

Bettmann/CORBIS

3. cultivate, cultivating, cultivation, cultivated

Growing up, Elvis was surrounded by the music of the American South. He listened to the Grand Ole Opry on the radio; he ____________________ a taste for gospel and sang in a church choir; and he studied African-American blues artists. Although these artists were largely unrecognized by white audiences of the time, many people of musical ____________________ borrowed from the great heritage of the blues. Elvis's knowledge of blues inspired him to ____________________ an intensely personal style. Some accused him of ____________________ a sexy image—and gave him the nickname "Elvis the Pelvis."

4. withstand, withstood

Elvis had to ____________________ many attacks by critics. In his early days, he was criticized by racists, who did not like his inclusion of blues music. Later, his reputation ____________________ the attacks of those who felt he built his fame on stealing the work of such magnificent blues artists as Muddy Waters and B. B. King. Yet Elvis also gathered accolades. Twice he was awarded the Grammy for gospel music.

5. mitigated, mitigating

   Tremendous success was ________________ by personal problems. His marriage failed, and, by the end of his life, he was probably addicted to mood-controlling pills. Yet Elvis's abiding love for his mother, even after her death, was a ________________ factor that counterbalanced his flaws. His songs are still popular today. Can you hum the tunes of "Love Me Tender," "Hound Dog," "All Shook Up," and "Don't Be Cruel"?

■ *Find the Example*

Choose the example that best describes the action or situation.

1. The birth years, in chronological order, of people born in successive years _______
   a. 1990, 1992, 1994 b. 1990, 1991, 1992 c. 1990, 1992, 1991

2. One mitigating factor in procrastination _______
   a. illness b. opportunity c. laziness

3. Discreet adulation _______
   a. a crowd screaming "We love you" to a rap artist
   b. a dream of beating a famous golfer
   c. a bedroom with a poster of a favorite star

4. Something that has withstood a mammoth force _______
   a. a huge office building destroyed by a landmine
   b. an abandoned shed on a deserted island
   c. a house still standing after a tornado

5. A copious amount of this would help grain cultivation _______
   a. sun b. rock c. wind

Chapter Exercises

■ *Practicing Strategies: Context Clues of Opposition*

In each sentence, one difficult word is italicized. Use context clues of opposition to make an intelligent guess about its meaning in the sentence.

1. She thought she would be *recompensed*, but she was never paid.

   Recompensed means ________________________.

2. This *peerless* painting is without equal.

   Peerless means ______________________________.

3. *Undaunted* by the cold weather, a crowd gathered outside to listen to the president's inauguration address.

   Undaunted means ______________________________.

4. Alpa displayed *fortitude* in climbing the mountain, for nothing could make her quit.

   Fortitude means ______________________________.

5. This *diminutive* type of hummingbird almost never grows to be more than three inches.

   Diminutive means ______________________________.

6. Her *sporadic* efforts at studying lacked regularity.

   Sporadic means ______________________________.

7. The man's reputation for *rectitude* was ruined when he was convicted of stealing money from his neighbors.

   Rectitude means ______________________________.

8. He is a *consummate* salesman, but his brother has no skill whatsoever.

   Consummate means ______________________________.

Items 9 and 10 are taken from newspaper sources.

9. Even if your son doesn't act sad, it doesn't mean that this doesn't bother him. Fifteen-year-old boys are famously *reticent* about their feelings.

   Reticent means ______________________________.

10. The perfect composition of the drawings clearly results from deliberation, the very opposite of anything *extemporaneous*.

    Extemporaneous means ______________________________.

■ *Companion Words*

Complete each sentence with the best word. You may use choices more than once. Choices: myself, about, to, in, of, amount, circumstances, for.

1. After a succession ________ career failures, Harry Truman achieved success as a politician, becoming U.S. president.

2–3. I would like ________ indulge ________ by sleeping all day.

4. Government-issued picture identification is mandatory ________ boarding planes.

5. There is a copious ________ of salt in most frozen foods.

6. When the mayor became complacent ________ his reelection, he lost.

7. The calendar lists holidays ________ chronological order.

8. "Sanitation engineer" is a euphemism ________ "janitor."

9. There were mitigating ____________ that explained her absence.

10. We have had snow ________ ten successive days!

■ *Writing with Your Words*

To practice effective writing, complete each sentence with an interesting phrase that indicates the meaning of the italicized word.

1. Students who take *copious* notes ____________________________

   ____.

2. I would never want to *jeopardize* ____________________________

   ____.

3. If you *fabricate* the truth ____________________________

   ____.

4. The *zealous* student ____________________________

   ____.

5. The *obsolete* computer ____

____.

6. Four-year-olds are often not *discreet* because they __________________

____.

7. The *chivalrous* knight ____

____.

8. When I reach the *pinnacle* of success, __________________________________

____.

9. It's important to be *meticulous* when ____________________________

____.

10. For several *successive* years, ____

____.

■ *Making Connections*

To connect new vocabulary to your life, write extended responses to these questions.

1. Describe your favorite indulgence.
2. Do you think discretion is important in public officials, or should they expose wrongdoing? Defend your answer.
3. Give an example of someone who is adulated by the public and describe what his or her admirers do.

Passage

Christian—The Lion Who Didn't Forget

Can a wild animal really act like a human being and remember his friends and protectors? If you doubt it, read the story of Christian.

The London of 1969 was a place where the unusual was usual. Hippies roamed the streets, and "Swinging London" was known for free lifestyles, crazy clothes, and wild parties. It was here, and then, **(1)** that two young men decided to **indulge** themselves by buying an unusual pet—a lion. In today's world, this would be unthinkable. **(2)** The sale of wild animals could not **withstand** the outcry from animal rights groups. But in 1969, the luxury department store Harrods was **complacent** about its position as a retail leader, so it sold creatures usually found in the jungle without concern.

Besides, this young lion cub had already tried to escape. A lion on the loose would have **jeopardized** the reputation of the entire store, not to mention people's lives. When John Rendall and Anthony Bourke offered to buy the animal, salespeople breathed a sigh of relief.

The adorable baby cub soon became the darling of the neighborhood. Like most cats, he slept a lot, usually in the furniture shop where his owners worked. He used a litter box, **(3)** and was **meticulous** about keeping himself clean. **(4)** The local minister **chivalrously** allowed the cub to run in a nearby gated church yard, so Rendall and Bourke named him Christian. **(5)** His playful and affectionate nature **mitigated** the fear people felt about lions.

However, as the months passed, Christian's size **augmented** rapidly. He grew from 35 to 185 pounds within a year. He ate a **copious** amount; two solid meals, two liquid meals, and supplements were required every day. As Christian's size and appetite grew to **mammoth** proportions, the owners decided they could no longer keep him. **(6)** They could not **procrastinate**: It was **mandatory** to find a way for Christian to live in the wild.

By chance two people who had been involved in **(7)** the movie *Born Free*, which had gathered **accolades** from animal rights activists, walked into the furniture store, and saw the lion. They suggested that the owners contact George Adamson, who had handled the lions used in the movie. He had gained the **adulation** of wildlife enthusiasts with his intelligent and sensitive treatment of the animals.

Adamson suggested that Christian be returned to the wild in Kenya. But this required much negotiation with the government. Meanwhile, Christian had become too big for life in London. So he was moved to a large house in the country, surrounded by land, near the sea. Country life required adjustments. **(8)** Christian's tolerance for cold water had to be **cultivated** gradually. When he first put his paw into the sea, he shivered and quickly withdrew it.

After a few months the arrangements for travel to Kenya were completed, and Christian was packed in a crate. Rendall and Bourke made the trip to Africa and accompanied him to the Kora game park. However, realizing that Adamson was an expert, **(9)** they gave him full **discretion** in handling their former pet and returned to London. Under Adamson's **zealous** care, Christian gradually became a wild animal living in the game park.

After a while, though, Rendall and Bourke grew lonely for Christian, and decided to visit Kenya. Christian was now living the life of a lion—a lion that kills for food. Would he remember them? Would he attack?

So it was with fear that they stood in the game park, waiting for Christian to approach. Recognizing them, Christian came up cautiously. As he sniffed the air, Rendall and Bourke tensed. Then it happened. Christian ran toward them, stood on his hind legs, and hugged them. The greeting was lion style. Christian wrapped his front paws around their shoulders and licked them. The video that captures this moment was made more than thirty years ago, using **(10)** technology that is now **obsolete.** But it is so moving that it has become a You-Tube hit, viewed by millions.

For two **successive** years, 1972 and 1973, the men went back to see their former pet. Then, as Christian became wilder, they stopped.

What happened to Christian? It is believed that he lived a long and successful life, and may have even been the head of his pride (or group of lions). He probably died of natural causes. George Adamson was not as lucky: he was ambushed and murdered by bandits. But the work he did with Christian lives on, and has touched the heart of millions who have viewed the video. Rendall and Bourke have written a book entitled *A Lion Called Christian* that records their experiences. The lion who lived in the center of Swinging London has become a symbol of animal rights across the world.

■ *Exercise*

Each numbered sentence corresponds to a sentence in the passage. Fill in the letter of the choice that makes the sentence mean the same thing as its corresponding sentence in the passage.

1. The two men decided to _______ themselves by buying an unusual pet.
   a. hurt b. be foolish about c. laugh at d. be nice to

2. The sale of wild animals could not _______ the outcry.
   a. conquer b. bear c. hope for d. publicize

3. He was also _______ about keeping himself clean.
   a. the best b. better than the owners c. reasonable d. careful

4. The local minister _______ allowed the cub to run in a nearby gated church yard.
   a. foolishly b. mysteriously c. courteously d. lately

5. Christian's playful and affectionate nature _______ the fear.
   a. delayed b. increased c. did away with d. weakened

6. They could not _______.
   a. keep him b. delay c. lie d. have him get bigger

7. The movie *Born Free* had gathered _______.
   a. softened words b. praise c. tolerance d. noble sentiments

8. Christian's tolerance for cold water had to be _______.
   a. increased b. conquered c. developed d. given as a special treat

9. They gave Adamson full _______ in handling their former pet.
   a. assistance b. delay c. amounts of money d. power

10. The technology is now _______.
   a. everywhere b. manufactured c. of the highest quality
   d. no longer used

■ *Discussion Questions*

1. How was Christian like a house cat, and how was he different?
2. Detail two ways in which Rendall and Bourke benefited from the kindness of others in handling Christian.
3. Did Rendall and Bourke handle Christian in a responsible manner? Explain your answer.

INSIGHT INTO IDIOMS

Rhyme and Repetition

Many idioms combine two words that sound almost alike. Most of these are informal. Feel free to use them in everyday speech, but not in formal conversation and writing. Often they are fun to pronounce. Try saying "I'll *hob-nob* with the *hoity-toity*" out loud, and see if the sounds make you laugh.

a. To *dilly dally* means to move slowly, or delay.
b. People who change their minds easily are called *wishy-washy*.
c. To *hob-nob* means to be friendly with, or associate closely with.
d. *Hoity-toity* means snobbish.
e. Something that contains many things that don't fit together is said to be a *hodgepodge*.
f. Something with false or silly ideas is called *claptrap*.
g. If you are nervous or jumpy, you might be described as having the *heebie jeebies*.

Practice chapter words one more time by filling in the letter of the correct idiom into the blank before each sentence.

_______ 1. To *cultivate* the friendship of the rich and famous, you must __________ with them.

_______ 2. I don't believe those *fabrications*; they are pure __________.

_______ 3. The cook's meals are a __________ of ingredients that don't go together, but at least the food is always *copious*.

_______ 4. One of my friends is *complacent* about most things, but his brother acts as if he constantly has the __________.

_______ 5. After receiving the *adulation* of the crowds, the athlete became __________, and forgot about his old friends.

Links to more lists of English idioms and their meanings can be found at the Student Companion Website for this book: **www.cengage.com/devenglish/richek8e**.

REVIEW

Chapters 1–4

■ *Reviewing Words in Context*

Read the passage, then complete each sentence with the best word. Use each choice only once.

THE "TROUBLE TWINS"

Courtesy author

a. adroitly
b. articulate
c. belligerent
d. chagrined
e. chronological
f. conservative
g. contemplate
h. enigma
i. epitome
j. exuberant
k. fraternal
l. frugal
m. intrepid
n. ludicrous
o. meticulous
p. thwarted

Background: Sophia and Rocio, students in the author's class, are identical twins who have been together since they shared a cradle. They sometimes find that they are independently humming the same song or thinking the same thoughts. Here is more about them.

1. Rocio and Sophia are identical twins, not ____________________, twins.

2. Both have ____________________ personalities; they are bubbly and get excited over things.

3. In addition, they both are ____________________ people who express themselves well.

4. In ____________________ order, Sophia, who was born five minutes before Rocio, came first.

5. Their wonderful relationship is the ____________________ of how sisters should get along.

6. Being twins made them feel secure, so they grew up to be ____________________ and afraid of nothing.

7. In fact, it is difficult for them to ____________________ what life would be like if they didn't have each other.

8. However, there are some differences between them; Rocio is ____________________ and shops carefully, but Sophia spends money freely.

9. Rocio, who is more ____________________, values marriage and family more highly than Sophia, who values independence.

10. They are both skilled musicians who can move their fingers____________________ when playing the violin and piano.

11. When they were young, their mother ____________________ their desire to look different from each other by dressing them the same. People teased them by calling them the "Trouble Twins."

12. To most people, it is a(n) ____________________ which twin is Rocio and which is Sophia.

13. However, if you examine their faces with ____________________ care, you can see that Rocio, who is called "la gorda" ("fat one"), has slightly rounder cheeks than Sophia, who is called "la flaca" ("thin one").

14. Once a ____________________ playmate, who was angry with Rocio, started to fight with Sophia!

15. More recently, Sophia's boyfriend was ____________________ when he realized he was trying to kiss Rocio!

■ *Passage for Word Review*

This passage continues the discussion of names that appear in Chapter 1. Complete the passage by supplying the words that make the best sense. Use each choice only once.

a. accorded
b. affluent
c. augmented
d. boisterous
e. clarify
f. cosmopolitan
g. discretionary
h. emulating
i. fabricated
j. indulging
k. mandatory
l. obsolescent
m. stoic
n. successive
o. supplanted
p. venerable

WHERE DID OUR SURNAMES COME FROM?

They come first in official lists; they identify us in a directory. We pass them on to each **(1)** ____________________ generation. What would we do without our last names, or "surnames"? Long ago, however, people were known by only one name. In the early Middle Ages, most people lived in small communities and, with only one Robert or Susan in the neighborhood, no last names were needed.

As the number of city dwellers **(2)** ____________________, though, last names were needed to tell them apart. So, as the population grew, more and more people got surnames. With ten or twelve Johns in a city, it was necessary to use surnames in order to identify them and **(3)** ____________________ which one you were talking about. The custom first became fashionable among the rich. Then, poor people, **(4)** ____________________ wealthy ones, also began using them. Today, of course, last names are **(5)** ____________________ for everyone. They are needed for everyday tasks like filling out forms and receiving mail.

Where did our last names come from? Many came from jobs. The most common surname in the United States, Smith, has a **(6)** ____________________ history. It was first recorded in Old English, and comes from "blacksmith," people who forged iron, especially for horseshoes. Today, however, automobiles have almost entirely **(7)** ____________________ the horse for travel. The profession of a blacksmith is **(8)** ____________________. Coopers made barrels, Millers ground wheat into flour, and you can probably guess what Carpenters and Taylors (tailors) did. Over time, however, these names lost their meanings, and very few Smiths living today would be able to make horseshoes!

Other last names were taken from places. Abraham Lincoln's last name means "from the lake colony." And there are two places in England named Washington. One was the origin of George Washington's surname.

A third source of names is one's father's name. Three of the five most popular names in the United States have the meaning of "son": Johnson and Jones mean "son of John." Williams means "son of William." In addition, the Scottish "Mc" or "Mac" means "son," so the name MacDonald was once **(9)** ____________________ to the son of a Donald. Similarly, Ramirez means "son of Ramon" and Gutierrez means "son of Gutierre" (Walter, in English).

A fourth source of names was the use of nicknames. People must have been **(10)** ____________________ in a bit of fun when they gave tall people the names Longfellow or Lang. A stranger hearing the name of Short or Moody would know exactly what to expect from appearance or behavior.

The name Rich would be given to a(n) **(11)** ____________________ person. Red might refer to a hair color or to a person who was a showoff. However, the meanings of some of these names have changed. The name Stout, now meaning a bit overweight, once referred to a noisy and bad-tempered person likely to become **(12)** ____________________ at gatherings. A(n) ____________________ person, who never complained, might be given the name "Perry," which means stone.

Having a surname was once **(13)** ____________________, but in today's world it is required. There are many different customs for giving last names. **(14)** A(n) ____________________ person, who has traveled throughout the world, has probably observed many ways in which last names are formed. A single name may be **(15)** ____________________ from two names. In Spanish-speaking countries, for example, a mother's last name is added to a father's with a hyphen. For example, Eugenio Cortez-Portillo has a father whose surname is Cortez and a mother whose surname is Portillo. In China, last names are put first. Thus the last name of Mao Zedong was Mao. In Russia, a father's name is given as a "patronymic" middle name. Alexander Fekson's son Gennady is *Gennady Alexandrovich Fekson*. Alexander's daughter Sophia is *Sophia Alexandrovna Fekson*. The most respectful way to address a Russian is to use a first name and patronymic, as in *Gennady Alexandrovich*.

■ *Reviewing Learning Strategies*

Dictionary Skills Complete each sentence with the answer that fits best.

1. If a word's pronunciation shows two accented syllables, the lighter one ___________

   a. receives more stress b. receives less stress
   c. receives equal stress to the darker one

2. An etymology gives the ___________ of a word.

   a. pronunciation b. meaning c. history

3. The word *Archaic* indicates that a certain meaning is ___________.

   a. no longer used b. used in archery c. used in slang

Context Clues Using context clues, guess the meaning of the italicized words.

4. The *portmanteau word* "smog" is formed from the words *fog* and *smoke*.

   Portmanteau word means ___________________________________.

5. The *nouveaux riche,* or newly rich, often like to show off their money.

   Nouveaux riche means ___________________________________.

6. I developed an *aversion* to coleslaw after I got sick from eating it.

   Aversion means ___________________________________.

7. The bike messenger's *alacrity* at delivering messages has earned him the nickname "Speedy."

   Alacrity means ___________________________________.

8. The *noxious* gas caused sickness and death.

   Noxious means ___________________________________.

9. The *refractory* mule refused to move from the spot, despite our urging.

   Refractory means ___________________________________.

10. Since dinosaurs died out centuries ago, they are no longer *extant*.

    Extant means ___________________________________.

PART 2

Word Elements

In Part 1 of this book, you learned about context clues. Part 2 focuses on **word elements**, the parts of words that have their own meanings. Unlike context clues, which provide hints from the sentence, word elements give hints within the word itself. For example, the parts *re-* (meaning "back") and *tract* (meaning "pull") are the two elements in the word *retract* (meaning "to pull back"). If you break an unknown word into separate elements, you can often figure out its meaning. If you then combine context clues with word element clues, you will have a powerful approach to understanding new words.

Prefixes, Roots, and Suffixes

There are three kinds of word elements: prefixes, roots, and suffixes. A **prefix** is a group of letters that is attached to the beginning of a word root. A **root** is the central, or main, portion of a word. A **suffix** is a group of letters that is attached to the end of a root. An example of a word that contains all three elements is *impolitely: im-* is the prefix, *polite* is the root, and *-ly* is the suffix. Now let us look at each element separately.

Prefixes

A prefix such as *im-* attaches to the beginning of a root. The hyphen at the end of *im-* shows where the root attaches. When a prefix joins a root, the result is a new word with a different meaning. In the word *impolite,* for example, the prefix *im-* means "not." When *im-* is joined to the root *polite,* the new word formed by the prefix and root means "not polite." Next, we can see what happens when the prefix *co-,* which means "together," is joined to two familiar word roots.

co- (together) + *exist* = *coexist* (to exist together)

co- (together) + *operate* = *cooperate* (to work or operate together)

In both of these examples, the prefix *co-* changes the meaning of the root word.

Roots

A root is the central portion of a word, and it carries the basic meaning. There are two types of roots: base word and combining root. A **base word** is simply an English word that can stand alone, such as *polite* or *operate*, and may be joined to a prefix or a suffix. **Combining roots** cannot stand alone as English words; they are derived from words in other languages. For example, the combining root *ject* is derived from the Latin word *iacere*, which means "to throw." Although the root *ject* is not an English word by itself, it can combine with many prefixes to form words. Two examples are *reject* and *eject*.

e- (a prefix meaning "out") + *ject* (a root meaning "throw") = *eject*

re- (a prefix meaning "back") + *ject* (a root meaning "throw") = *reject*

How do a prefix and a root create a word with a new meaning? Sometimes the new word's meaning is simply the combination of its root and prefix. Thus, *eject* means "to throw out." At other times the meaning of a word is somewhat different from the combined prefix and root. *Reject* does not mean "to throw back"; rather, it means "not to accept." These two meanings are related; we could imagine that someone who did not accept something might throw it back. In fact, "to throw back" gives an imaginative mental picture of *reject*. Prefixes and roots often give an image of a word rather than a precise definition. This image can help you remember the meaning of a word. The formation of several words from *ject* is illustrated below.

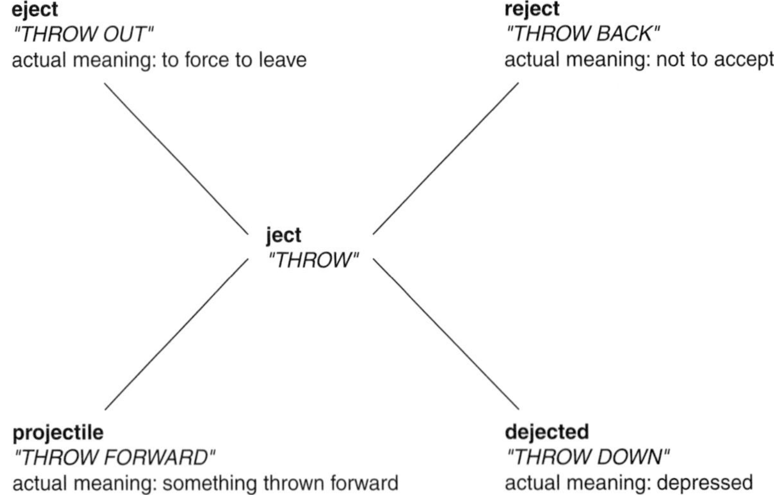

Suffixes

A suffix, such as *-ly,* is added to the end of a root. The hyphen at the beginning shows where the root attaches. Most suffixes change a base word from one part of speech to another. (See the table on pages 5 and 6.) For example, *-able* changes a verb (*reach*) to an adjective (*reachable*). Suffixes may also indicate a plural, as in *boys,* or a past tense, as in reach*ed.* A few suffixes extend the basic meaning of a word root. The root *psych* ("mind") and the suffix *-logy* ("study of") are joined to form *psychology* ("the study of the mind").

Many common words contain word elements. Each of the following words consists of a prefix, a root, and a suffix: *reaction, unlikely, exchanges, reviewing,* and *invisibly.* Can you identify each element?

Answers are on page 399.

Using Word Elements

Word elements provide valuable clues to the meanings of unknown words, but they must be used carefully.

Some word elements have more than one spelling. For example, the root *ject* can be spelled *jet* (as in *jet* and *jettison*). The prefix *anti-* is also spelled *ant-* (as in *antacid* and *antagonist*). Some spelling differences make words easier to pronounce. Others reflect the history of a word element. Fortunately, spellings usually vary by only one or two letters. Once you learn to look for the common letters, you should be able to identify word elements easily.

Some word elements have more than one meaning. For example, the combining root *gen* can mean both "birth" and "type." This book gives all the common meanings of many combining roots, prefixes, and suffixes, and some hints about when to use them. When you encounter word elements that have more than one meaning, remember to use the context clues you learned in Part 1 of this book. If you combine your knowledge of word elements with context clues, you can usually determine the most appropriate meaning.

Finally, when you see a certain combination of letters in a word, those letters may not always form a word element. For instance, the appearance of the letters *a-n-t-i* in a word does not mean that they always form the prefix *anti-*. To find out whether or not they do, you must combine context clues with your knowledge of word elements. To illustrate this, *a-n-t-i* is used in two sentences below. Which sentence contains the prefix *anti-* (meaning "opposite" or "against")?

> This *antianxiety* pill will help calm you down.
>
> We *anticipate* you will come.

The answer is the first sentence; *antianxiety* (calmness) is the opposite of *anxiety.* (The *anti-* in *anticipate* is actually a varied spelling of the prefix *ante-*, meaning "before.")

The use of word elements is an excellent way to increase your vocabulary. Prefixes, roots, and suffixes can help you unlock the meanings of thousands of difficult words. The chapters in Part 2 of this book present many different word elements. Each one is illustrated by several new words that will be valuable to you in college. If you relate these words to the word elements they contain, you will remember both more effectively.

As you work through the word elements in Part 2, keep in mind the context clues that you learned in Part 1. Together, word elements and context clues give you very powerful strategies for learning new words.

CHAPTER

Word Elements: Prefixes

The rich cultural heritage that the ancient Greeks and Romans left to us includes many word elements that are still used in English. This chapter introduces prefixes from ancient Greek and from Latin, the language of the ancient Romans. Learning these prefixes will help you determine meanings of many unfamiliar words.

Chapter Strategy: Word Elements: Prefixes

Chapter Words:

Part 1

anti-	antidote	*re-*	resilient
	antipathy		revelation
	antithesis		revert
equi-	equilibrium	*sub-*	subdue
	equitable		subordinate
	equivocal		subvert

Part 2

auto-	autobiography	*im-, in-* (*il-, ir-*)	impartial
	autocratic		incongruous
	autonomous		ingenious
ex-	eccentric		interminable
	exorbitant		invincible
	exploit		
	extricate		

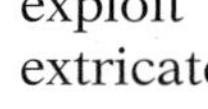

Visit the Student Companion Website at **www.cengage.com/devenglish/richek8e** to test your knowledge of these words before you study, hear each word pronounced, find additional practice exercises, and access more information on words and topics.

Did You Know?

Where Does English Come From?

The origins of language are lost in the mists of time. Archaeologists have found examples of ancient jewelry, weapons, and art, but no one knows how or why people first spoke. Linguists suspect, however, that most of the languages of Europe, the Middle East, and India are descended from a common source. This possible parent language, called *Indo-European,* would have been spoken at least 5,000 years ago. The Indo-European root *mater* (mother), for example, shows up in many languages.

Languages No Longer Spoken		*Modern Languages*	
Ancient Greek	mētēr	English	mother
Latin	mater	German	mutter
Old English	modor	Italian	madre
		Spanish	madre
		French	mère
		Polish	matka

Most of our English vocabulary descends from Indo-European roots through several languages, like Old English, that are no longer spoken. English has also been enriched by many other languages that are not Indo-European, such as Arabic (*chemistry*), Hebrew (*amen*), and the West African language of Fula (*yam*).

However, much of the higher-level vocabulary of modern English comes from the Indo-European languages of ancient Greek and Latin. (These are often called the *classical languages*.) Knowledge of the Greek and Latin word elements used in English will help you master thousands of modern English words.

Who were these ancient Greeks and Romans?

The civilization of the ancient Greeks flourished between 750 and 250 BCE. Greece was a land of small, separate city-states that created the first democracies and the first concept of citizenship. Sparta and Athens were two important city-states. While the citizens of Sparta excelled in warfare, Athens became a center of art and learning. Athenians produced the first lifelike sculpture, wrote the first tragedies and comedies, and learned philosophy from Socrates and Plato. Unfortunately, ancient Greek civilization also had its dark side. The economic system was based on slavery, and only a small percentage of the population (men who were not slaves) could be full citizens. Women were given few political rights. Tragic wars between city-states also marred Greek history.

In contrast to the divided Greek city-states, the city of Rome steadily took over first the whole of Italy, and then more territory, until it finally ruled over a huge empire. From about 200 BCE to 450 CE, the Roman

Empire, centered on the Mediterranean Sea, brought its way of life to large parts of the world, including most of Europe and parts of Africa. The Romans introduced a highway system, a postal service, water supplies, public baths, and border patrols to many less advanced areas. Some of their ancient aqueducts (structures that carry water) are still in use! They also spread the Latin language that they spoke.

But, like ancient Greece, Rome had its problems. After the first emperor, Augustus, died, murder became common in the Roman court. Several emperors were poisoned, stabbed, or smothered. Meanwhile, officials and the army continued to rule the empire efficiently.

Can you answer these questions about the Greeks and Romans?

1. An epic poem, the *Iliad,* tells of a Greek war that started when Helen, the daughter of Zeus, was stolen from her husband. Helen is often called "Helen of __________."
   a. Crete b. Sparta c. Troy d. Athens
2. __________ was a famous Roman leader who said, "I came, I saw, I conquered."
   a. Augustus Caesar b. Brutus c. Cato d. Julius Caesar
3. Cleopatra, queen of Egypt, did *not* have a romance with __________.
   a. Mark Antony b. Julius Caesar c. Augustus

Answers are on page 399.

Learning Strategy

Word Elements: Prefixes

The learning strategy in this chapter concentrates on *prefixes,* word elements attached to the beginning of word roots. The seven prefixes presented are very common, so learning them will help you master many difficult words. One dictionary lists over four hundred words that use *ex-* and more than six hundred formed from *in-* or *im-*.

Prefix	*Meaning*	*Origin*	*Chapter Words*
Part 1			
anti-, ant-	against; opposite	Greek	antidote, antipathy, antithesis
equi-, equa-	equal	Latin	equilibrium, equitable, equivocal
re-	back; again	Latin	reconcile, resilient, revelation, revert
sub-	below, under, less; part of	Latin	subconscious, subvert, subdue, subside

Part 2

auto-	self	Greek	autobiography, autocratic, autonomous
ex-, e-, ec-	out of; former	Latin	eccentric, exorbitant, exploit, extricate
im-, in-	not; in	Latin	impartial, incongruous, ingenious, interminable, invariably, invincible

When prefixes join word roots, the prefixes give clues to word meaning. Let us look first at how prefixes can combine with base words that can stand alone.

anti- (against) + *war* makes *antiwar,* meaning "against war"

The *antiwar* protesters demonstrated in Washington, D.C.

sub- (below) + *soil* makes *subsoil,* meaning "a layer of earth beneath the top soil."

The light rain did not penetrate the *subsoil.*

auto- (self) + *suggestion* makes *autosuggestion,* meaning "a suggestion made to yourself."

Some people use *autosuggestion* when they try to stop smoking.

Use prefixes to form new words, then write in the word and its meaning.

re- (again) + *possess* makes ____________, meaning ____________.

in- (not) + *essential* makes ____________, meaning ____________.

equi- (equal) + *potential* makes ____________, meaning ____________.

Answers are on page 399.

Now let's look at how prefixes join combining roots (roots that cannot stand alone as English words). Sometimes they form English words whose meanings are the combined meanings of the prefix and root.

anti- (against) + *-pathy* (feeling) makes *antipathy,* which means "feeling against," or hatred.

Have you ever felt *antipathy* toward someone?

At other times, the meaning of a word is not precisely the combined meanings of a prefix and a combining root. Still, these word elements will give you valuable clues to meaning. For example, the Latin root *vert* (to turn) combines with two prefixes that you will study in this chapter to make different English words. The idea of "turn" appears in both. The first word, *revert,* is close to, but not exactly, the meaning of the prefix and root. The second word, *subvert,* requires more imagination to relate to its word parts.

re- (back) + *vert* (turn) makes *revert,* which translates to "turn back."

Revert does not actually mean "turn back," but the meaning is close. Its definition is "to return to a habit or condition." Perhaps you know a person who *reverted* to smoking after having quit.

sub- (under) + *vert* (turn) makes *subvert,* or "to turn from under."

Subvert departs even more from the meanings of its word parts. *Subvert* means to make something worse by corrupting it or trying to overthrow it. Traitors seek to *subvert* their countries' governments, as they work within ("from underneath, turning") those systems.

As you can see, prefixes and roots may not give the *entire* meaning of an unknown word, but they do provide excellent hints. If you combine the use of context clues with the use of word elements, you can often determine the precise meaning of an unfamiliar word.

Here are the meanings of the roots and prefixes of two words. Write in the meaning of each word in the sentence.

reiterate, from *re-* (again) and *iterāre* (to repeat).

Do I have to *reiterate* the directions I just gave?

Reiterate means ____.

incredulous, from *in-* (not) and *cred* (believe)

As she continued to listen to the weird story, she grew increasingly *incredulous*.

Incredulous means ____.

Answers are on page 399.

Prefixes

Part 1

The four prefixes presented in Part 1 of this chapter are described here.

anti-, ant- (against; opposite)

The two meanings of *anti-* are related and therefore easy to remember. *Antiaircraft* missiles are fired **against** aircraft, and *antigambling* laws make gambling illegal. New English words continue to be formed with *anti-* since people always seem to find things to protest **against.**

equi-, equa- (equal)

Equi- is used in many English words. Two homes that are *equidistant* from a school are the same, or **equal,** distance from that school. *Equivalent* sums of money have the same, or **equal,** value. For example, one dollar is *equivalent* to four quarters. Two **equally** powerful forces may be called *equipotent.*

re- (back; again)

Re- has two distinct meanings. It usually means "again" when it is attached to other English words (or base words). For example, when *re-* is added to the base words *start* and *do,* it forms *restart* (start **again**) and *redo* (do **again**). However, when *re-* is added to combining roots, which cannot stand alone, it often means "back." *Recede,* for instance, means "to go **back**" and comes from the Latin word elements *re-* (back) and *cēdere* (to go).

sub- (below, under, less; part of)

In the word *substandard, sub-* means "below": "**below** the standard." A *subcompact* car is smaller (or **less**) in size than a compact. In addition, *sub-* can also refer to a classification that is "part of" something else, such as a *subtotal,* which is **part of** a total. In biology, animals from one species may be further classified into several *subspecies.*

Words to Learn

Part 1

anti-, ant-

1. **antidote** (noun) ăn′tĭ-dōt′

   From Greek *anti-* (against) + *didonai* (to give) (to give a remedy against something harmful)

   a. a substance that acts against a poison or a medical problem

   Hikers in the desert should carry an **antidote** for snake bites.

   b. something that acts against a harmful effect

   A great party was just the **antidote** I needed after a stressful day at work.

   Producing fuel-efficient cars is one **antidote** to global warming.

▶ *Common Phrases*
antidote to; antidote for

Medications with Anti-

The prefix *anti-* is widely used in medicine. Health-care professionals prescribe *antibiotics* such as penicillin and neomycin to kill organisms that can cause disease. The word *antibiotic* comes from *anti-* and *bio,* meaning "life." We take an *antihistamine* to stop the sneezing and runny nose of a cold or an allergy. *Antihistamine* comes from *anti-* plus *histi,* the ancient Greek word element meaning "tissue," or body substance. Immunizations against smallpox, measles, polio, and tuberculosis allow us to form *antibodies* that prevent these diseases. Currently, medical researchers are trying to locate substances that will form *antibodies* against the deadly viruses that cause as AIDS, SARS, BSE, avian flu, and swine flu.

2. **antipathy** (noun) ăn-tĭp′ə-thē (plural: **antipathies**)

    From Greek: *anti-* (against) + *patho* (feeling)

    great hatred, opposition, or disgust

    Debbie felt deep-seated **antipathy** to the man who had cheated her family out of money.

    Increased contact between the two cultures gradually decreased the **antipathy** between them.

3. **antithesis** (noun) ăn-tĭth′ĭ-sĭs (plural: **antitheses**)

    From Greek: *anti-* (against) + *tithenai* (to put)

    opposite; direct contrast

    Censorship is the **antithesis** of freedom of expression.

    The actor's real-life charm and fashionable clothes made him the **antithesis** of the slob he played on the TV soap opera.

    ► *Common Phrases*
    antithesis of; antithetical to

    ► *Related Word*
    antithetical (adjective) (ăn′-tĭ-thĕt′ĭ-kəl) Rigid thinking is *antithetical* to creativity.

equi-, equa-

4. **equilibrium** (noun) ē′kwə-lĭb′rē-əm

    From Latin: *equi-* (equal) + *libra* (balance)

    balance between forces; stability

    Traditional Chinese philosophy values keeping the forces of yin (passivity) and yang (activity) in **equilibrium**.

The tightrope walker almost lost his **equilibrium**.

When he found he had been laid off from his job, the man lost his **equilibrium** and began to cry.

▶ *Common Phrase*
in equilibrium

NOTE: The concept of balance can be used to describe both non-physical conditions, such as evenness of temperament or forces, and physical conditions, such as the ability to walk along a narrow curb without falling.

5. **equitable** (adjective) ĕk′wĭ-tə-bəl

From Latin: *equi* (equal)

fair; just

The judge divided the divorcing couple's money in an **equitable** fashion.

Civil rights laws were written to provide **equitable** treatment to people of all backgrounds and ethnic groups.

NOTE: In *equitable,* the word element *equi* is used as a root.

▶ *Related Words*

equity (noun) (ĕk′wĭ-tē) Children are sensitive, so teachers should try to treat each one with *equity*, without picking favorites.

inequitable (adjective) (ĭn-ĕk′wĭ-tə-bəl′) Because funds are usually based on local taxes, schools in poor and rich neighborhoods receive *inequitable* funding. (*Inequitable* means "not equitable.")

Long-Delayed Equity

A popular hit of the 1960s, "The Lion Sleeps Tonight," featured high "eeeeees" that are sung above the haunting melody. The song was written by Solomon Linda, who lived in South Africa. It recalled his childhood memories of protecting cattle from lions. Although the song was a best seller, the apartheid laws that discriminated against blacks meant that he received almost no money for the hit song. In 1962, he died in poverty. In 2006, however, a successful lawsuit gave his children 25 percent of all royalties, past and present. At last, Linda's family has received a measure of *equity,* although it is too late for him.

NOTE: The term *equity* also refers to the financial worth of something. The *equity* one has in a house is the value of a house, minus the mortgage.

6. **equivocal** (adjective) ĭ-kwĭv′ə-kəl

From Latin: *equi-* (equal) + *vox* (voice) (When something is equivocal, it seems as if two equally strong voices are sending different messages.)

a. open to different interpretations, often misleading, or avoiding the truth

Equivocal results from testing during pregnancy left the parents unsure if the baby would suffer from cystic fibrosis. (There is no intention to mislead in this sentence.)

The president's **equivocal** reply, "I will serve our national interest," did not answer the question of whether he would support a war. (In this sentence, there is an intention to mislead, or avoid the truth.)

b. doubtful, uncertain

Although her books are bestsellers, her position as a great writer is **equivocal**.

▶ *Related Words*

equivocate (verb) (ĭ-kwĭv′ə-kāt′) "I might have been around the area," the suspect *equivocated*, when asked where he was on the night of the robbery.

equivocation (noun) I was annoyed by my boss's continual *equivocation* whenever I asked for some vacation time.

re-

7. **resilient** (adjective) rĭ-zĭl′yənt

From Latin: *re-* (back) and *salire* (to jump)

Able to recover quickly from problems; easily adjusting to change

After the vicious attacks of 9/11 killed many employees, the **resilient** company of Cantor Fitzgerald started to rebuild.

The **resilient** citizens began rebuilding their town as soon as the floodwaters went down.

▶ *Related Word*

resilience (noun) Refugees from war and violence often show great *resilience* in starting new lives in other countries.

8. **revelation** (noun) rĕv′-lā′shən

From Latin: *re-* (back) + *vēlāre* (to veil) This makes *revēlāre,* "to draw back the veil." (When a veil is drawn back, something surprising or even shocking may be discovered.)

dramatic disclosure; surprising news

The Islamic holiday of Ramadan marks God's **revelation** of the Koran to the prophet Mohammed. (Here, *revelation* has a positive, religious meaning.)

Fans were shocked by the **revelation** that the pop star had hired another singer to record her songs. (Here *revelation* has a negative meaning.)

▶ *Related Word*
reveal (verb) (rĭ-vēl′) Mystery novels usually *reveal* the murderer's identity in the last few pages.

9. **revert** (verb) rĭ-vûrt′

From Latin: *re-* (back) + *vert* (turn)

to return to a former practice, habit, or condition

The abandoned farmland **reverted** to its natural prairie state.

Whenever his brother was around, my boyfriend **reverted** to childish behavior.

After her divorce, Lakesha **reverted** to her maiden name.

▶ *Common Phrases*
revert to; revert back to

▶ *Related Word*
reversion (noun) The athlete's *reversion* to drugs disqualified him from the tryouts.

sub-

10. **subdue** (verb) səb-do͞o′

From Latin: *sub-* (under) + *duc* (lead) (Someone who is subdued is led by, or placed under, the control of another.)

a. to conquer or bring under control

The Romans **subdued** land from Egypt to Scotland.

Police were called in to **subdue** rioters after the championship game.

Unable to **subdue** his emotions, the clerk hugged the boss who had given him a big raise.

b. to make less intense or noticeable

The soft lighting **subdued** the bright colors in the room.

▶ *Related Word*
subdued (adjective) The *subdued* voices of golf tournament sportscasters contrast with the shouts of football announcers.

11. **subordinate** (adjective, noun) sə-bôr′də-nĭt; (verb) sə-bôr′də-nāt

From Latin: *sub-* (under) + *ōrdĭnāre* (to arrange in order)

a. less important; of lower rank (adjective) sə-bôr′də-nĭt

All other U.S. courts hold **subordinate** positions to the Supreme Court.

b. a person of lower rank or importance (noun) sə-bôr′də-nĭt

Bosses should treat their **subordinates** with respect.

The assistant is a **subordinate** of the boss.

c. to place in a lower or less important position (verb) sə-bôr′də-nāt

Parents often **subordinate** their own wishes to their children's needs.

▶ *Common Phrases*
subordinate to (adjective); a subordinate of (noun)

NOTE: The pronunciation of the verb *subordinate* differs from the adjective and noun forms.

▶ *Related Word*
subordination (noun) Rejecting their *subordination* to Great Britain, American colonists formed an independent country.

12. **subvert** (verb) səb-vûrt′

From Latin: *sub-* (under) + *vert* (turn) (to turn from beneath)

to weaken or undermine; to destroy slowly

Vicious gossip can **subvert** a person's reputation.

Constant complaining by one worker **subverted** everyone's morale.

▶ *Related Words*
subversion (noun) Refusing citizens the right to vote is a *subversion* of democracy.
subversive (adjective) Is burning the U.S. flag a *subversive* activity?

Exercises

Part 1

■ *Definitions*

Match the word and definition. Use each choice only once.

1. equitable _______
2. revert _______
3. resilient _______
4. subdue _______
5. equilibrium _______
6. antithesis _______
7. antipathy _______
8. equivocal _______
9. revelation _______
10. antidote _______

a. conquer
b. doubtful
c. beneath awareness
d. return to a former habit
e. something that acts against a poison
f. hatred
g. surprising news
h. fair
i. balance; stability
j. less important in rank
k. opposite
l. able to recover quickly

■ *Meanings*

Match each prefix to its meaning. Use each choice only once.

1. re- _______
2. equi-, equa- _______
3. anti-, ant- _______
4. sub- _______

a. under, below, part of
b. again, back
c. equal
d. against

■ *Words in Context*

Complete each sentence with the best word. Use each choice only once.

a. antidote	d. equilibrium	g. resilient	j. subdue
b. antipathy	e. equitable	h. revelation	k. subordinate
c. antithesis	f. equivocal	i. revert	l. subvert

1. Calcium chloride injections can serve as a(n) ______________ to harm from black widow spider bites.

2. Since the evidence was ____________________, jury members felt they could not convict the man.

3. Although Eric was the ____________________ of everything Cherise had been looking for, she fell in love with him.

4. Her ____________________ for her ex-husband was so great that she refused to talk to him.

5. Using a tranquilizer gun, the forest rangers were able to ____________________ the bear that invaded our campsite.

6. Soldiers who are not loyal to the army can ____________________ the morale of others.

7. In a(n) ____________________ arrangement, the two partners each took half of the profits.

8. The CEO was so busy that her ____________________ had to handle many details for her.

9. The ____________________ boxer got right back up after he was knocked down, and started to fight.

10. Children experiencing stress may ____________________ back to sucking their thumbs long after they have quit the habit.

■ *Using Related Words*

Complete each sentence with the correct form. Use each choice only once.

From Roman Republic to Empire

1. subverted, subversion

For almost five hundred years, until about 40 BCE, Rome was a republic governed by the Roman Senate. However, continual fighting among senators ____________________ this system of government. Further ____________________ took place as great conquerors brought glory and gold to Rome from the territories they subdued. Such conquerors, it was said, started to think of themselves as emperors.

Ancient Rome was ruled by the Senate until about 40 BCE.

Bettmann/CORBIS

2. subordinate, subordination

After achieving much political success, Julius Caesar set out to **subordinate** Gaul (now France and Belgium) to the Romans. He achieved this **subordination** and returned home a hero. However, several senators became convinced that he was about to make himself emperor, and they murdered him.

3. revelation, revealed

While Augustus, Caesar's nephew, was in Illyria, a letter from his mother brought the shocking **revelation** that Caesar had been killed. His mother warned Augustus to flee. Instead, his decision **revealed** his character: he immediately went to Rome. This courage later helped him become Rome's first emperor. For the next several hundred years, Rome remained an empire.

4. equivocal, equivocation

Although Augustus was an excellent ruler, some of his followers hold more **equivocal** positions in history. Many were weakened by lives of luxury, and a few may even have been insane. Caligula, for example, without the slightest bit of ___equivocation___, made his favorite horse a royal official. Nero played the fiddle as Rome burned. As time went by, the power of Roman emperors weakened.

5. antithesis, antithetical

About two hundred years after Augustus' death, a series of "barbarian" invasions greatly weakened Rome. A lack of technology and art made the invaders' cultures ___antithetical___ to the highly civilized Roman culture. The destructive violence of the attacks was the ___antithesis___ of the principles on which the Roman Empire stood. The invasions continued for the next two hundred years, and the last emperor of Rome was forced to resign in 476 CE.

■ *Find the Example*

Choose the example that best describes the action or situation.

1. An antidote to antipathy ___a___
a. making friends with an old enemy b. meeting an old friend from high school c. continuing to fight political battles

2. The antithesis of equilibrium ___c___
a. balancing on a beam b. peace and happiness c. feeling dizzy

3. Subversion of something equitable ___b___
a. talking about your enemy's faults b. cheating people you make a fair contract with c. a fair wrestling match

4. A revelation of resilience ___b___
a. recovery from an illness that is predicted by a physician b. surprise announcement of recovery from injuries c. giving up when a person is diagnosed with a serious illness

5. Subduing a subordinate ___c___
a. making your boss give you a raise b. asking a cashier for more change c. making your employee be quiet

Prefixes

Part 2

The following three prefixes are introduced in Part 2 of this chapter.

auto- (self)

This prefix comes from the Greek word for **self**. The word *automobile* comes from *auto-* and *mobile,* meaning "moving." When the automobile was invented, it was named for the amazing sight of something moving all by **itself.**

ex-, e-, ec- (out of; former)

When *ex-* is combined with a base word, it usually means "former" or "in the past." The words *ex-wife* (**former** wife) and *ex-president* (**former** president) show *ex-* used in this sense. The hyphens in these words give a hint that the **former** meaning is being used. When *ex-* is used with a combining root, it usually means "out of," as in *exhale* (to breathe **out**). The words introduced in this lesson join *ex-* to combining roots, so *ex-* means "out of" in all these words. However, remember that *ex-* can also mean "former."

im-, in- (not; in); *il-, ir-* (not)

When spelled *im-* or *in-*, this prefix may have one of two meanings. The most common meaning of *im-* and *in-* is "not," as in the words *impure* (**not** pure) and *indecent* (**not** decent). *Im-* and *in-* can also mean "**in**," as in *inhale* (to breathe **in**) and *import* (to carry **into** a country). The *im-* spelling is used before the letters *b, m,* and *p.* This prefix is also spelled *ir-* before roots that begin with *r* as in *irregular.* Finally, it is spelled *il-* before roots that begin with *l,* such as *illegal.* The *il-* and *ir-* spellings always mean "not."

Words to Learn

Part 2

auto-

13. **autobiography** (noun) ô′tō-bī-ŏg′rə-fē (plural: **autobiographies**)

From Greek: *auto-* (self) + *bio* (life) + *graph* (write)

account of a person's life written by that person

African-American athlete, singer, and actor Paul Robeson wrote an **autobiography** detailing his life as a performer and political activist.

▶ *Related Word*

autobiographical (adjective) Many of rapper Eminem's songs are *autobiographical*.

Celebrities and Their Autobiographies

Can you match these famous people with the titles of their autobiographies?

1. 50 Cent	a. *Dreams from My Father*
2. Howard Stern	b. *From Pieces to Weight*
3. Danica Patrick	c. *Driven from Within*
4. Michael Jordan	d. *Crossing the Line*
5. Donda West	e. *Raising Kanye*
6. Barack Obama	f. *Private Parts*

Answers are on page 399.

14. **autocratic** (adjective) ô′tə-kră′tĭk

From Greek: *auto-* (self) + *krates* (ruling)

having absolute power; domineering

Mao Zedong, the **autocratic** ruler of China from 1949 to 1976, published a book that became required reading for millions of people.

My father's **autocratic** parenting style meant that whatever he said we had to do.

▶ *Related Words*

autocrat (noun, person) (ô′tə-krăt′) Peter the Great was an *autocrat* who ruled Russia from 1682 to 1725.

autocracy (noun) (ô-tŏk′rə-sē) Chileans rejected the *autocracy* of General Augusto Pinochet Ugarte when they voted for a multiparty leadership in 1989.

15. **autonomous** (adjective) ô-tŏn′ə-məs

From Greek: *auto-* (self) + *nomos* (law)

self-governing; independent

Vatican City is an **autonomous** country that rules itself, but sits within the country of Italy.

People need to be self-supporting before they can truly be **autonomous**.

► *Related Word*
autonomy (noun) Slaves lack *autonomy.*

ex-, e-, ec-

16. **eccentric** (adjective) ĕk-sĕn′trĭk

From Greek: *ek-* (out) + *kentron* (center)

odd; different from normal or usual

The **eccentric** performer Michael Jackson was known for wearing one white glove at all times.

► *Related Word*
eccentricity (noun) (ĕk′-sĕn-trĭs′ə-tē) One of Thomas Jefferson's *eccentricities* was soaking his feet in cold water every morning.

Tony's appearance was *eccentric*.

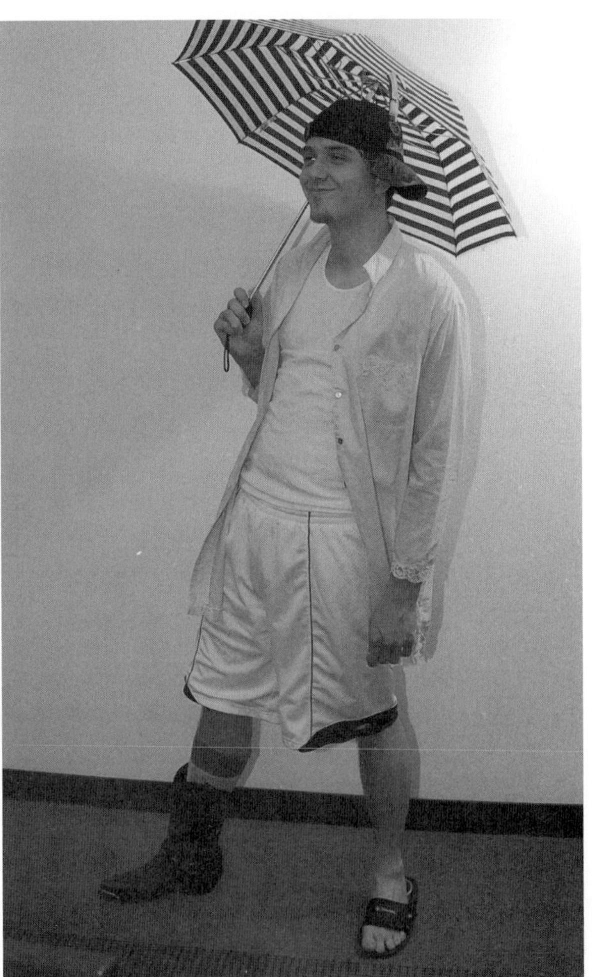

Courtesy author

17. **exorbitant** (adjective) ĭg-zôr′bĭ-tənt

From Latin: *ex-* (out) + *orbita* (path)

expensive; unreasonable; exceeding proper limits

A $500 fine is **exorbitant** to pay for a parking ticket.

We would not borrow money from a bank that charged **exorbitant** interest rates.

▶ *Related Word*

exorbitance (noun) We were shocked by the *exorbitance* of the prices that the resellers wanted for football tickets.

18. **exploit** (verb) ĭk-sploit′; (noun) ĕks′ploit′

From Latin: *ex-* (out) + *plicāre* (to fold), making *explicāre* (to unfold) (When we *exploit* something, we "fold it out" and make it work for us.)

a. to take advantage of; to use (verb) ĭk-sploit′

Company owners **exploited** coal miners, who worked long hours in dangerous conditions for little pay. (Here *exploit* has a negative meaning.)

Alaska **exploits** its rich oil and natural gas reserves while trying not to harm the environment.

b. great adventure; great deed (noun) ĕks′ploit′

The **exploits** of pirates seem romantic in movies, but in reality, they are brutal crimes.

▶ *Related Word*

exploitation (noun) (ĕk′sploi-tā′shən) Consumers have protested the *exploitation* of child labor in clothing factories.

NOTES: (1) *Exploit* and *exploitation* often suggest taking unfair advantage (as in the exploitation of minorities). However, the words can mean simply "to take advantage of" or "to use wisely." (2) Notice the difference in pronunciation stress between *ex-ploit′* (verb) and *ex′ploit* (noun).

19. **extricate** (verb) ĕk′strĭ-kāt′

From Latin: *ex-* (out) + *tricae* (difficulties), making *extricāre* (to disentangle, to free)

to free or escape from difficulty; to disentangle

Four sets of cutting tools were needed to **extricate** the passenger from the overturned truck.

Once you get involved in an argument, it can be hard to **extricate** yourself.

▶ *Common Phrase*
to extricate (oneself) from

▶ *Related Word*
extrication (noun) (ĕk′strĭ-kā′shən) The *extrication* of his appendix left a small scar.

im-, in-

20. **impartial** (adjective) ĭm-pär′shəl

From Latin: *im-* (not) + *pars* (part)

fair; just; not biased

To ensure that the scholarship board remained **impartial**, names of students were removed from applications.

The judge instructed the jury to consider the facts in an **impartial** manner.

▶ *Common Phrase*
impartial toward

▶ *Related Word*
impartiality (noun) (ĭm′pär-shē-ăl′ə-tē) It is difficult to judge a good friend with *impartiality*.

21. **incongruous** (adjective) ĭn-kŏng′gro͞o-əs

From Latin: *in-* (not) + *congruere* (to agree)

out of place; not consistent or in harmony

The eighty-year-old great-grandfather and the twenty-five-year-old model made an **incongruous** couple.

The modern furniture looked **incongruous** in the ancient castle.

▶ *Related Word*
incongruity (noun) ĭn′kŏn-gro͞o′ĭ-tē News reporters noted the *incongruity* of the woman's mild manner and the terrible crime she was charged with.

An Incongruous Pair

Mzee, a tortoise (type of turtle), and Owen, a hippopotamus, formed a close mother-son relationship at a nature preserve in Kenya. This *incongruous* pair came together after Owen was rescued from floods following the catastrophic tsunami in 2004. Mzee, who is male, played a mother's role for Owen. From Mzee, Owen learned what was safe to eat in his new home, and the two became inseparable. In return, Owen protected Mzee, chasing away animals and people he felt were threatening his "mother."

Owen and Mzee: An *incongruous* pair

AP Photo

22. **ingenious** (adjective) ĭn-jēn′yəs

From Latin: *in-* (in) + *gen* (born), making *ingenium* (inborn talent)

clever; inventive

An **ingenious** engineer invented air conditioning to prevent temperature changes from affecting the paper in a printing plant.

Critics believe the soft drink's success depended more on **ingenious** advertising than on taste.

► *Related Word*

ingenuity (noun) (ĭn′jə-nōō′ĭ-tē) Human *ingenuity* has led to hundreds of uses for duct tape, including catching insects, preserving crumbling guard rails, removing warts, and making prom outfits.

Want more uses of duct tape? Look for links posted at the Student Companion Website at **www.cengage.com/ devenglish/richek8e.**

23. **interminable** (adjective) ĭn-tûr′mə-nə-bəl

From Latin: *in-* (not) + *terminus* (end, boundary)

endless; too long

Even a short walk seems **interminable** when you have a blister on your toe.

NOTES: (1) *Interminable* has a negative connotation. (2) This word often describes something that seems endless rather than something that actually is endless.

24. **invincible** (adjective) ĭn-vĭn′sə-bəl

From Latin: *in-* (not) + *vincibilis* (conquerable)

unable to be conquered or defeated

After winning every match of the season, the soccer team seemed **invincible**.

▶ *Related Word*

invincibility (noun) (ĭn-vĭn′sə-bĭl′ĭ-tē) Superman is known for his *invincibility*—except when Kryptonite is around.

Exercises

Part 2

■ *Definitions*

Match the word and definition. Use each choice only once.

1. interminable __l__
2. extricate __g__
3. invincible __k__
4. incongruous __b__
5. ingenious __f__
6. exploit __e__
7. impartial __h__
8. autocratic __i__
9. exorbitant __d__
10. autobiography __c__

a. self-ruling
b. not in harmony
c. the story of one's own life
d. very expensive
e. to take advantage of
f. clever
g. to free from difficulty
h. not biased
i. having absolute power
j. odd
k. not able to be conquered
l. endless; too long

■ *Meanings*

Match each prefix to its meaning. Use each choice only once.

1. auto- __a__
2. ex-, e-, ec- __c__
3. im-, in- __b__

a. self
b. in; not
c. out; former

■ *Words in Context*

Complete each sentence with the best word. Use each choice only once.

a. autobiography	e. exorbitant	i. incongruous
b. autocratic	f. exploit	j. ingenious
c. autonomous	g. extricate	k. interminable
d. eccentric	h. impartial	l. invincible

1. The famous escape artist Houdini could ___g, extricate___ himself from a packing crate that had been nailed shut and placed under water.

2. Did that star write her ___a, autobiography___ alone, or did someone help her?

3. Mexico is now a(n) ___c, autonomous___ country, but was once a colony of Spain.

4. The time I spent waiting for the results of my medical test seemed ___k, interminable___.

5. It is wrong to ___f, exploit___ laborers by not paying them on time and forbidding them to join unions.

6. In a(n) ___j, ingenious___ plan to prevent houses in the Netherlands from flooding, residents construct homes that float in the water.

7. Nazi Germany seemed ___l, invincible___ as its forces swept over mainland Europe, conquering wherever they invaded.

8. The sophisticated computer system seemed ___i, incongruous___ with the dirt floor and straw roof of the hut.

9. The ___d, eccentric___ man lived on a diet of cooked carrots, spinach salad, and liver sausage.

10. The landlord wanted a(n) ___e, exorbitant___ rent of $10,000 per month for the small apartment.

■ *Using Related Words*

Complete each sentence with the correct form. Use each choice only once.

FACT AND FICTION FROM ANCIENT GREECE

1. incongruously, incongruous

   It might sound ____________________ for a scientist to make a famous discovery while sitting in a bathtub. But that's where Archimedes discovered an important principle of physics. Even more ____________________, this distinguished scientist yelled "Eureka!" (I have found it!)

2. autonomy, autonomous

   In 490 BCE, Darius, king of the vast Persian empire, decided to conquer the city-state of Athens and end its ____________________. Against all odds, Athens defeated the Persian army on the Plain of Marathon and remained ____________________. Pheidippides ran twenty-six miles to deliver news of the victory to Athens. Since then, a race of twenty-six miles, or any long, difficult contest, has been called a "marathon."

3. impartial, impartiality

   The philosopher Socrates was a famous teacher in ancient Athens. Unfortunately, when he criticized city leaders, they brought him to trial for corrupting youth. The trial was so emotional that it was impossible to be ____________________ in the debate. In 399 BCE, the authorities condemned Socrates to die by drinking the poison hemlock. Although the city elders stated that they had acted with ____________________, others disagreed.

4. exploitation, exploited

   You have most likely heard of Aesop's fables. Aesop, who was probably a slave, lived in ancient Greece in about 500 BCE. In one of his fables, a couple had a goose that laid one golden egg each day.

When the couple ____________________ their good fortune wisely, they grew wealthier. However, one day they decided to get all the gold immediately. They killed the goose, only to find that there was no gold inside it. Thus, their attempt at greedy ____________________ cost them dearly. From this fable comes the phrase "to kill the goose that lays the golden egg."

5. eccentric, eccentricity

Modern voting machines have led to many errors, but imagine how ____________________ a modern voter would consider the ancient Athenian method of voting on pieces of pottery. The Athenians voted to expel dangerous citizens by writing their names on pieces of broken clay jars. This ____________________ has given us a modern English word. The clay pieces were called *oster,* and to snub or exclude someone is now "to ostracize."

■ *Reading the Headlines*

Here are some headlines that might appear in newspapers. Read each and answer the questions. (Remember that small words, such as *is, are, a,* and *the,* are often left out of headlines.)

ECCENTRIC INVENTOR AND BASKETBALL STAR SEEM LIKE INCONGRUOUS BUSINESS PARTNERS

1. Is the inventor odd? ______
2. Do the two people seem like they belong together? ______

NEW EXPLOITS IN EXTRICATING HIMSELF FROM DISASTER GIVE MOUNTAIN CLIMBER REPUTATION FOR INVINCIBILITY

3. Did the mountain climber get himself out of trouble? ______
4. Does it seem like he can be defeated? ______

AUTOCRATIC LEADER REFUSES TO GRANT IMPARTIAL OBSERVERS THE AUTONOMY TO JUDGE WHETHER ELECTIONS ARE FAIR

5. Does the leader hold a lot of power? _______

6. Are the observers fair minded? _______

7. Are the observers free to judge? _______

EXORBITANTLY PRICED AUTOBIOGRAPHY SEEMS INTERMINABLE TO READ

8. Is the autobiography expensive? _______

9. Does the autobiography seem short? _______

10. Did someone write about himself or herself? _______

Chapter Exercises

■ *Practicing Strategies: New Words from Word Elements*

Use your knowledge of prefixes to determine the meanings of these words and complete each sentence. Use each choice only once.

a. antiaircraft	e. autoinoculation	i. reconsider
b. antifreeze	f. equator	j. refill
c. anti-intellectual	g. illegal	k. subcontractor
d. autobrake	h. income	l. subchief

1. You must stop those ____________________ activities and follow the law!

2. I wish you would ____________________ your decision, now that you know more about the problem.

3. Some advanced airplanes have ____________________ systems, which stop the plane while the pilots perform other tasks.

4. Money that comes in to you is called ____________________.

5. We wanted to talk to the leader, but instead we had to talk to the

   ____________________.

6. The ____________________ guns were designed to shoot down enemy planes.

7. The general supervisor hired a(n) ____________________ to do the plumbing.

8. The ____________________ divides the Earth equally into the Northern and Southern Hemispheres.

9. I poured ____________________ into my radiator to prevent the water from turning to ice.

10. In an ____________________ campaign, the autocrat arrested doctors, lawyers, and teachers.

■ *Practicing Strategies: Combining Context Clues and Word Elements*

In each sentence, one prefixed word is italicized. Use the meaning of the prefix and the context to make an intelligent guess about its meaning.

1. The child's writing was *illegible*, and we had to ask her to read it to us.

   Illegible means ____.

2. Despite the fact that he had never attended school, the *autodidact* had a wealth of knowledge.

   Autodidact means ____.

3. At the time of an *equinox,* there are twelve hours of daylight and twelve hours of darkness.

   Equinox means ____.

The next two items are taken from newspaper sources.

4. The facility has acute care for people who require continuous management of serious illnesses and *subacute* care for people who need frequent medical attention and skilled nursing care.

   Subacute means ____.

5. The Night Ministry's outreach van, an aged school bus *refitted* as a mobile soup kitchen, pulled up to a stretch of West 63rd Street.

   Refitted means ______________________________.

■ *Practicing Strategies: Using the Dictionary*

This entry is taken from an online source. Read it and answer the questions that follow.

bloom[1] definition
bloom (blo͞om)

noun

1. flower; blossom
2. flowers collectively, as of a plant
3. the state or time of flowering
4. a state or time of best health or greatest beauty, vigor, or freshness; prime
5. a youthful, healthy glow (of cheeks, skin, etc.)
6. the grayish, powdery coating on various fruits, as the plum, grape, etc., and on some leaves
7. any similar coating, as on new coins
8. a mass of planktonic algae in lakes, ponds, or the sea, as in the development of red tides

intransitive verb

1. to bear a flower or flowers; blossom
2. to reach a prime condition, as in health, vigor, beauty, perfection, etc.; flourish
3. to glow with color, health, etc.

transitive verb

Archaic: to cause to bloom, flower, or flourish

Etymology: ME *blom* < ON *blomi,* flowers and foliage on trees < IE **bhlō-*, var. of base **bhel-*, to swell, sprout > blade, bleed, L *flos,* flower, Gr *phyllon,* leaf

1. Which common word in the dictionary key contains a vowel pronounced like the *oo* in *bloom*? ______________________

2. What is the part of speech and number of the definition that best fits this sentence: "We gathered the most beautiful bloom and placed it in a vase." ______________________

3. What is the definition of *bloom* that is no longer in use?

   ____

4. What is the part of speech and number of the definition that best fits this sentence? "The apple tree *bloomed* with flowers.

   ____

5. In which language did *bloom* originate? ______________________

■ *Companion Words*

Complete each sentence with the best word. You may use choices more than once, and some items may have more than one correct answer. Choices: to, of, from, in, for, back, about

1. Hatred is the antithesis ________ love.
2. Dimercaprol is used as an antidote ________ arsenic poisoning.
3. The first-class seaman is a subordinate ________ the admiral.
4. A good stereo system keeps high and low notes ________ equilibrium.
5. Eating pork is antithetical ________ the beliefs of Jews and Muslims.
6. We extricated ourselves ________ the stuck elevator by climbing out.
7. The revelations ________ huge executive bonuses shocked the public.
8. The exploits ________ Robin Hood have been the subject of many movies.
9. In the army, the private is subordinate ________ the sergeant.
10. Please don't revert ________ to biting your nails.

■ *Writing with Your Words*

To practice effective writing, complete each sentence with an interesting phrase that indicates the meaning of the italicized word.

1. If I had to *subdue* a lion, ________________________________

   ____.
2. One policy that I think is *equitable* is ________________________________

   ____.
3. First she lost her *equilibrium*, and then ________________________________

   ____.
4. I was shocked by the *revelation* that ________________________________

   ____.

5. When I saw the *exorbitant* price of the sneakers, ______________________________.

6. I felt *exploited* when ______________________________.

7. One habit I never want to *revert* back to is ______________________________.

8. The world needs an *ingenious* solution to the problem of ______________________________.

9. The *resilient* woman ______________________________.

10. The *invincible* soccer player ______________________________.

■ *Making Connections*

To connect new vocabulary to your life, write extended responses to these questions.

1. In your experience, are student employees treated equitably at work? Give examples.
2. Describe a situation in which a person was autocratic.
3. How much autonomy do you feel a teenager should be granted? Give examples and reasons for your position.

Passage

Food of the People

It has fed our nation for more than seventy years, inspiring poetry and song. It has even been listed among the one hundred greatest inventions of the twentieth century. Yet it has come under attack for its nutritional value as well as its appearance. What is it? The SPAM® Family of Products, of course!

Lenscap/Alamy

The SPAM Family of Products was first produced in 1935. A few years later, **(1)** Hormel Foods Corporation (formerly Geo. A Hormel & Company) invented an **ingenious** process that allowed meat to be preserved in a can without refrigeration. But sales didn't really take off until the company changed the name of the product. It ran a contest and chose the entry of "Spam." The person who coined the name received $100. Although this sum would not be considered **equitable** payment by today's standards, it was quite a bit of money at the time.

The seemingly **interminable** economic depression of the 1930s **(2)** made the price of many fresh meats **exorbitant**. Canned meat, like SPAM, was a cheaper alternative. So with its new, appealing name, SPAM found its way into many U.S. homes. A can of SPAM was easy to get, store, and prepare.

World War II (1939–1945) made SPAM luncheon meat a truly common food. With its new, square-cornered cans, designed to meet military needs, SPAM could easily be shipped to soldiers. **(3)** The high-calorie food quickly **subdued** hunger and supplied protein. SPAM fed the armies of many nations. In his **autobiography**, *Khrushchev Remembers,* the former head of the Soviet Union credited SPAM with saving the Russian army from starvation. And, back in the United States, when other meats were rationed, SPAM could be bought in unlimited quantities.

SPAM luncheon meat continued to feed troops in other wars. Jess Loya, a Vietnam veteran, remembers that **(4)** SPAM was an **antidote** to his homesickness. Opening a can would remind him of his childhood when, living with a single father, he ate it often.

With its former gelatin-like coating and odd, boxlike shape, SPAM has long been a source of conversational fun. **(5)** Its pink color, similar to ham but more intense, seems to spark strong reactions of either **antipathy** or devotion. Advertisements have added to the popularity of SPAM. Radio featured "SPAMMY™ the Pig" and the musical "Hormel Girls," who toured the United States. In 1940, SPAM became quite possibly the subject of the world's first singing commercial. Sung to the tune of "My Bonny Lies Over the Ocean," it went "SPAM, SPAM, SPAM, SPAM, Hormel's new miracle meat in a can. Tastes fine, saves time. If you want something grand, ask for SPAM."

Although Hormel called it "the miracle meat in a can," others have referred to it as "the mystery meat." This is unfair because, **(6)** as **impartial** observers have pointed out, the ingredients are listed on each can. (They are chopped pork shoulder with ham meat added, salt, water, sugar, and sodium nitrite.) In these more health-conscious times, the calorie count and high percentage of fat have also become a concern. In fact, Hormel Foods now makes SPAM Lite and SPAM Oven Roasted Turkey.

SPAM is manufactured in several countries. In fact, in Korea SPAM is sold in stylish gift boxes. **(7)** It may seem **incongruous** to see SPAM alongside expensive watches and perfume, but South Koreans consider it a great treat. Within the United States, Hawaiians eat the most SPAM per capita, averaging four cans per person each year. SPAM can be prepared in many ways, including grilled, baked, and microwaved, or it can be eaten cold right from the can. There are thousands of recipes that include SPAM. Cooking contests featuring SPAM are popular throughout the United States.

It may come as a **revelation** that some uses for SPAM Products have nothing to do with food. Joey Green has become famous for using it to polish furniture and bathroom fixtures. Reporter James Barron, however, noted that it left a greasy film. Others have found that SPAM can spackle a wall, fill holes in a canoe, and soothe a black eye. **(8)** These uses seem **eccentric**, but amusing.

SPAM has been the subject of poetry, including haiku, a form of verse originally from Japan. One author writes:

> Pretty pink Spam ham
> Shining on the white platter.
> Where did my fork go?

Sonnets and limericks have also been written to SPAM.

With all the fun and nutrition that SPAM has given us over the years, it is good to know that it still sells well. **(9)** SPAM is **resilient** enough to remain unaffected by criticism. Sales remain **invincible** to humorous put-downs and even insults. **(10)** Hormel Foods continues to be an **autonomous**, family-originated company. The continuing popularity of the SPAM Family of Products is illustrated by the fact that if all the cans ever sold were laid end to end, they would circle the Earth at least twelve times!

■ *Exercise*

Each numbered sentence corresponds to a sentence in the passage. Fill in the letter of the choice that makes the sentence mean the same thing as its corresponding sentence in the passage.

1. Hormel Foods Corporation invented a(n) ______ process.
   a. interesting b. speedy c. independent d. clever

2. The price of many fresh meats was ______.
   a. increased b. unfair c. expensive d. a shock

3. The high-calorie-count food quickly ______ hunger.
   a. extended b. conquered c. maximized d. revealed

4. SPAM was a(n) ______ his homesickness.
   a. a reminder of b. cure for c. secondary to d. extension of

5. Its pink color seems to spark strong reactions of ______ or devotion.
   a. unhappiness b. loyalty c. hatred d. love

6. ______ observers have pointed out that the ingredients are listed on each can.
   a. Bossy b. Strange c. Nameless d. Unbiased

7. It may seem ______ to see SPAM alongside expensive watches and perfume.
   a. natural b. inventive c. out of place d. not acceptable

8. These uses seem ______, but amusing.
   a. out-of-place b. hateful c. adventurous d. odd

9. SPAM ______.
   a. is very profitable b. is of doubtful health value c. is opposed
   d. is able to adjust to changes

10. Hormel Foods continues to be a(n) ______, family-originated company.
    a. out-of-place b. odd c. adventurous d. independent

■ *Discussion Questions*

1. On balance, do you think SPAM has had good or bad effects? Explain your answer.
2. Describe two things that appeal to you about SPAM and two things you find unappealing.
3. Why do you think SPAM has drawn so much attention?

Another Meaning for Spam

Spam has a newer meaning: distributing unwanted advertisements by e-mail is called *spamming*. The name originated with *Monty Python's Flying Circus*, when comedians sang, "SPAM, SPAM, SPAM" to drown out conversation. In the same way, *spam* is said to overwhelm personal e-mail messages.

You can find more information on SPAM through the Student Companion Website at **www.cengage.com/ devenglish/richek8e.**

INSIGHT INTO IDIOMS

Expressions for Beginnings, Endings, and Time

Beginnings, endings, and time form the basis for many idioms. One such idiom describes the common situation of being just in time—with not a minute to spare. We use the idiom *just in the nick of time* to describe arriving or finishing something at the last possible moment. Have you ever caught a bus *in the nick of time*?

What is a *nick*? Until recently, most clocks and watches were driven by two small wheels with notches, or *nicks,* in them. The nicks on one wheel caught on nicks on another wheel, moving as frequently as every second. You may actually have a watch with nicks. If so, it needs to be wound up every few days.

Here are more idioms about time:

a. To *start from scratch* means to start from the beginning.

b. To *wind up* means to end something.

c. A person who is *at the end of his rope* is desperate, and doesn't know what to do.

d. If a woman *takes her time* she does things slowly, at her own rate.

e. A person who has *time on his hands* has extra time.

f. Something that is *behind the times* is out of date or no longer in fashion.

g. When we say it's *high time,* we indicate that something is overdue or late, and should be done immediately.

Practice chapter words one more time by filling in the letter of the correct idiom into the blank before each sentence.

______ 1. The boss has exploited his workers for years, and it's _________ they got a raise.

______ 2. Because my sister always _________ dressing and putting on makeup in the bathroom we share, the wait to use it is interminable.

______ 3. The clothes in that store are the antithesis of new fashion; they are _________.

______ 4. When he suddenly lost his equilibrium and started to scream, we realized he was _________.

______ 5. We hope that the wrestler subdues his rival quickly so that the match will _________ early.

Links to more lists of English idioms and their meanings can be found at the Student Companion Website for this book: **www.cengage.com/devenglish/richek8e.**

CHAPTER 6

Word Elements: People and Names

Words that come from names fill the English language. The *diesel* engine, the *Ferris* wheel, and *nicotine* were named for their discoverers. In this chapter you will learn more words formed from names. In addition, the chapter presents combining roots that relate to people and two prefixes that come from names in Greek mythology.

Chapter Strategy: Roots; Word Elements About People

Chapter Words:

Part 1

anthrop	anthropological misanthrope philanthropist	*nom, onym*	nominal pseudonym renowned
gen	congenital degenerate genesis	*viv*	viable vital vivacious

Part 2

pan-	pandemonium panorama	*Name Words*	boycott gargantuan martial maverick odyssey quixotic spartan tantalize
psych-	psyche psychosomatic		

Visit the Student Companion Website at **www.cengage.com/devenglish/richek8e** to test your knowledge of these words before you study, hear each word pronounced, find additional practice exercises, and access more information on words and topics.

Did You Know?

Which Words Come from Names?

Many English words are taken from names in classical myths. The ancient Greeks and Romans had well-developed and colorful mythologies that reflected the violence and passion of life in a time when humans were largely at the mercy of disease and natural forces.

The mythological king of the gods, Jupiter, ruled thunder—a fearful force to ancient people. His many exploits included dethroning his father and turning himself into a swan in order to seduce a young girl. He loved nasty jokes. The word *jovial,* meaning "merry," comes from Jove, another name for Jupiter.

Mercury, often shown with wings on his feet, was the rapid messenger of the gods. The metal *mercury,* used in thermometers, is a quick-moving liquid at room temperature. A quick-tempered person is often called *mercurial.* Venus, or Aphrodite, was the goddess of love. An *aphrodisiac* is a drug or food that is said to increase sexual desire.

Other words come from the names of real people. The Earl of *Sandwich* (1718–1792) loved to gamble so much that he refused to leave the game, even to eat. Instead he had meat brought to him between two pieces of bread. U.S. Union Civil War general Ambrose Burnside, a fashion leader, allowed his hair to grow down the side of his face, inventing a style we still call—reversing Burnside's name—*sideburns.* George Washington Gale Ferris invented the *Ferris wheel* for the 1893 Columbian Exposition in Chicago. The idea for the *Frisbee* came from the easy-to-catch pie tins manufactured by the Frisbee company in Bridgeport, Connecticut.

Groups of people also contribute words. The coffee drink *cappuccino* comes from the Italian Capuchin order of Roman Catholic monks.

The names of places have also been used for words. The word *dollar* comes from *taler,* shortened from *Joachimstal,* the city in Bohemia where it was first used. *Peach* is taken from the Latin word for Persia (now Iran), where this fruit originated. *Tangerine* came from Tangier, in Morocco.

Even imaginary places have lent their names to English. In about 1500, a Spanish novelist described a beautiful, imaginary island inhabited by strong women. When exploring the Americas, a Spaniard used the novelist's word to name a real place of great natural beauty, at first thought to be an island. It is called *California*.

In this chapter, you will learn several words derived from names. Perhaps one day a word will be coined from your name!

Words from People and Places

Can you match the word to its person or place of origin?

1. Oscar	a. name of the engineer who invented this fuel
2. chauvinist	b. a country club in suburban New York
3. tuxedo	c. legendary soldier very devoted to Napoleon
4. Atlas	d. uncle of the secretary of the Motion Picture Academy
5. diesel	e. mythical being supporting the world on his shoulder

Answers are on page 399.

Learning Strategy

Word Elements: Roots; Word Elements About People

This first part of Chapter 6 discusses roots and how they function in words. Four roots related to people are used as examples. The second part of the chapter continues with prefixes, presenting two taken from names.

Element	*Meaning*	*Origin*	*Function*	*Chapter Words*
Part 1				
anthrop	human	Greek	root	anthropological, misanthrope, philanthropist
gen	birth; type	Greek; Latin	root	congenital, degenerate, genesis
nom, onym	name	Latin; Greek	root	nominal, pseudonym, renowned
vit, viv	life	Latin	root	viable, vital, vivacious
Part 2				
pan-	all	Greek	prefix	pandemonium, panorama
psych-, psycho-	mind; soul	Greek	prefix	psyche, psychosomatic

A root is the word element that carries the central meaning of a word. Although prefixes and suffixes may alter the meaning of a root, they do not carry as much meaning as the root itself.

Remember that there are two kinds of root—base word and combining root. Base words can stand alone as English words. They may or may not have prefixes and suffixes attached to them. *Work* is an example of a base word.

Combining roots cannot stand alone as English words. They require a prefix, a suffix, or at least a change in spelling in order to form a word. Most of the roots you will study in this book are combining roots that come from ancient Greek and Latin. Although they were words in these ancient languages, they appear in modern English only as word elements.

The root *anthrop* (human) is an example of a combining root. It forms a word when it is attached to a prefix (*misanthrope*) or a suffix (*anthropological*).

Nom or *onym,* meaning "name," is another example of a combining root. This root has more than one spelling because it comes from both Latin and Greek. It forms over thirty English words. Slight changes in spelling give us the words *name* and *noun;* adding a suffix gives us *nominate*; adding different prefixes gives us *antonym* and *synonym.*

Every word formed from the root *nom* or *onym* carries a meaning related to "name." Sometimes the meaning is directly stated; at other times the root gives a hint rather than supplying a full meaning. The word *name* has the same meaning as the root *nom* or *onym;* thus, the word and the root are directly related. Other words have an indirect relationship to *nom* and *onym:*

A *noun* is a word that names a person, place, idea, or thing.

To *nominate* is to name somebody to a position or to name somebody as a candidate in an election.

A *synonym* is a word that means the same thing as another word; two synonyms name the same thing. (*Syn-* means "same.")

An *antonym* is a word opposite in meaning to another word; two antonyms name opposite things. (As you learned in Chapter 5, *ant-* means "opposite.")

Word Roots

Part 1

The four roots presented in Part 1 of this chapter are all related to people and their lives.

anthrop (human)

The root *anthrop* comes from the Greek word for "human," *anthropos.* You may have taken a course in *anthropology,* the study of **human** life.

gen (birth; type)

Because *gen* forms more than fifty English words, it is an extremely useful root. *Gen* has two meanings: "birth" and "type." The ancients felt that these meanings were related because when someone was **born,** he or she was a certain **type** of person. *Gen* means **birth** in the word *gene,* which refers to the hereditary information in each cell of a living plant or animal. We are all **born** with our genes. Recently, an enormous *genome* research project defined the function of all human genes. Another word, *generation,* refers to people who are **born** during the same time period.

Gen means "type" in the word *gender,* which tells what **type** of person you are, male or female. Perhaps you buy *generic* foods at the grocery. These have no brand names and are of a general **type.** Context clues will help you to determine whether *gen* means "birth" or "type" when you see it in a word.

nom, onym (name)

This root comes from both Latin and Greek. *Nomen* is Latin for "name," and the word originally appeared in Greek as *onoma.*

vit, viv (life)

In Latin, *vita* means "life." *Vit* forms such words as *vitamin,* chemicals necessary for human **life.** Manufacturers have used this root in brand names, such as *Vitalis,* which is supposed to add **life** to your hair. *Victuals* (pronounced and sometimes spelled informally as *vittles*) means "food." It comes from the Latin verb *vivere,* "to live"—food enables us to **live.**

Words to Learn

Part 1

anthrop

1. **anthropological** (adjective) ăn′thrə-pə-lŏj′ĭ-kəl

From Greek: *anthrōpos* (human being)

referring to the study of human beings and their cultures

Through **anthropological** research, Margaret Mead discovered the rites of passage to adulthood in Samoan tribes.

▶ *Related Words*

anthropologist (noun) Franz Boas, an important early *anthropologist*, studied many native American languages.

anthropology (noun) In one application of *anthropology,* research into ancient Peruvian canals is improving modern-day farming methods.

2. **misanthrope** (noun) mĭs′ən-thrōp′

From Greek: *misein* (to hate) + *anthrop* (human)

a person who hates or distrusts other people

A failure in business and personal life, the **misanthrope** resented the happiness of others.

▶ *Related Words*

misanthropic (adjective) (mĭs′ən-thrŏp′ĭk) *Misanthropic* gorilla researcher Dian Fossey preferred the company of animals to people.

misanthropy (noun) Known for his *misanthropy,* the billionaire refused to give even a dime to charity.

ArenaPal/Topham/The Image Works

MCA-Universal Pictures/Photofest

Ebenezer Scrooge and the Grinch are *misanthropic* characters.

Scrooge and the Grinch

Two famous characters exemplify *misanthropy*. Ebenezer Scrooge, created by Charles Dickens in the classic novella *A Christmas Carol,* mistreats his employee and wishes ill to everybody, especially at Christmas. Scrooge has become famous for his classic expression "Bah, Humbug!" A more modern *misanthrope,* the Grinch, actually steals Christmas. The Grinch was created by children's author Theodor Geisel, better known as Dr. Seuss.

3. **philanthropist** (noun) fĭ-lăn′thrə-pĭst

   From Greek: *philos* (loving) + *anthrop* (human)

   one who wishes to help humanity; a person who makes large gifts to charity

   The **philanthropist** donated money to construct a new hospital.

▶ *Related Words*

philanthropic (adjective) (fĭl′ən-thrŏp′ĭk) Many sports stars have foundations that make *philanthropic* gifts to help needy children.

philanthropy (noun) The *philanthropy* of the American Jewish community helped build the state of Israel.

Philanthropy *from the Humble*

The *philanthropy* of Mexican Americans toward Mexico, the country of their origin, has become legendary. In fact, donations from the United States, which totalled $23.98 billion in 2007, are Mexico's second largest source of foreign income. Often this money comes from humble people who generously give of the little they have. A documentary called *The Sixth Section* shows the improvements people living in Newburgh, New York have made in the lives of people in Boquerón, Puebla, Mexico.

gen

4. **congenital** (adjective) kən-jĕn′ĭ-təl

   From Latin: *com-* (together; with) + *gen* (birth) (If something is *congenital,* you are born with it.)

   existing at birth

   People who suffer from microtia, a **congenital** problem, have ears that are not fully developed.

A Website for the Disabled

Jay Cohen, born with the *congenital* condition of spinal muscular dystrophy, has dedicated his life to helping others with disabilities. His site, **www.disabledonline.com** gives information on education, employment, legal developments, and entertainment to individuals with disabilities. It also features a chat room. You can access the site through the Student Companion Website at **www.cengage.com/devenglish/richek8e.**

NOTE: *Congenital* can also mean doing something as a habit, as in "He is a *congenital* liar."

5. **degenerate** (verb) dĭ-jĕn′ə-rāt; (adjective, noun) dĭ-jĕn′ər-ĭt

From Latin: *de-* (worsen) *gen* (type)

a. to become worse; to deteriorate (verb) dĭ-jĕn′ə-rāt

The calm meeting unexpectedly **degenerated** into a fist fight.

b. becoming worse (adjective) dĭ-jĕn′ər-ĭt

The patient's **degenerate** lung condition was due to his life-long smoking habit.

c. a corrupt or vicious person (noun, adjective) dĭ-jĕn′ər-ĭt

In TV police dramas, the cops are always chasing thieves, thugs, and other **degenerates**. (noun)

Only a **degenerate** person could like the horrifying violence in that movie. (adjective)

▶ *Related Words*

degeneration (noun) Wet macular *degeneration* is a visual problem caused by problems in the retina of the eye.

degenerative (adjective) Multiple sclerosis is a *degenerative* condition that worsens with time.

6. **genesis** (noun) jĕn′ĭ-sĭs (Plural: **geneses**)

From Greek: *gen* (birth) (*Genesis* meant "birth" or "origin" in ancient Greek.)

origin; beginning

Pre-Hispanic customs are the **genesis** of many Mexican holiday traditions.

Careful observation is the **genesis** of many scientific discoveries.

The first book of the Bible, the book of **Genesis**, describes the creation of the world.

▶ *Common Phrase*
genesis of

nom; nym

7. **nominal** (adjective) nŏm′ə-nəl

From Latin: *nom* (name)

a. in name only

Although Queen Elizabeth II is the **nominal** ruler of England, the prime minister and Parliament hold most of the power.

b. very small

Astrid made a **nominal** donation of $1 to the charity.

8. **pseudonym** (noun) so͞od′n-ĭm′

From Greek: *pseudes* (false) + *onym* (name)

fictitious name; a chosen name

Stephen King has published novels under the **pseudonym** of Richard Bachman.

A list of rap stars whose **pseudonyms** contain "Lil" includes Lil' Bow Wow, Lil C, Lil' Fats, Lil' Flip, Lil' Keke, Lil' Papa, Lil Romeo, and Lil Poison.

NOTE: The word *pseudonym* often refers to authors or artists. In contrast, *alias,* which usually refers to names assumed by criminals, has a negative connotation.

▶ *Common Phrases*
under the pseudonym of; using the pseudonym

Match the Celebrity Pseudonym and Real Name

1. Superman	a. Clark Kent
2. Queen Latifah	b. Dana Owens
3. 50 Cent	c. [symbol]
4. Prince	d. Sean John Combs
5. Snoop Dogg	e. Curtis James "Boo Boo" Jackson III
6. Diddy	f. Cordozar Calvin Broadus, Jr.

Answers are on page 399.

Lists of famous people and their pseudonyms, can be accessed through the Student Companion Website at **www.cengage.com/devenglish/richek8e**.

9. **renowned** (adjective) rĭ-nound′

From Latin: *re-* (again) + *nom* (to name) (A person who is "named repeatedly" becomes famous.)

famous; well regarded

Renowned physicist Albert Einstein figured out the relationship between mass and energy.

Hawaii is **renowned** for its beautiful beaches.

▶ *Related Word*
renown (noun) Louis Braille won *renown* for inventing a system of raised dots that enables the blind to read.

▶ *Common Phrase*
renowned for

vit; viv

10. **viable** (adjective) vī-′ə-bəl

From Latin: *vit* (life), becoming French *vie* (life)

capable of living; capable of success; workable

Mosquito eggs remain **viable** for four years, awaiting enough rain to hatch.

Despite the recession, the neighborhood restaurant was able to remain **viable** by offering inexpensive lunches.

▶ *Related Word*
viability (noun) The business plan lacked *viability.*

11. **vital** (adjective) vīt′l

From Latin: *vit* (life)

a. referring to life

The monitor measured **vital** signs like pulse and blood pressure during the operation.

b. necessary; essential

Oxygen is **vital** to animal life.

It is **vital** for the secret service to closely guard a U.S. president.

c. lively; full of life; busy

Seattle's **vital** downtown area attracts many tourists.

▶ *Common Phrases*
vital to, vital for

▶ *Related Word*
vitality (noun) (vī-tăl′ĭ-tē) A program of moderate exercise increases *vitality*. (*Vitality* means "life energy.")

12. **vivacious** (adjective) vĭ-vā′shəs

From Latin: *viv* (to live) (*Vivax* meant "lively.")

lively; full of spirit

No photo could capture the **vivacious** spirit of the high school cheerleader.

▶ *Related Word*
vivacity (noun) (vĭ-văs′ə-tē) The opera singer's *vivacity* enabled her to play Carmen, who captured the hearts of so many men.

NOTE: *Vivacious* is usually used to describe women.

Vivacious people often laugh and gesture.

Courtesy author

Exercises

Part 1

■ Definitions

Match the word and definition. Use each choice only once.

1. Genesis is _______.
2. Someone renowned is _______.
3. Degenerate means _______
4. Something congenital is _______.
5. A pseudonym is _______.
6. A vivacious person is _______.
7. A misanthrope is _______
8. A philanthropist is _______.
9. A viable idea is _______.
10. A person in nominal control is _______.

a. necessary
b. to become worse
c. a charitable person
d. famous
e. present at birth
f. a person who hates others
g. workable
h. lively
i. not really in power
j. a chosen name
k. a beginning
l. the study of human beings

■ Meanings

Match each word element to its meaning. Use each choice only once.

1. vit, viv _______
2. anthrop _______
3. gen _______
4. nom, onym _______

a. birth; type
b. human
c. life
d. name

■ *Words in Context*

Complete each sentence with the best word. Use each choice only once.

a. anthropology	e. degenerate	i. renowned
b. misanthrope	f. genesis	j. viable
c. philanthropist	g. nominal	k. vital
d. congenital	h. pseudonym	l. vivacious

1. Much research in ____________________ has dealt with the cultures of primitive tribes.

2. Many babies who weigh only a few pounds at birth are ____________________ and grow into healthy adults.

3. Pablo Picasso is ____________________ for his sculptures and paintings.

4. The company's founder is now only its ____________________ head, since his daughter makes all the decisions.

5. In team sports, cooperation is ____________________ to success.

6. Andrew Carnegie, a(n) ____________________, donated money to establish libraries.

7. In arthritis, a long-term condition, pain often increases as joints ____________________.

8. Some people are born with hemophilia, a(n) ____________________ condition that slows the ability of blood to clot.

9. Paul Hewson performs under the ____________________ Bono with the band U2.

10. The ____________________ of writing dates back 3,500 years to the Sumerians.

■ *Using Related Words*

Complete each sentence with the correct form. Use each choice only once.

Tales and Traditions from The Ancient Greeks

1. misanthrope, misanthropic

   In the ancient Greek classic the *Odyssey,* Odysseus, the hero, has to choose between sailing near two ____________________ monsters. Scylla, the first ____________________, is a six-headed horror that eats human beings. Charybdis is a whirlpool that sucks in ships. He chooses Scylla. Today, to face two bad choices is referred to as being "between Scylla and Charybdis."

2. renown, renowned

   When Odysseus, the ____________________ hero, goes to fight in the Trojan War, he entrusts his son's education to a tutor of great ____________________, named Mentor. Today a coach or adviser is often called a "mentor."

3. vital, vitality

   In Greek mythology, the hero of the *Iliad,* Achilles, was ____________________ to the success of the Greeks in conquering Troy. At his birth, Achilles's goddess mother wanted to make her son immortal, so she dipped him in the River Styx to preserve his ____________________. However, the heel she held him by was not touched by the protective water. As battle raged in Troy, an arrow struck Achilles in that heel, killing him. A point of weakness is now called an "Achilles heel."

4. anthropological, anthropologist

   Originally staged by the ancient Greeks, the Olympic Games took place from 776 to 394 BCE. In the 1800s, Frenchman Pierre de Coubertin spent his life reviving them. The modern Olympics, begun in 1896, are now a tradition. John MacAloon, an

____________________, studies the meaning of the games. He concludes that, from an ____________________ point of view, they give a sense of national identity and allow people throughout the world to participate in a common event.

5. vivacious, vivacity

In one of Aesop's fables, as a ____________________ girl walked to town carrying a jug of milk on her head, she thought of how the milk would make cream that she could sell to buy eggs. The eggs would make chickens, and she could sell the chickens for a gown, which would attract a rich husband. As she fantasized, her ____________________ overcame her. She tossed her head and spilled the milk. From this story comes the proverb "Don't count your chickens before they're hatched."

■ *Find the Example*

Choose the example that best describes the action or situation.

1. Degeneration of a vital organ _______
   a. finger with an infection that gets worse and worse
   b. progressive heart disease c. sudden tumor in the head

2. Most probable genesis of a misanthrope _______
   a. loving mother b. criminal conviction c. child abuse

3. Study of a renowned anthropologist _______
   a. prize-winning paper on the flight of bees
   b. book on Indonesian culture by famous professor
   c. paper on Peruvian customs that is widely rejected

4. Vivacious philanthropist _______
   a. dancing star building a beautiful home
   b. serious scientist donating to help stop global warming
   c. lead rock singer giving money for world peace

5. A viable child with congenital lung condition would probably _______
   a. live without problems. b. die. c. live with problems.

Prefixes and Name Words

Part 2

Part 2 of this chapter first presents two prefixes that come from characters in Greek mythology. Then several words taken directly from names are introduced.

pan- (all)

The prefix *pan-* is the Greek word for "all." It appears in two names from Greek mythology. Pan was the god of woods, fields, and shepherds. He had the lower body of a goat and the upper body of a man. He got his name because, as Homer wrote, "he delighted **all.**" Pandora (*pan-*, **all,** + dōron, gifts) was the first woman. The gods gave her a box that she was told not to open, and sent her to Earth. Curious, she disobeyed, and out flew **all** the world's troubles. Only Hope remained inside the box. (Like Eve in the Bible, Pandora was a woman blamed for causing **all** the world's problems.) The prefix *pan-* is used in such words as *pan-American,* which refers to **all** of the Americas: North, South, and Central.

psych-; psycho- (mind; soul)

The Greek word *psyche* originally meant "breath" and referred to the soul or the spirit of a person. This is personified in Greek mythology as Psyche, a beautiful mortal who was loved by Eros (or Cupid), the god of love. Eros visited Psyche every night but told her never to look at him. One night, overcome by curiosity, Psyche held a lamp up to Eros as he slept. A drop of oil dripped on his shoulder, waking him, and he fled. As Psyche searched frantically for Eros, she performed many difficult tasks to win the favor of the gods. To reward her, they made her immortal and allowed her to marry Eros. Psyche, with her beauty and dedication, symbolizes the soul. Her immortality shows how the human soul finally goes to heaven. In modern words, *psych-* usually means "mind" rather than "soul." *Psychobiology* is the study of the biology of the **mind.** In some words, *psych* functions as a root. Perhaps you have taken a class in *psychology,* the study of the **mind.**

Words to Learn

Part 2

pan-

13. **pandemonium** (noun) păn′də-mō′nē-əm

From Greek: *pan-* (all) + *daimōn* (demon)

Chaos; wild disorder and noise

Pandemonium broke loose as soldiers started shooting into the crowd of demonstrators.

14. **panorama** (noun) păn′ə-răm′-ə

From Greek: *pan-* (all) + *horan* (to see)

a. a wide, unbroken view over a large area

From our hotel room balcony, we could see a breathtaking **panorama** of Miami Beach.

b. a wide-ranging survey

The short book offers a **panorama** of art history.

▶ *Related Word*

panoramic (adjective) The viewing deck of New York's Empire State Building offers *panoramic* scenes of the city.

NOTE: *Panorama* can refer either to a physical view of something or a wide "view" in one's mind.

▶ *Common Phrase*

panorama of

psych-

15. **psyche** (noun) sī′kē

From Greek: *psych-* (mind; soul)

mental state; soul

Try not to let this defeat affect your **psyche**.

Maslow's pyramid of needs shows that physical needs and needs for safety, love, self-esteem, and personal achievement govern the human **psyche**.

NOTE: *Psyche* usually refers to the part of the mind that is not rational and that is related to feelings such as self-esteem and happiness.

16. **psychosomatic** (adjective) sī′kō-sō-măt′ĭk

From Greek: *psycho-* (mind) + *soma* (body)

referring to physical disorders that are caused by the mind

Physicians thought that ulcers were **psychosomatic**, until they discovered the bacteria that caused them.

Name Words

17. **boycott** (verb, noun) boi′kŏt′

a. to refuse to use or buy something as an act of protest (verb)

In the 1970s and 1980s, public **boycotts** of grapes resulted in better conditions for farm workers.

b. the act of boycotting (noun)

Many nations were alarmed when North Korea decided to **boycott** international talks on nuclear disarmament.

▶ *Common Phrase*
boycott of

Captain Boycott

The Irish potato famine of the mid-1800s made farmers so poor that a law was passed in 1881 to reduce their rents. Captain Charles C. Boycott, a cruel English land agent, angered people by insisting on the original payments, thus forcing many farmers out of business. In response, the Irish Land League *boycotted* him by refusing to do further business with him.

18. **gargantuan** (adjective) gär-găn′cho͞o-ən

huge; immense

The skylines of Singapore and Seoul are filled with **gargantuan** skyscrapers.

I couldn't finish the **gargantuan** "super burrito."

The lottery prize was a **gargantuan** one hundred million dollars.

A Gargantuan Tale

Gargantua and Pantagruel is a series of stories written by French author François Rabelais between 1532 and 1562. Gargantua is a giant with an appetite to match. At one point, he eats five people in a salad! He arranges his hair with a *gargantuan* comb 900 feet long.

19. **martial** (adjective) mär′shəl

referring to war or soldiers

The museum had a fine collection of swords, revolvers, and other **martial** items.

▶ *Common Phrases*

martial law After the attempted revolt, the dictator placed the country under *martial law*. (Martial law is rule by military authorities imposed on a civilian population.)

martial arts *Martial arts* were included in the Olympics for the first time in 2004. (*Martial arts* are sports such as karate and tae kwon do that teach one how to defend oneself.)

Mars—Month and Planet

Mars, the Roman god of war, gives his name to the month of March. He is also the source of the name for Mars, a planet that appears faintly red, suggesting blood. Except for Earth, each of the planets in our solar system is named for a Greek or Roman god. Closest to the sun is *Mercury,* the quickly rotating planet named for the messenger god. *Venus,* named for the god of love, is followed by *Earth* and *Mars. Jupiter* is named for the king of the gods. *Saturn* is Jupiter's father, and *Uranus* is his grandfather. *Neptune* is ruler of the sea. Finally, *Pluto,* the planet farthest from the sun, honors the gloomy god of the underworld, the region of the dead. (In 2006, however, Pluto was taken off the list of planets.)

The planets were named for Greek and Roman gods.

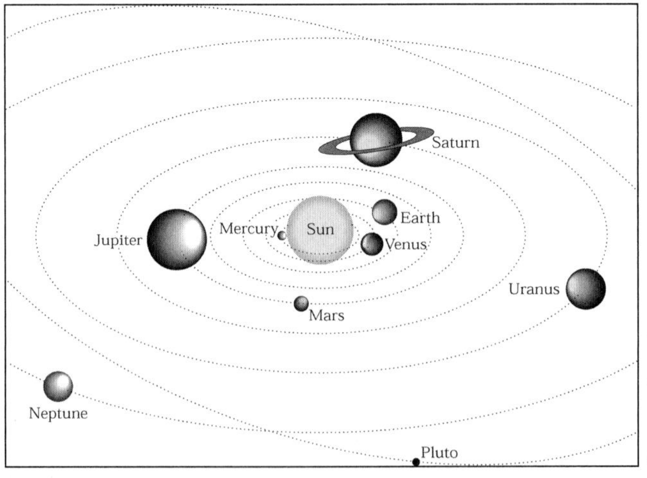

20. **maverick** (noun, adjective) măv′ər-ĭk

a. an independent-minded person who refuses to follow accepted rules and guidelines (noun)

Winston Churchill was a **maverick** who changed political parties twice in his career.

b. independent-minded (adjective)

Against the guidelines of his church, the **maverick** church elder urged that women be allowed to become ministers.

Maverick of Texas

In the 1800s, cattlemen began branding their calves to indicate ownership. Samuel Maverick, a Texan rancher of independent spirit, refused to follow the custom. This annoyed the other ranchers, who called all unbranded cattle *mavericks*. Eventually, the word was used to describe independent people like Maverick himself. Maverick led a colorful life, fighting duels, spending time in prison, and serving in the Texas legislature.

21. **odyssey** (noun) ŏd′ĭ-sē

a long and adventurous journey

Ernesto 'Ché' Guevara's 1952 motorcycle **odyssey** through South America changed his ideas about social justice.

As the result of a spiritual **odyssey** that led him to join the Nation of Islam, Malcolm Little changed his name to Malcolm X.

Homer's *Odyssey*

The *Odyssey,* a classic ancient Greek poem by Homer, details the journey of Odysseus (also known as Ulysses) back home from the Trojan War. His adventures include a shipwreck, a visit to the underworld, the irresistible songs of the dangerous Sirens, and a choice between meeting two monsters, Scylla and Charybdis. In honor of this hero, an intense physical or spiritual journey is called an *odyssey*.

22. **quixotic** (adjective) kwĭk-sŏt′ĭk

noble but not practical; having unreachable ideals; idealistic

In a **quixotic** attempt to stop the loggers from destroying a forest, Maribel tied herself to a tree.

The Original Don Quixote

Miguel de Cervantes published his classic novel *Don Quixote* in 1605. In it, an old man, Don Quixote, decides to become a wandering knight and does noble but foolish deeds. He duels with a windmill that he thinks is a giant. He mistakes an inn for a castle and a peasant girl for a noble lady. His squire (helper), Sancho Panza, sees how ridiculous all of this is, but remains loyal to his master.

Although *Don Quixote* was written in Spanish, many of its famous phrases are used in modern-day English. These include "in a pickle," "too much of a good thing," "a wink of sleep," "a stone's throw," "smell a rat," "honesty is the best policy," "turn over a new leaf," and "faint heart never won fair lady."

Mary Evans Picture Library/Alamy

Don Quixote traveled with his squire, Sancho Panza.

23. **spartan** (adjective) spär′tn

lacking in comfort; requiring self-discipline

Our **spartan** campsite had no electricity or plumbing.

The athlete's **spartan** routine required three hours of exercise and five hours of practice each day.

Sparta: A Tough Place to Grow Up

The ancient Greek city of Sparta was known for its devotion to athletics and the art of warfare. Spartans valued physical stamina, rough living, and bravery. So *spartan* was their training process that boys were taken away from their families and put in training camps when they were seven years old.

NOTE: The word *spartan* is sometimes capitalized.

24. **tantalize** (verb) tăn′tə-līz

to tempt and then deny satisfaction

Dad **tantalized** us by saying "I have a secret!"

The thief was **tantalized** by the heavily guarded truck filled with cash.

► *Related Word*
tantalizing (adjective) We wanted to buy the *tantalizing* cupcakes in the bakery window, but it was closed.

► *Common Phrase*
tantalized by

The Temptations of Tantalus

The mythical being Tantalus displeased Zeus, the king of the gods. To punish him, Zeus placed him in a pool of water, but whenever Tantalus reached down to drink, the water would rush away. A vine of grapes hung nearby, but if Tantalus reached out, it would move beyond his reach. Thus Tantalus was *tantalized* by drink and food he could never have.

Exercises

Part 2

Definitions

Match the word and definition. Use each choice only once.

1. A quixotic person is ______.
2. A maverick is ______.
3. An odyssey is ______.
4. A psychosomatic illness has ______.
5. A martial man is ______.
6. Pandemonium is ______.
7. A spartan life is ______.
8. Something gargantuan is ______.
9. A panorama is ______.
10. To boycott is ______.

a. not to buy or use
b. a mental cause
c. tempt but deny satisfaction
d. idealistic
e. without comforts
f. an independent-minded person
g. warlike
h. confusion
i. a wide view
k. huge
l. mental state or soul
m. a long trip

Meaning

Match each word element to its meaning. Use each choice only once.

1. pan- ______
2. psych- ______

a. mind; soul
b. all

■ *Words in Context*

Complete each sentence with the best word. Use each choice only once. You may have to capitalize some words.

a. panorama	e. boycott	i. odyssey
b. pandemonium	f. gargantuan	j. quixotic
c. psyche	g. martial	k. spartan
d. psychosomatic	h. maverick	l. tantalize

1. ____________________ broke loose as the starving people rushed to get bags of food.

2. Community churches urged members to ____________________ stores that were unfair to employees.

3. The ____________________ refused to follow company procedures.

4. Depressing thoughts troubled Keisha's ____________________.

5. Don't ____________________ the dog by showing him the snack you are about to eat.

6. Professional football players were annoyed when they had to stay at

   a(n) ____________________ college dorm rather than a luxurious hotel.

7. Raisa's ____________________ as an immigrant brought her from the Ukraine, to Italy, to Argentina, and finally to the United States.

8. The ____________________ rollercoaster was the tallest thing in the amusement park.

9. Lan's ____________________ headaches disappeared when her abusive boss left the company.

10. The woman wasted her time working on a(n) ____________________ campaign to provide free tuition to all college students.

■ *Using Related Words*

Complete each sentence with the correct form. Use each choice only once.

1. panorama, panoramic

From the top of the Colorado's Mesa Verde, the traveler sees a

____________________ view of valleys once farmed by the ancient Anasazi people. Over centuries, their homes changed from fireplaces with roofs to large stone apartment buildings. From the cliffs they inhabited, these people enjoyed the same

____________________ that tourists see today.

2. martial, martial arts

You have probably heard of ____________________ like judo and karate, but have you heard of Capoeira? Afro-Brazilians invented it when most of them were slaves. Capoeira served the

____________________ function of defense, but, perhaps to fool slave owners, it appeared to be a dance.

3. psyche, psychosomatically, psychosomatic

How much does the ____________________ govern the body? A study done at Ohio State University found that healing may be

affected by ____________________ factors. Wounds inside the mouth healed more slowly during exam time, indicating that the

body is ____________________ affected by stress.

4. tantalizes, tantalizing, tantalized

New insights from psychology offer us information on the causes of

unhappiness. Psychologists find that being ____________________ by the riches of others harms our psyches. Less-well-off people tend to be troubled if they live near very rich ones. They see a

____________________ life they cannot afford, and this leads to envy. So, psychologically, it may be better not to know people

whose lifestyle ____________________ us.

■ *Reading the Headlines*

Here are some headlines that might appear in newspapers. Read each and answer the questions. (Remember that small words, such as *is, are, a,* and *the,* are often left out of headlines.)

COUNTRY HOLDS GARGANTUAN PARADE OF MARTIAL FORCES

1. Was the parade small? ______

2. Did the parade feature military forces? ______

MAVERICK UNION LEADER CALLS FOR BOYCOTT OF CHAIN STORE

3. Is the leader independent? ______

4. Does the leader want people to buy at the chain store? ______

QUIXOTIC ATTEMPT AT SPARTAN LIFESTYLE IS MEANT TO HELP GLOBAL WARMING

5. Is it realistic to expect the lifestyle to greatly affect global warming?

   ______

6. Is the lifestyle elegant? ______

LIVING IN CONSTANT PANDEMONIUM WILL AFFECT PSYCHE

7. Are these lives calm? ______

8. Is a mental state being affected? ______

HARDSHIPS OF ODYSSEY CAUSED PSYCHOSOMATIC ILLNESSES

9. Was a trip taken? ______

10. Are these illnesses caused by the mind? ______

Chapter Exercises

■ *Practicing Strategies: New Words from Word Elements*

Use your knowledge of word elements to determine the meanings of these words and complete each sentence. Use each choice only once.

a. anonymous	e. genotype	i. patronymic
b. anthropocentric	f. homonym	j. psychogenic
c. genealogy	g. nomenclature	k. revive
d. generation	h. pan-global	l. vivarium

1. Since *pater* is a root meaning "father," a(n) ____________________ name comes to you through your father or paternal relative.

2. Since *homo* means "the same," a word that is pronounced, or named, the same way as another is called a(n) ____________________.

3. A ____________________ condition originates in the mind.

4. The point of view that human beings are the center of the universe is sometimes called ____________________.

5. Since *-logy* means "study of," ____________________ is the study of your ancestors or your family history.

6. A ____________________ is a container that holds live animals.

7. Scholars often use scientific ____________________ when referring to plants and animals.

8. When animals or plants seem to come back to life again, we say they ____________________.

9. Dances from around the planet were featured at the ____________________ celebration.

10. *A* means "without," so a(n) ____________________ song is one for which we don't know the name of the composer.

■ *Practicing Strategies: Combining Context Clues and Word Elements*

In each sentence, one italicized word contains a word element that you have studied in this chapter. Use the meaning of the word element and context to make an intelligent guess about its meaning in each sentence.

1. Authors of children's books often use *anthropomorphism,* representing bees or flowers or kittens as having human intelligence.

   Anthropomorphism means ______________________________.

2. Loud noises can *engender* hearing loss.

   Engender means ______________________________.

3. It is impossible to find a *panacea* for all the problems of humanity.

   Panacea means ______________________________.

The next two items are taken from newspaper sources.

4. Malone said the term "mailroom" is a *misnomer* in the newspaper industry because its functions are not limited to the distribution of mail.

   Misnomer means ______________________________.

5. Under natural selection, beneficial genes become more common in a population as their owners have more *progeny*.

   Progeny means ______________________________.

■ *Companion Words*

Complete each sentence with the best word. You may use choices more than once, and some items may have more than one correct answer. Choices: of, for, to, under, by, into

1. We were tantalized __________ the photos of the expensive vacation villa.
2. Bacteria are vital __________ food digestion.

3. Indian statesman Gandhi was renowned ________ his philosophy of nonviolence.

4. After Indonesia was placed ________ martial law, President Suharto resigned.

5. The genesis ________ the steam engine dates to the ancient Greeks.

6. The view from the mountaintop is a panorama ________ forests.

7. A boycott ________ department stores helped workers to unionize.

8. The poorly organized rock festival degenerated ________ chaos.

9, 10. Marshall Mathers performs ________ the pseudonym ________ Eminem.

■ *Writing with Your Words*

To practice effective writing, complete each sentence with an interesting phrase that indicates the meaning of the italicized word.

1. During the *martial* drills, ____________________

____________________.

2. To test the *viability* of my idea for a business, ____________________

____________________.

3. The *maverick* ____________________

____________________.

4. Carrying a *gargantuan* load ____________________

____________________.

5. The *misanthrope* said, ____

____.

6. My dream *odyssey* consists of ____

____.

7. I am *tantalized* by ____

____.

8. If I could choose a *pseudonym*, ______________________________________

____.

9. We *boycotted* the company because ____________________________________

____.

10. His *spartan* diet ____

____.

■ *Making Connections*

To connect new vocabulary to your life, write extended responses to these questions.

1. Describe a quixotic cause that you would like to undertake. Why is it quixotic?
2. Describe your idea of a beautiful panorama.
3. Describe a time that you or someone you know has lived in spartan conditions.

Passage

The Greek Myth of Winter

Myths are part of the cultural heritage the ancient Greeks and Romans gave to us. This one is about how winter began. In modern times, science has explained the causes of violent weather and changes of season, but such events puzzled ancient people. Perhaps to gain a sense of control, they created tales about the world around them. Note, too the "mother in law" in this story.

Ancient Greeks and Romans told stories of gods who ate, loved, and hated just as we do, but on a larger scale. **(1)** Because these gods had **gargantuan** powers, their smallest wish could mean disaster or good fortune for the entire world. A **misanthropic** god might send deadly storms; **(2)** a **philanthropic** one might share the secrets of fire.

(3) One ancient Greek tale of human-like gods deals with the **genesis** of winter. According to the ancient Greeks, the world was once a warm, green paradise where the goddess Demeter provided summer throughout the year. But one day, Persephone, Demeter's beautiful and **vivacious** daughter, wandered away from her friends to explore a field of flowers. Unfortunately, Hades, the god of the underworld, was visiting the Earth and enjoying a **panoramic** view of the very same place. With one look at Persephone, Hades instantly fell in love. **(4)** A rather **degenerate** character, Hades simply carried her off to the underworld and made her his bride.

(5) Pandemonium broke out when word of Hades's crime reached the other gods. Demeter frantically tried to get her daughter back, begging Zeus, king of the gods, to order her return. But although Zeus was **renowned** for his power, **(6)** Hades, a **maverick** among the gods, refused to return Persephone.

In her desperation, Demeter forgot to provide the world with the **(7)** warmth and sunshine **vital** to growing crops, and the Earth plunged into winter. Plants died and humans faced starvation. Demeter's grief was causing the death of the human race! Zeus appealed to Hades, who finally agreed to let Persephone return home, as long as she had not eaten anything.

What had Persephone been doing while Demeter was trying to release her? Sitting unhappily in the underworld, **(8)** she had led a **spartan** existence, refusing all the luxuries that Hades offered. She had eaten no food—except for four pomegranate seeds. Alas! **(9)** Persephone had eaten only a **nominal** amount, but she had eaten something. Hades did not have to let her go.

(10) Fortunately, Zeus and Demeter quickly thought of a **viable** compromise. For eight months of the year, Persephone would live with her mother, and for four months she would live with Hades. Just as Persephone's life was divided, Demeter decreed that for eight months the Earth would have warm weather, and for four months it would have winter.

And that is how, according to the ancient Greeks, winter began.

■ *Exercise*

Each numbered sentence corresponds to a sentence in the passage. Fill in the letter of the choice that makes the sentence mean the same thing as its corresponding sentence in the passage.

1. These gods had _______ powers.
   a. huge b. idealistic c. mental d. important

2. A _______ god might share the secrets of fire.
   a. necessary b. generous c. kindly d. tempting

3. One ancient Greek tale deals with the _______ of winter.
   a. chill b. beginning c. mental state d. hard conditions

4. Hades was a rather _______ character.
   a. vicious b. noble c. famous d. human-hating

5. _______ broke loose.
   a. Hatred b. War c. Psychological problems d. Disorder

6. Hades was a _______ among the gods.
   a. mind b. rebel c. warrior d. survivor

7. Warmth and sunshine were _______ crops.
   a. necessary for b. workable with c. lacking for d. useless to

8. Persephone had led a(n) _______ existence.
   a. uncomfortable b. sick c. warlike d. unhappy

9. Persephone had eaten a _______ amount.
   a. sickly b. healthy c. famous d. small

10. Zeus and Demeter thought of a _______ compromise.
    a. necessary b. confusing c. tricky d. workable

Discussion Questions

1. Was Zeus's power limited? Explain your answer.
2. Why do you think the Greeks represent their gods as super-powerful humans?
3. Describe a human situation that would bring forth the emotions that Demeter felt.

Insight into Idioms

Expressions About the Body

Many idioms are related to the human body. Some describe how we feel when the experiences of our minds cause reactions in our bodies. Have you ever felt that you had *butterflies in your stomach?* Not surprisingly, this idiom means to be nervous. Other idioms refer to imaginative uses of our bodies. If you've ever listened to someone who needed to talk, you *lent them an ear.*

a. *Gave her the cold shoulder* means ignored her.

b. A person who *gets cold feet* becomes so nervous that he or she loses the courage to do something.

c. When people refuse to honor a promise or commitment, they *back out*.

d. Something that scared a person *made his blood run cold* (or *made his hair stand on end*).

e. If people wait until they calm down, they *cool their heels.*

f. If you listen to something, you *lend an ear*.

g. If you did not listen to something, the information *went in one ear and out the other.*

Practice chapter words one more time by filling in the letter of the correct idiom into the blank before each sentence.

____ 1. The people in the mayor's office were in a state of *pandemonium*, so she made them _________ before she would see them.

____ 2. Elroy wants to ask the *vivacious* waitress out, but he _________ because he thinks she will reject him.

____ 3. As the *gargantuan* monster came toward Gerald, it _________.

____ 4. Anna's *psyche* would be injured if her friend _________ at a party.

____ 5. It is *vital* that you don't _________ out of your promise to babysit, for I must go to this meeting.

Links to more lists of English idioms and their meanings can be found at the Student Companion Website for this book: **www.cengage.com/devenglish/richek8e**.

CHAPTER 

Word Elements: Movement

Modern life seems to keep us in constant motion. Even our information travels at a fast pace. Communications sent through e-mail and text messaging take just a few seconds to reach any place in the world. This chapter presents words based on movement. Each of the six roots and two prefixes deals with an action. These word elements form many widely used English words.

Chapter Strategy: Word Elements: Movement

Chapter Words:

Part 1

duc, duct	conducive deduction induce	*stans, stat*	stature status quo staunch
ject	dejected eject jettison	*tain, ten*	abstain tenacious tenuous

Part 2

tract	distraught extract retract	*circum-*	circumscribe circumspect circumvent
vers, vert	adversary diversion inadvertently	*trans-*	transcend transitory traverse

Visit the Student Companion Website at **www.cengage.com/devenglish/richek8e** to test your knowledge of these words before you study, hear each word pronounced, find additional practice exercises, and access more information on words and topics.

Did You Know?

How Did Inventions Get Their Names?

What would life be like if we could not hop on a bus, switch on a light bulb, refrigerate our leftovers, or turn a faucet handle for water? If we went back in time to 1700, we would have to live without cars, electricity, refrigeration, and running water.

Three hundred years ago, people traveled on foot or rode horses on unpaved roads with deep ruts. A twenty-mile trip took all day; today the same trip takes less than an hour. Because there were no stoves or refrigerators, people cooked over open fires. Meat was either eaten immediately or preserved as sausage. Disease-ridden water killed hundreds of thousands.

In today's world, automobiles, trains, and airplanes provide rapid transportation. We use freezers and refrigerators to preserve our food, as well as temperature-regulated stoves and microwave ovens to cook it with precision. Many diseases have been controlled, and average life expectancy has almost doubled.

The past one hundred years have been especially productive times for inventors. Such widely used devices as the computer, television (and the remote control), automatic clothes dryer, computer, mobile phone, zipper, paper clip, microwave, Post-it® note, digital camera, and the electronic reader were all invented after 1911.

Each invention brought a new word into English. Often, scientists and inventors took names from ancient Greek and Latin. This tradition started in 1611 when a Greek poet suggested a name for Galileo's new invention, using two Greek word elements, *tele-* (far) and *scope* (look). The invention is the *telescope*. Modern inventors continue to create names from ancient Greek and Latin word elements.

The inventions and discoveries listed below make your life easier and safer. The name of each one contains classical word elements.

Invention	*Classical Word Elements*	*Approximate Date of Invention*
microscope	*micro-* (small) + *-scope* (look)	1665
anesthetic	*an-* (without) + *aisthēsis* (feeling)	1850
bicycle	*bi-* (two) + *kuklos* (wheel)	1862
telephone	*tele-* (far) + *-phone* (sound)	1880
automobile	*auto-* (self) + *movēre* (to move)	1885
refrigerator	*re-* (again) + *frigus* (cold)	1890
television	*tele-* (far) + *visus* (sight)	1925
computer	*com-* (together) + *putāre* (to reckon)	1940
microwave	*micro-* (small) + *wafian* (wave)	1963

Learning Strategy

Word Elements: Movement

The word elements in this chapter describe movements, such as leading *(duct)*, pulling *(tract)*, and turning *(vert)*. Each element forms at least fifty English words, so learning them will help you dramatically expand your vocabulary.

Element	*Meaning*	*Origin*	*Function*	*Chapter Words*
Part 1				
duc, duct	lead	Latin	root	conducive, deduction, induce
ject	throw	Latin	root	dejected, eject, jettison
stans, stat	standing; placed	Latin; Greek	root	stature, status quo, staunch
tain, ten	stretch, extend; hold	Latin	root	abstain, tenacious, tenuous
Part 2				
tract	pull	Latin	root	distraught, extract, retract
vers, vert	turn	Latin	root	adversary, diversion, inadvertently
circum-	around	Latin	prefix	circumscribe, circumspect, circumvent
trans-	across	Latin	prefix	transcend, transitory, traverse

Many of the word elements in this chapter started out describing physical movement, but over the years acquired related, nonphysical meanings. The word element *ject* (throw) illustrates how word elements and meanings relate. If you think about the meanings of the word elements that follow, you will be able to picture each word's meaning in your mind.

> The word elements *de-* (down) and *ject* (throw) make *deject,* or "throw down." The word *dejected* actually means depressed, or how we feel when our mood is "thrown down."

The word elements *e-* (out of) and *ject* (throw) make *eject,* or "throw out of." When a candy bar is *ejected* from a vending machine, it is "thrown out."

Circumstance is another word whose elements give us a mental picture. It combines the prefix *circum-* and the root *stans. Circumstances* are things that are "standing" *(stans)* "around" *(circum-)* an event; in other words, they surround it. Circumstances that might "stand around" and keep you from studying are noise in the library or a friend who wants to talk.

Word Roots

Part 1

The four word roots of movement presented in Part 1 are as follows:

duc, duct (lead)

This root appears in many words. The *ducts* in a building **lead** air and water to different rooms. A *conductor* **leads** an orchestra so that all the players stay together. (*Con-* means "together.") European noblemen are called *dukes* because long ago their ancestors **led** troops into battle.

ject (throw)

This root appears as *jet,* a stream of water or air **thrown** into space. *Ject* can also represent the idea of **throwing** rather than the physical action itself. Although the word elements of *reject* actually mean "to **throw** back," the word itself has the related but nonphysical meaning of "not to accept."

stans, stat (standing; placed)

This root indicates a lack of movement, as in *statue. Stans* and *stat* can also refer to **standing** in an abstract, nonphysical way. For example, one's *status* is one's **standing** or placement in society. *Circumstance,* mentioned earlier, also contains this root.

tain, ten (stretch, extend; hold)

The many meanings of *ten, tain* are related. When we **hold** something, we can **stretch** and **extend** it. The word *thin* comes from *ten,* and we can imagine making something *thin* by **holding** it and then **stretching** it. This root means **hold** in the word *contain* ("to **hold** together"). *Tain, ten* can also mean **hold** in a nonphysical sense. For example, a *tenet* is a belief that somebody **holds.**

Words to Learn

Part 1

duc, duct

1. **conducive** (adjective) kən-do͞o′sĭv

   From Latin: *con-* (together) + *duc* (lead)

   contributing to; leading to

   Candlelight and soft music are **conducive** to romance.

   Loud music in a restaurant isn't **conducive** to conversation.

   ▶ *Common Phrase*
   conducive to

2. **deduction** (noun) dĭ-dŭk′shən

   From Latin: *de-* (away) + *duct* (lead)

   a. something subtracted from a total

   A **deduction** was taken from the bill after the customer found a fly in her soup.

   b. a conclusion drawn from evidence

   From the delicious smells coming from the kitchen, we drew the **deduction** that Keisha was baking cookies.

   ▶ *Related Words*
   deduct (verb) The teacher *deducted* points for turning in papers late.
   deductible (adjective) Some medical expenses are tax *deductible*.
   deduce (verb) (dĭ-do͞os′) When LeShawn saw a ring on the finger of the pretty woman's hand, he *deduced* she was married.
   deductive (adjective) Darwin used *deductive* reasoning to formulate his theory of evolution.

   NOTE: When *deduction* means "subtraction," it is related to *deduct* and *deductible*; when *deduction* means "conclusion," it is related to *deduce* and *deductive*.

3. **induce** (verb) in-do͞os′

   From Latin: *in-* (away) + *duc* (lead)

   to persuade; to help bring about

The yoga teacher **induced** her students to relax by asking them to close their eyes and breathe deeply.

Because some medicines **induce** sleep, you should not take them before you drive.

▶ *Related Word*
inducement (noun) The college offered full scholarships as *inducements* to top high school athletes.

ject

4. **dejected** (adjective) dĭ-jĕk′tĭd

From Latin: *de-* (down) + *ject* (throw)

depressed; downcast

Albert became **dejected** when he realized he didn't have enough money to buy the house that he wanted.

▶ *Related Word*
dejection (noun) A mood of *dejection* hung over the defeated candidate's headquarters.

5. **eject** (verb) ĭ-jĕkt′

From Latin: *ex-* (out) + *ject* (throw)

to force to leave; to expel

When my computer would not **eject** the DVD, I called the help desk.

After the protesters tried to interrupt the congressional session, they were **ejected** from the Capitol.

▶ *Related Word*
ejection (noun) Seconds before the plane crashed, an automatic *ejection* device saved the pilot.

6. **jettison** (verb) jĕt′-ĭ-sĕn

From Latin: *ject* (throw)

to throw out forcefully; to throw overboard

Shortly after takeoff, the space shuttle **jettisoned** the empty fuel tank into the ocean.

The network **jettisoned** the reality show after its ratings fell.

NOTE: *Jettison* can apply to nonphysical things, as in to "jettison an unworkable plan."

stans, stat

7. **stature** (noun) stăch′ər

   a. high level of achievement and honor

   Albert Einstein was a scientist of great **stature.**

   b. physical height

   A condition called achondroplasia prevents people from developing a normal adult **stature.**

U.S. Presidents of Great Stature

Two U.S. presidents demonstrated great *stature* in both senses of the word. George Washington stood six feet two inches tall, a very unusual height in the 1700s. More important, he led the troops in the American Revolution and, as the first U.S. president, unified the former colonies. He also established presidential rather than royal customs; for example, we don't bow to presidents. Abraham Lincoln, six feet four inches tall, led the union through the terrible Civil War (1861-5). After it ended, he urged mercy for those who had been defeated. Historians rate both Lincoln and Washington as great presidents—and presidents of great size.

8. **status quo** (noun) stā′təs kwō′

   From Latin: *stat* (standing, placed) *quo* (in which), making "the condition in which"

   the existing conditions; present state of things

   The increasing number of women ministers and rabbis shows a change in the **status quo.**

   The new CEO plans to maintain the **status quo** for a year before making changes.

9. **staunch** (adjective) stônch

   From Latin: *stans* (standing), through the French word *étanche* (watertight, firm) (Something *staunch* stands firm and strong.)

   a. faithful; firmly supporting

   My **staunch** friend stood by me through my difficult divorce.

   The mayor was a **staunch** supporter of equal rights.

b. healthy; strong

Mountain climbing requires a **staunch** constitution.

A **staunch** defense saved the town from attack.

► *Related Word*

staunchness (noun) African-American Rosa Parks's *staunchness* in refusing to move to the back of a bus made her a hero in the Civil Rights movement.

tain, ten

10. **abstain** (verb) ăb-stān′

From Latin: *abs-* (away) + *tain* (hold) ("To hold away from" is not to do something.)

a. not to do something by choice

After monks take a vow of silence, they **abstain** from speaking.

b. to register a vote of no opinion; to withhold a vote

Seven people voted yes, seven voted no, and seven **abstained.**

► *Common Phrase*

abstain from

► *Related Words*

abstinence (noun) (ăb′stə-nəns) The month-long Muslim holiday of Ramadan requires *abstinence* from food during daylight hours. (*Abstinence* usually refers to self-denial.)

abstention (noun) (ăb-stən′shən) Union members approved the contract by a vote of 102 to 79, with five *abstentions.* (*Abstention* usually refers to a vote.)

11. **tenacious** (adjective) tə-nā′shəs

From Latin: *ten* (hold)

firmly holding; gripping; stubbornly persistent

The dog kept a **tenacious** grip on Yara's shoes.

The **tenacious** newspaper reporter pursued every lead to gather facts about her story.

A Tenacious *Author*

As a poor, single mother, J. K. Rowling sat day after day writing a manuscript in a café because she could not afford to heat her apartment. When it was finished, she submitted it to twelve publishers, who all turned it down. Finally, a thirteenth one accepted it, and the book *Harry Potter* was born. Today this *tenacious* woman is the wealthy author of one of the best-known series of books in our time.

Despite the terrible wind, Alma held on to her umbrella with a *tenacious* grip.

Courtesy author

▶ *Related Word*

tenacity (noun) The cyclist showed **tenacity** in her twenty-year fight to create a neighborhood bike path.

12. **tenuous** (adjective) tĕn′yo͞o-əs

From Latin: *tenuis* (thin), derived from *ten* (stretched)

a. weak and at risk; having little truth or validity

After posting losses for three quarters, the company's financial position was **tenuous.**

Your argument that all speed limits should be eliminated is, at best, **tenuous.**

b. thin

The **tenuous** strands of a spider's web are surprisingly strong.

Exercises

Part 1

■ *Definitions*

Match the word and definition. Use each choice only once.

1. jettison _______	a. the present state of things
2. status quo _______	b. weak; having little truth
3. tenacious _______	c. gripping
4. tenuous _______	d. contributing to
5. conducive _______	e. depressed
6. dejected _______	f. persuade; help bring about
7. deduction _______	g. something subtracted
8. staunch _______	h. to throw out
9. stature _______	i. attendance
10. induce _______	j. faithful; firmly supporting
	k. not to do
	l. level of achievement and honor

■ *Meanings*

Match each word root to its meaning. Use each choice only once.

1. ject, jet _______	a. hold
2. tain, ten _______	b. lead
3. duc, duct _______	c. throw
4. stans, stat _______	d. standing; placed

■ *Words in Context*

Complete each sentence with the best word. Use each choice only once.

a. conducive	e. ejection	i. staunch
b. deduction	f. jettison	j. abstain
c. induce	g. stature	k. tenacity
d. dejected	h. status quo	l. tenuous

1. You need to ____________________ from alcohol for twenty-four hours before the medical test.

2. I am a(n) ____________________ supporter of workers' rights to organize unions, and have supported this cause for thirty years.

3. The honored judge held a position of great ____________________ in her community.

4. The man became ____________________ after he lost his job.

5. Mind-altering drugs can make one's hold on reality ____________________.

6. If our lifeboat starts to sink, people will have to ____________________ their luggage to make it lighter.

7. The manufacturer tried to ____________________ people to buy cars by giving discounts.

8. There would be quite a change in the ____________________ if all money were divided equally among people.

9. From the awful smell coming from the open refrigerator, we drew the ____________________ that there was rotten food inside.

10. A(n) quiet, comfortable environment is ____________________ to effective studying.

■ *Related Words*

Complete each sentence with the correct form. Use each choice only once. You may have to capitalize some words.

1. dejection, dejected

   Charles Gray has been developing a supercar that gets eighty miles per gallon. The project, started in the 1980s, has had a history of bureaucratic tangles. ______________ because of its lack of success, Gray built his own car, which uses nitrogen for fuel.

Although problems remain, Gray refuses to give in to __________, and perhaps someday he will be able to produce this truly efficient vehicle for others.

2. abstain, abstinence

Because the AIDS virus can spread through shared needles, the Chicago Recovery Alliance gives drug addicts free needles in exchange for used ones. Officials would rather that people practiced

______________ from heroin. But if they cannot force people to

______________, the Alliance at least wants to stop the spread of AIDS by needles.

3. tenacious, tenacity, tenaciously

Inventor Jerome Lemelson, who held the most patents in the United States after Thomas Edison, displayed tremendous

______________ in court battles he fought against companies who stole his many of ideas. Lemelson was forced to fight

______________ for years to protect his rights to inventions such as the technology for video camcorders, bar code scanners,

and the Hot Wheels toy. When, after a ______________ struggle, he finally became affluent, he funded a yearly prize for inventions, as well as several university programs to encourage invention.

4. ejection, ejected, eject

The simple paper clip has hundreds of uses, including helping to

______________ disks from computers. In fact, the clip is a big

help in the ______________ of almost any small item from a tight space. Clips are also used as bookmarks, money holders, cuff links, and playthings. It is estimated that only one in every five is used to hold paper. Invented by Norwegian Johan Vaaler, they have also been a symbol of freedom. During World War II, Norwegians wore them to symbolize their hope that the Nazis who were occupying

their land would soon be ______________.

5. deduce, deductions, deductive

   Sherlock Holmes, an English detective created by Sir Arthur Conan Doyle, was a master of ______________ reasoning. His ______________ of a criminal's identity could be drawn from inspecting such items as cigar ashes or the soles of shoes. The famous, but fictional, detective was said to be based on a real-life Scottish doctor, Joe Bell, who could ______________ a patient's problem from an amazingly small amount of evidence.

■ *Reading the Headlines*

Here are some headlines that might appear in newspapers. Read each and answer the questions. (Remember that small words, such as *is, are, a,* and *the,* are often left out of headlines.)

PUBLIC TOLD TO ABSTAIN FROM TAKING PILL THAT INDUCES DEJECTION

1. Should the public take the pill? _______
2. Does the pill have an effect on people? _______
3. Does the pill make people happy? _______

A LOOK AT TEAM SUPPORTS DEDUCTION THAT MEMBERS ARE NOT CHOSEN FOR GREAT STATURE

4. Has team leadership announced whether it bases its choices on stature? _______
5. Are team members very tall? _______

TENACIOUS PARENTS WIN YEAR-LONG FIGHT TO HAVE BULLY EJECTED

6. Do the parents give up easily? _______
7. Was the bully forced to leave? _______

AFTER STAUNCH SUPPORT FOR REFORM WITHIN ONE PARTY, TENUOUS AGREEMENT BETWEEN PARTIES SIMPLY EXTENDS STATUS QUO

8. Was there weak support for reform within the party? _______

9. Is the agreement fully confirmed? _______

10. Does it seem like things will remain the same? _______

Prefixes of Movement

Part 2

Part 2 continues with more word elements that show movement: first, two additional roots, *tract* (pull) and *vert* (turn); and then two prefixes, *circum-* (around) and *trans-* (across).

tract (pull)

Tractor, a machine that **pulls** a plow through the soil, is a common word formed from this root. Like many movement roots, *tract* is also used in words that no longer carry the physical meaning of **pull.** For example, when we *distract* someone's attention, we "**pull** it away" in a mental rather than a physical sense.

vers, vert (turn)

Vert can mean **turn** in a direct sense. When we *invert* a cup, we **turn** it upside down. This root can also hint at a nonphysical meaning of **turn.** When we *advertise,* we "**turn** (*vert*) attention toward" a product.

circum- (around)

Circum- is a prefix meaning **around.** The distance **around** a circle is its *circumference.* Like other movement word elements, *circum-* can indicate the idea, rather than the action, of **around**. For example, a library book that *circulates* "goes **around**" and is read by many people.

trans- (across)

Transcontinental jets go **across** a continent—as from New York to Los Angeles. The prefix *trans-* can also suggest the idea of **across** rather than actual physical movement. When we *translate* something, it goes **across** languages, or from one language to another.

Words to Learn

Part 2

tract

13. **distraught** (adjective) dĭs-trôt′

From Latin: *dis-* (apart) + *tract* (pull) (*Tract* changed to *traught* in Middle English.)

crazy with worry or distress; extremely upset

The baker became **distraught** when her assistant dropped the wedding cake.

Our fear increased when we saw that the **distraught** man had a gun.

The child was **distraught** over his parents' divorce.

NOTE: *Distracted,* which comes from the same word elements as *distraught,* has a less extreme meaning. It can be used simply for "confused" or "not attentive."

14. **extract** (verb) ĭk-străkt′; (noun) ĕk′străkt

From Latin: *ex-* (out) + *tract* (pull)

a. to pull out; to draw out (verb) ĭk-străkt′

A dehumidifier can **extract** water from the air.

Computer experts can sometimes **extract** lost data from a ruined hard drive.

b. something that is drawn or taken out (noun) ĕk′străkt

Pyrethrum, an **extract** of the chrysanthemum flower, can be used to repel mosquitoes.

c. a piece of writing selected from a larger whole (noun) ĕk′străkt

Extracts from Columbus's 1492 journal are required reading for the history course.

NOTE: When pronouncing the verb *extract,* accent the second syllable; for the noun form, accent the first.

▶ *Related Word*

extraction (noun) The *extraction* of salt from ocean water may be done by evaporation.

A poor immigrant of Haitian *extraction* rose to be a famous scientist. (Here, *extraction* means "ancestry.")

Extract *of the Aztecs*

Vanilla extract, a popular flavoring for baked goods, is drawn from the pods of orchids. The ancient Aztecs of Mexico used it to flavor xocolatl (chocolate) drinks. Spanish explorer Hernando Cortés was introduced to this vanilla and chocolate drink at the court of the Aztec ruler Montezuma. He brought it to Europe, where it soon became popular. Vanilla extract is widely used in perfume. It can also mask unpleasant smells, repel bugs, and relieve the pain of minor burns.

15. **retract** (verb) rĭ-trăkt′

From Latin: *re-* (back) + *tract* (pull)

to withdraw a promise or statement; to pull something back

The suspect **retracted** his confession.

When a tortoise is frightened, it **retracts** its head into its shell.

▶ *Related Word*

retraction (noun) The company issued a *retraction* of its error-filled profits statement.

vers, vert

16. **adversary** (noun) ăd′vər-sĕr′ē (plural: **adversaries**)

From Latin: *ad-* (toward) + *vert* (turn) (When we "turn toward" an enemy or adversary, we prepare to fight.)

opponent; foe

Both **adversaries** fought hard to win the tennis match.

In the Civil War, former slaves proved to be brave **adversaries** of the Confederate Army.

▶ *Related Word*

adversarial (adjective) The U.S. legal system is an *adversarial* one, in which a defense argues against a prosecution.

NOTE: *Adversary* connotes a stubborn and determined foe.

Match the Adversaries

Can you match these adversarial pairs?

1. Aliens	a. Mark Antony
2. Harry Potter	b. Luke Skywalker
3. Shrek	c. The Duke of Wellington
4. Darth Vader	d. Monsters
5. Tweety Bird	e. Lord Voldemort
6. Napoleon	f. Prince Charming
7. Octavian	g. Sylvester

Answers are on page 399.

17. **diversion** (noun) dĭ-vûr′zhən

From Latin: *dis-* (away) + *vert* (turn)

a. something that turns one's attention away

Talking on cell phones is a dangerous **diversion** for drivers.

The small attack from the front served as a **diversion** while the main army charged the enemy from the sides.

b. something that entertains

A good book can provide **diversion** on an airplane ride.

c. a turning aside

The city's marathon resulted in the **diversion** of traffic to side roads.

► *Related Words*

divert (verb) The beautiful scenery *diverted* my attention from the road.

diversionary (adjective) While I used the *diversionary* tactic of engaging our neighbor in conversation, my sister rescued our ball from his yard.

Tony's attention was *diverted* from the conversation.

Courtesy author

18. **inadvertently** (adverb) in′əd-vûr′tnt-lē

From Latin: *in-* (not) + *ad-* (toward) + *vert* (turn) (When you are "not turned toward" something, events often happen inadvertently, or accidentally.)

unintentionally; by accident

Smokers who fall asleep with a lit cigarette can **inadvertently** cause a fire.

Greg **inadvertently** forwarded the e-mail to everyone in his address book.

► *Related Word*

inadvertent (adjective) We corrected the waitress's **inadvertent** addition mistake and paid the amount we actually owed.

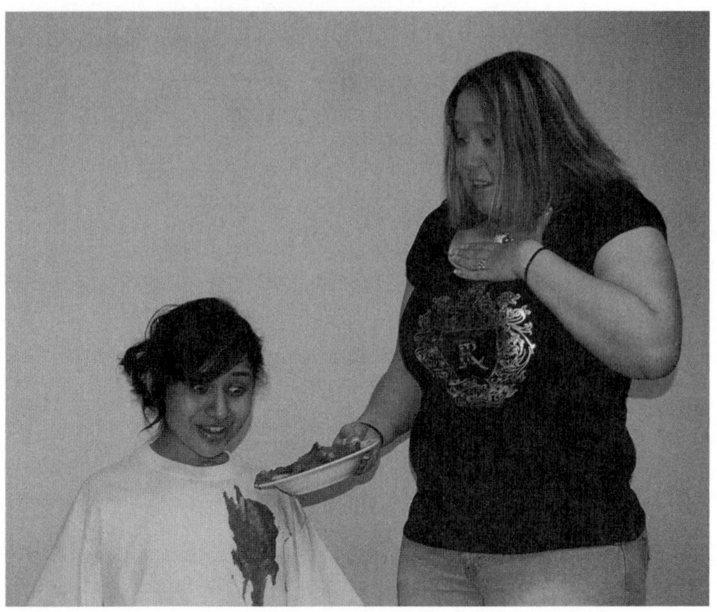
Courtesy author

Chris *inadvertently* spilled spaghetti all over Lucia's shirt.

circum-

19. **circumscribe** (verb) sûr′kəm-skrīb′

From Latin: *circum-* (around) + *scrib* (write)

to limit; to restrict; to enclose

To **circumscribe** the department head's power, the CEO took some responsibilities away from her.

The garden was **circumscribed** by a high wall.

20. **circumspect** (adjective) sûr′kəm-spĕkt′

From Latin: *circum-* (around) + *spec* (look) (To be circumspect is "to look around," or be careful.)

cautious; careful; considering results of actions

The **circumspect** job seeker made sure there were no embarrassing pictures of her on friends' web pages.

Circumspect people avoid spreading gossip.

▶ *Related Word*

circumspection (noun) The media consultant advised the baseball star to practice *circumspection* and not criticize teammates publicly.

21. **circumvent** (verb) sûr′kəm-vĕnt′

From Latin: *circum-* (around) + venīre (to come)

to avoid; to outwit

To **circumvent** the long lines at stores, Bea ordered the item through the Internet.

Computer hackers **circumvented** the computer security system and stole millions.

▶ *Related Word*

circumvention (noun) *Circumvention* of child support payments continues to be a social and legal problem.

trans-

22. **transcend** (verb) trăn-sĕnd′

From Latin: *trans-* (across) + *scandere* (to climb) (When we transcend something, we "climb across" limits and overcome them.)

to overcome; to go above limits

Marian Anderson was able to **transcend** racial prejudice and become the first African American soloist at New York's Metropolitan Opera.

Our friendship **transcends** cultural barriers.

▶ *Related Word*

transcendent (adjective) Michelangelo's *transcendent* Sistine Chapel ceiling has awed viewers for over five hundred years. (*Transcendent* means going beyond ordinary limits especially in excellence.)

23. **transitory** (adjective) trăn′sĭ-tôr′ē

From Latin: *trans-* (across) + *īre* (to go), making *transīre* ("to go across" or to pass through quickly)

short-lived; existing briefly; passing

Romantic relationships based only on physical attraction are often **transitory.**

The **transitory** drop in oil prices soon gave way to another rise.

24. **traverse** (verb) trə-vûrs′

From Latin: *trans-* (across) + *vert* (turn) (Note that *traverse* uses two word elements taught in this lesson.)

to travel across or through

The trail **traverses** woods, wetlands, and prairie.

Exercises

Part 2

■ *Definitions*

Match the word and definition. Use each choice only once.

1. transcend _______
2. adversary _______
3. circumscribe _______
4. circumspect _______
5. transitory _______
6. diversion _______
7. extract _______
8. distraught _______
9. traverse _______
10. inadvertently _______

a. short-lived
b. to overcome
c. opponent
d. to withdraw
e. to avoid
f. to limit
g. cautious
h. crazy with worry
i. accidentally
j. something that is taken out
k. to cross
l. something that draws attention away

■ *Meanings*

Match each word element to its meaning. Use each choice only once.

1. trans- _______
2. vers, vert _______
3. tract _______
4. circum- _______.

a. across
b. pull
c. around
d. turn

■ *Words in Context*

Complete each sentence with the best word. Use each choice only once.

a. distraught
b. extract
c. retract
d. adversary
e. diversion
f. inadvertently
g. circumscribe
h. circumspect
i. circumvent
j. transcend
k. transitory
l. traverse

1. After a hard-fought handball match, I shook hands with my _________________.

2. Because even discarded e-mail can be recovered, be ____________________ about the messages you send.

3. Ayesha was ____________________ when she realized her wallet had been stolen.

4. If you press the button, the blade of the knife will ____________________ into the holder.

5. Some tourists ____________________ the entire Colorado river in boats, but others leave before the river's end.

6. If we ____________________ our yard by building a fence, our dog won't bother our neighbors.

7. We can ____________________ the traffic jam by taking a side street.

8. Her headache was ____________________ and vanished after a few minutes.

9. Ming was able to ____________________ her poverty and troubled childhood by graduating from college and getting a good job.

10. Now that I have studied, I'm ready for a(n) ____________________ like seeing a movie.

■ *Using Related Words*

Complete each sentence with the correct form. Use each choice only once. You may have to capitalize some words.

Inventions and Discoveries

1. transcend, transcending, transcendent

For many people, competing in sports competitions can be a __________________ experience. But how can you ____________ the difficulty of losing your legs? Oscar Pistorius, whose legs were amputated when he was less than a year old, vied for a place on the South African track team in the 2008 Olympics. ____________________ his disability with the help of an artificial Cheetah® Flex Foot running leg, Oscar is able to compete with able-bodied athletes.

2. extracted, extract, extraction

   William Blackstone, from Bluffton, Indiana, built the first washing machine as a present for his wife. It swished clothes around in soapy water and ____________________ the dirt. Then, to remove the soap, the clothes were rinsed in clean water. Finally, a separate "wringer" was used for the ____________________ of excess water. Later, John Chamberlain invented a single machine that was able to wash, rinse, and ____________________ water, like the washing machines of today.

3. inadvertent, inadvertently

   In 1928, while Sir Alexander Fleming was researching bacteria, he went on vacation. During his absence, a test-tube lid ____________________ slipped off, and his sample was killed by an unknown mold. Fleming returned and was just about to throw the sample out when he realized that the mold might be able to kill harmful bacteria. In this ____________________ manner, he discovered the important antibiotic, penicillin.

4. retraction, retract

   The scientist Galileo earned fame for his theories of astronomy. But convinced that his work was not consistent with the Bible, the Catholic Church forced him to ____________________ his findings. Even after his ____________________, though, the Pope condemned Galileo and forced him to live alone until he died. In 1992, Pope John Paul II formally acknowledged that the Church had made a mistake in condemning Galileo.

■ *Find the Example*

Choose the example that best describes the action or situation.

1. Adversary whose power has been circumscribed _______
   a. defeated rival b. friend fired from a job
   c. enemy who won an election

2. Retracting an extract _______
   a. accepting congratulations for the most excellent part of a speech
   b. admitting that a paragraph in a book was incorrect
   c. apologizing for a speech that was insulting to others

3. A person would be most distraught if she inadvertently lost _______
   a. her umbrella. b. her university identification.
   c. her daughter.

4. Something a person can circumvent or traverse _______
   a. a class in calculus b. a hill c. a skyscraper

5. The most transitory diversion _______
   a. a two-minute trip to buy food b. a one-thousand-page novel
   c. a three-minute film clip on YouTube

Chapter Exercises

■ *Practicing Strategies: New Words from Word Elements*

Use your knowledge of word elements to determine the meanings of these words and complete each sentence. Use each choice only once.

a. abduct	e. circumsolar	i. intractable
b. Antivert	f. circulatory	j. static
c. aqueducts	g. detention	k. tenor
d. avert	h. injection	l. transcontinental

1. *Aqua* means "water"; the ancient Romans built __________________ to lead water to their cities.

2. When you are put in __________________ in high school, you are "held" in a special office.

3. Something that is __________________ stands still, rather than moving.

4. When we get a(n) __________________, medicine is "thrown into" our bodies.

5. A famous __________________ train system connected New York to California.

6. The __________________ system conducts blood "around" the body.

7. Since *anti* means "against," a medicine named ________________ helps fight against dizziness, a feeling that the world is "turning" around you.

8. The singing voice of ________________ got its name because originally it "held" a song's melody.

9. People who are ________________ cannot be "pulled" to a different point of view, or have their minds changed.

10. Many stars go in ________________ paths, around the sun.

■ *Practicing Strategies: Combining Context Clues and Word Elements*

In each sentence, one word is italicized. Use the meaning of the word element and the context to make an intelligent guess about its meaning.

1. The truck had to make many stops, and so it took a *circuitous* rather than a direct route.

   Circuitous means ________________________________.

2. Because of the blockage, blood in the artery reached a state of *stasis*.

   Stasis means ________________________________.

3. She *interjected* jokes into her serious speech.

   Interjected means ________________________________.

The next two items are taken from newspaper sources.

4. To keep the mix from drying between waterings, he adds a water-*retentive* polymer, such as Soil Moist.

   Retentive means ________________________________.

5. These days cruises that *circumnavigate* the globe are more popular and are attracting younger, more active travelers.

   Circumnavigate means ________________________________.

■ *Practicing Strategies: Using the Dictionary*

The following entry is taken from a print source. Read it and then answer the questions.

> **suit** (so͞ot) *n.* **1a.** A set of matching outer garments, esp. one consisting of a coat with trousers or a skirt. **b.** A costume for a special activity: *a diving suit.* **2.** A group of things used together; a set or collection. **3.** *Games* Any of the four sets of 13 playing cards (clubs, diamonds, hearts, and spades) in a standard deck. **4.** Attendance required of a vassal at his feudal lord's court or manor. **5.** *Law* A court proceeding to recover a right or claim. **6.** The act or an instance of courting a woman; courtship. **7.** *Slang* One who wears a business suit, esp. an executive. ❖ *v.* **suit•ed, suit•ing, suits**—*tr.* **1.** To meet the requirements of; fit. **2.** To make appropriate or suitable; adapt. **3.** To be appropriate for; befit. **4.** To please; satisfy. **5.** To provide with clothing; dress. —*intr.* **1.** To be suitable or acceptable. **2.** To be in accord; agree or match. **—*phrasal verb:* suit up** To put on clothing designed for a special activity. [ME *sute* < AN < VLat. **sequita*, act of following, fem. of **sequitus*, p. part. of **sequere*, to follow < Lat. *sequī*. See SUITOR.]

1. List the part of speech and definition number that fits the sentence "Did the service at the restaurant suit you?" ____________________
2. What is the phrasal verb for *suit*? ____________________
3. List the part of speech and definition number that fits the sentence "When the suit arrived, he insisted that the meeting begin."____________________
4. In which language did the word *suit* originate? ____________________
5. What is the part of speech and definition number that best fits the following sentence? "She rejected his suit because she didn't love him." ____________________

■ *Companion Words*

Complete each sentence with the best word. You may use choices more than once. Choices: from, of, to, over, in, by.

1. Warm family gatherings are conducive ________ happiness.
2. A revolution in the country brought about many sudden changes ________ the status quo.

3. The noisy teenagers were ejected ________ the concert.

4. Napoleon was the adversary ________ Wellington.

5. Please abstain ________ using cell phones during the performance.

6. She was distraught ________ her husband's illness.

7. At one time, marshmallows were made from the extract ________ the mallow plant.

8. Will free checking induce people ________ open a bank account?

9. The forest preserve was circumscribed ________ a large fence.

10. Nobel Prize winners are generally people ________ great stature.

■ *Writing with Your Words*

To practice effective writing, complete each sentence with an interesting phrase that indicates the meaning of the italicized word.

1. One difficulty I must *transcend* is ____________________

____.

2. After the hockey player was *jettisoned* from the team, ____________

____.

3. People *circumvent* long lines for tickets by ____________________

____.

4. The *transitory* hailstorm ____________________________

____.

5. My favorite *diversion* is ____________________________

____.

6. I *inadvertently* ____________________________________

____.

7. People who are *circumspect* ______________________________

____.

8. I would like to *circumscribe* the power of ________________

____.

9. His position on the team is *tenuous* because ______________

____.

10. One thing I would like to change in the *status* quo is __________

____.

■ *Making Connections*

To connect new vocabulary to your life, write extended responses to these questions.

1. Describe a time when you have felt distraught.
2. What brings out, or has brought out, your tenacity? Explain your answer.
3. Describe a problem you were able to circumvent.

Passage

Celebrity Fever

Oprah, Angelina, Brad, Jen, J.Lo, Beyoncé . . . Billions of people worldwide can identify exactly whom these names belong to. In fact, entire magazines, TV shows, blogs, and websites are devoted to them. What do they eat and wear? Will their relationships break up?

Celebrity worship is nothing new. In fact, anthropologists tell us that every culture has some form of it. So do the apes, chimpanzees, and monkeys that resemble humans. It seems that social animal groups, including humans, contain "alpha" males and females. These leaders have more prestige and power than the rest of the pack. Other, less powerful animals follow the higher-**status** alpha individuals. **(1)** From this, scientists have **deduced** that interest in celebrities is programmed into our genes.

There are many different ways of tracking the famous. Magazines like *In Touch, Us,* and *People,* networks like *E!*, and *EZines* give us constant updates on their activities and romances. Technology has also helped us to follow celebrities. In the 1990s, wire-tapping and long-range cameras revealed that Prince Charles of England was having an affair, and that his sister-in-law, "Fergie," was touching toes with a sweetheart. In today's world, the growth of fansites, blogs, and Twitter make conditions even more **conducive** to tracking the smallest events in the lives of our favorite stars.

Often, very famous people cannot escape being pursued by **(2)** reporters who **tenaciously** try to **extract** the most intimate details of their lives. **(3)** It is almost impossible to **circumvent** them. When "Brangelina" (Brad Pitt and Angelina Jolie) begged for privacy, they were greeted with laughter.

(4) We all have moments when we are not completely **circumspect,** and if you are a celebrity, it is almost certain that your **inadvertent** slips will be publicized within minutes. In fact, bad news is even more readable than good. A **dejected**-looking star on the cover of a tabloid sells lots of copies to supermarket customers. **(5)** The contestants on *American Idol* are routinely **jettisoned.** But despite their usually **transitory** fame, they are almost always followed by the media.

How does all this affect the billions of us who follow celebrity news? Interest can be healthy when the famous provide good models. Newscaster Katie Couric focused attention on the need for colon cancer screening. Rock stars Bono and Bob Geldof are social activists who were nominated for the Nobel Peace Prize in 2006. Celebrity news can also be a harmless amusement that **diverts** our attention from our own problems.

But not all interest is healthy. Many teenagers, to the despair of their parents, have copied the outfits of Sienna Miller or the hairstyle of David Beckham. **(6)** In fact, stars often put their names on fashion lines to **induce** sales. Anorexia, an eating disorder causing extreme weight loss, has been partially blamed on the influence of celebrities. In an effort to attain the "perfect" bodies of those they worship, young girls can starve themselves to death.

Or celebrity worship can lead to a sort of mass hysteria. In India, the 2006 death of superstar Rajkumar sent shock waves through the population. **(7) Distraught** fans attacked cars, pelting stones at them. Indian citizens have given the term *idol worship* a new meaning—the fans of one actress actually built a temple in her honor.

At times, celebrity worship can turn deadly. Pursuing reporters have been blamed for the car crash that killed Princess Diana of Britain in 1997. A fan claimed that Eminem's violent lyrics inspired him to commit murder. Celebrities themselves can also become the targets of fans. John Lennon was shot dead in the streets of New York. **(8)** Tennis star Monica Seles was stabbed by a fan of **adversary** Steffi Graf.

Celebrity worship has become troublesome enough that it is now a topic of research. Southern Illinois researcher James Houran and his colleagues identify three levels. The first, called "entertainment social," is harmless. As an example, **(9) staunch** fans may simply enjoy reading and talking about stars. The second is "intense personal." At this level, the connection **transcends** a simple interest and becomes a personal "bond" with the celebrity. So, a fan may feel that Jennifer Aniston is his soul mate.

At the third level, "borderline," a fan may **traverse** the line that separates mental health and insanity. **(10)** People who have only a **tenuous** grasp of reality can allow celebrity worship to take over their lives. This may turn fans into stalkers—or even killers. Lonely people, with little in their own lives, are particularly at risk. They may fantasize that Brad or J.Lo will leave their mate and find eternal happiness with the person who has worshipped them from afar for so long. Celebrity worship may be harmless fun—or it can be a deadly pursuit.

■ *Exercise*

Each numbered sentence corresponds to a sentence in the passage. Fill in the letter of the choice that makes the sentence mean the same thing as its corresponding sentence in the passage.

1. From this, scientists have _______ that interest in celebrities is programmed into our DNA.
   a. suggested b. felt c. argued d. concluded

2. Reporters tenaciously try to _______ the most intimate details.
   a. follow b. draw out c. closely note d. pay for

3. It is almost impossible to _______ them.
   a. avoid b. reason with c. cross d. pull back from

4. We have all had moments when we are not completely _______.
   a. careful b. happy c. entertained d. distressed

5. The contestants on *American Idol* are routinely _______.
   a. accidentally found b. insulted c. competing d. thrown out

6. In fact, stars often put their names on fashion lines to _______ sales.
   a. bring about b. publicize c. profit from d. finalize

7. _______ fans attacked cars.
   a. Violent b. Upset c. Amused d. Rejected

8. Monica Seles was stabbed by a fan of _______ Steffi Graff.
   a. famous b. upset c. rival d. strong

9. _______ fans may simply enjoy reading and talking about stars.
   a. Worried b. Faithful c. Playing d. Sad

10. People who have only a _______ grasp of reality can allow celebrity worship to take over their lives.
    a. short-lived b. weak c. false d. unrealistic

■ *Discussion Questions*

1. What similarity does the author see in the behavior of social animals and humans?
2. Why do you think that bad news about celebrities sells better than good news?
3. Do you think that public funds should be given to celebrities for security? Why or why not?

INSIGHT INTO IDIOMS

Actions

Can you bend over backwards? It is a yoga action that takes lots of training! Its origin is probably in northern India, where it was done to symbolize submission to God's authority. As an English idiom, to *bend over backwards* means to do everything possible to please someone else. Here are other idioms that make use of actions.

a. When a person *is axed,* he (or she) is fired from a job.
b. To *cut down to size* is to criticize a person who is overconfident.
c. To *draw the line* is to set a limit.
d. To *cover a lot of ground* is to give a lot of information.
e. When something is revealed only at the last minute, it is called a *cliffhanger*.
f. When an audience claps and cheers at a performance, it *bring the house down.*

Practice chapter words one more time by filling in the letter of the correct idiom into the blank before each sentence.

_____ 1. After the boss circumscribed the power of the supervisor who had been ordering us around, he felt he had been _________.

_____ 2. A person who _________ from his job and has to look for a new one will probably feel dejected.

_____ 3. You may try many things to defeat your adversary, but you should _________ at cheating.

_____ 4. The theater is filled with staunch friends of the actors, so they probably will _________ when the play ends.

_____ 5. My friend inadvertently revealed the ending of the movie, so it was no longer a(n) _________ for me.

Links to more lists of English idioms and their meanings can be found at the Student Companion Website for this book: **www.cengage.com/devenglish/richek8e**.

CHAPTER 8

Word Elements: Together and Apart

The poet John Donne wrote, "No man is an island." All of us connect with other people in our classes, jobs, pastimes, and family lives. To help describe these connections, Chapter 8 presents word elements that mean "together" and "apart." This chapter also introduces several words that came into English from other languages. Over centuries, as English speakers came in contact with people around the world, they "borrowed" words and brought them into English.

Chapter Strategy: Word Elements: Together and Apart

Chapter Words:

Part 1

co-, com-, con-:	coherent	*dis-*	discord
	collaborate		disparity
	communal		disseminate
	compatible	*sym-, syn-*	synchronize
	concur		synopsis
	contemporary		synthesis

Part 2

		Borrowed Words
greg	congregate	bravado
	egregious	charisma
	gregarious	cliché
sperse	disperse	cuisine
	intersperse	nadir
	sparse	zenith

Visit the Student Companion Website at **www.cengage.com/devenglish/richek8e** to test your knowledge of these words before you study, hear each word pronounced, find additional practice exercises, and access more information on words and topics.

Did You Know?

What Are Two Sources of English?

Modern English has roots in two languages: Old French and Old English. Old French was a Romance language; that is, it descended from Latin, which was spoken by ancient Romans. Old French is an ancestor of modern French. Old English, spoken in England from about 700 to 1150 CE, was a Germanic language, similar in many ways to the German spoken today. How did the two languages come together?

In 1066 William the Conqueror crossed the English Channel from Normandy, in northwestern France, to England. He then conquered England and made himself king. He replaced the English nobility with his Norman countrymen, who spoke a version of Old French. For many years, then, the ruling class of England spoke Old French, and the commoners continued to speak Old English. (He also left many descendants, including one of the editors of this book.)

Gradually, though, Old French and Old English merged into Middle English, which was spoken until the 1300s. This language then developed into modern English. But to this day, many rare, fancy English words (like the ones you find in vocabulary books) are of Old French origin and thus descend from Latin. In contrast, the common words of English usually come from Old English.

What does this mean to you? Perhaps you speak or have studied Spanish, Italian, French, or Portuguese. These are Romance languages, related to the Old French that William the Conqueror brought to England. If you speak a Romance language, you can easily learn many difficult English words. Often, all you need to do is to think of a *cognate,* a word that sounds the same and has the same meaning, from a Romance language. As an example, *furious* is an English word descended from Old French. The Spanish cognate is *furioso.*

Modern English is full of word pairs that have the same or similar meanings, but one word is derived from Old French and the other from Old English. Several of these word pairs are listed below. Notice that the words descended from Old French are longer and more difficult than their Old English pairs.

Old English (Germanic Origin)	*Old French (Romance Origin)*
drink	imbibe
talk	converse
give	donate
earth	terrain
top	pinnacle
brave	valiant

Links to lists of English words that were borrowed from other languages can be found through the Student Companion Website at **www.cengage.com/devenglish/richek8e**.

Learning Strategy

Word Elements: Together and Apart

Part 1 of this chapter presents three common prefixes that refer to being together or apart: *com-* and *syn-* mean "together"; *dis-* means "apart." These prefixes are very useful to know; each one is used to form more than one hundred English words.

Part 2 presents two roots that are related to the idea of together and apart, *greg* (flock, herd) and *sperse* (scatter).

Element	*Meaning*	*Origin*	*Function*	*Chapter Words*
Part 1				
co-, col-, com-, con-, cor-	together	Latin	prefix	coherent, collaborate, communal, compatible, concur, contemporary
dis-	apart; not	Latin; Greek	prefix	discord, disparity, disseminate
sym-, syn-	together; same	Greek	prefix	synchronize, synopsis, synthesis
Part 2				
greg	flock; herd	Latin	Root	congregate, egregious, gregarious
sperse	scatter	Latin	Root	disperse, intersperse, sparse

Prefixes

Part 1

The three prefixes presented in Part 1 are discussed in more detail here.

co-, col-, com-, con-, cor- (together)

This prefix is in several hundred English words. Its five spelling variations help us pronounce it more easily when it is attached to various roots. Each of the words formed with this prefix carries a sense of **together.** For example, a *coworker* is someone who works **together** with another worker. To *collect* means "to bring things **together.**" When people *communicate* or *correspond,* they come **together** through speech or writing. When two electrical wires establish *contact,* they come **together** by touching.

dis- (apart; not)

In most words, *dis-* means **not.** The word *distrust,* formed from the prefix *dis-* and the base word *trust,* means "**not** to trust." A person in *disgrace* is **not** in the "grace," or favor, of others. The informal word *dis* means **not** to respect, or "not to show respect for," as in "She *dissed* me." *Dis-* can also mean **apart.** Biology students sometimes *dissect* frogs, or cut them **apart**. A noisy student may *disrupt* a class, or break it **apart** into confusion.

sym-, syn- (together; same)

The two meanings of *syn-* and *sym-* are related, making them easy to remember. For example, *sympathy* is composed from *sym-* (**same**) and the root *path* (feeling). *Synagogue,* a place where Jewish people meet to worship, is composed from *syn-* (**together**) and *agein* (to lead).

Words to Learn

Part 1

co-, col-, com-, con-, cor-

1. **coherent** (adjective) kō-hîr′ənt

From *co-* (together) + *haērere* (to cling or stick)

logical; consistent; clearly reasoned

The action movie was exciting, but it lacked a **coherent** plot.

The city needs a **coherent** strategy for reducing crime.

▶ *Related Words*

coherence (noun) Lacking any *coherence,* the student's paper was simply a disorganized collection of sentences.

cohere (verb) The sticky bandage *cohered* to my skin. (*Cohere* means "to stick.")

incoherent (adjective) Myra was laughing so hard that her reply was **incoherent**. (*Incoherent* means "not coherent," or unable to be understood, as in "incoherent speech.")

2. **collaborate** (verb) kə-lăb′ə-rāt′

From Latin: *col-* (together) + *labōrāre* (to work)

to work together

Bill Hewlett and David Packard **collaborated** on a project that produced the first personal computer.

Richard Rogers **collaborated** with Oscar Hammerstein to produce Broadway musicals.

▶ *Related Words*

collaboration (noun) The giant wall mural was a **collaboration** by five artists.

collaborator (noun, person) Traitor Vidkun Quisling was a *collaborator* who helped the Nazis conquer and rule his home country of Denmark.

NOTE: The word *collaborator* can have the negative meaning of "one who aids an enemy that is occupying one's country."

▶ *Common Phrases*

collaborate with (others); collaborate on (a project)

Can you match these famous collaborators with their projects?

1. Williams, Stone, and Dorsey
2. Zuckerburg, Moskovitz, Hughes, and Saverin
3. Bert and Ernie
4. Dora and Diego
5. Ben and Jerry
6. Watson and Crick

a. discoverers of DNA
b. puppets on Sesame Street
c. ice cream firm founders
d. founders of Facebook
e. founders of Twitter
f. explorers

Answers are on page 399.

3. **communal** (adjective) kə-myo͞o′nəl

From Latin: *com-* (together) (*Communis* meant "shared," "public.")

referring to a community or to joint ownership

A single rude cell-phone user can disturb a large **communal** space.

Beachfronts and farmland in Mexico are often claimed by an *ejido,* which is a form of **communal** ownership.

▶ *Related Word*

commune (noun) (kŏm′-yo͞on) In a *commune,* people live together, sharing housing and incomes.

NOTE: The verb *commune,* with the second syllable accented, means to communicate closely, and is often used in phrases like "commune with nature."

4. **compatible** (adjective) kəm-păt′ə-bəl

From Latin: *com-* (together) + *path* (feeling)

harmonious; living in harmony

I checked to make sure that the application I downloaded was **compatible** with my five-year-old cell phone.

The **compatible** roommates shared a love of sports.

Peanut butter and jelly are **compatible** in ingredients in sandwiches.

► *Common Phrase*
compatible with

► *Related Words*
compatibility (noun) *Compatibility* is an important factor in a happy marriage.
incompatible (adjective) Working late nights as a waiter was **incompatible** with his early morning class schedule. (*Incompatible* means "not compatible.")

5. **concur** (verb) kən-kûr′

From Latin: *con-* (together) + *currere* (to run)

to agree

Experts **concur** on the harmful effects of smoking.

In a 2007 report, over 1,200 scientists **concurred** that human activity is causing global warming.

► *Common Phrases*
concur with (agree with) a person; concur on (agree on or about) something

► *Related Words*
concurrence (noun) The wire-tapping of U.S. citizens requires the *concurrence* of the Attorney General's office.
concurrent (adjective) If you want to see those two *concurrent* TV programs, you must tape one with your TiVo.® (*Concurrent* means "at the same time.")

6. **contemporary** (noun: adjective) kən-tĕm′pə-rĕr′ē (plural: **contemporaries**)

From Latin: *com-* (together) + *tempus* (time)

a. a person living at about the same time as another (noun)

Albert Einstein was a **contemporary** of Joseph Stalin.

Great artists are sometimes not appreciated by their **contemporaries.**

b. existing at the same time (adjective)

The Industrial Revolution and the rapid development of cities were **contemporary** events.

c. current; modern (adjective)

While English, Spanish, and Japanese are **contemporary** languages, Latin is not.

Contemporary mobile phones sometimes have hundreds of applications.

▶ *Related Word*

contemporaneous (adjective) The deaths of Thomas Jefferson and John Adams, on July 4, 1826, were *contemporaneous* events.

dis-

7. **discord** (noun) dĭs′kôrd′

From Latin: *dis-* (apart) + *cord* (heart)

a. strife; lack of agreement

Letting friends cut into a line may cause **discord** with those waiting behind.

The money dad left in his will caused **discord** when my sisters argued over how to divide it.

b. a harsh, disagreeable combination of sounds

The **discord** of orchestra members tuning their instruments was followed by a beautiful concert.

▶ *Related Word*

discordant (adjective) (dĭ-skôr′dnt) The beginning violin student filled the room with *discordant* sounds.

The Apple of Discord

According to a Greek legend, the goddess of *discord,* Eris, had not been invited to a wedding at which all the other gods were to be present. Enraged, she arrived at the party and threw onto the table a golden apple intended "for the most beautiful." Three goddesses, Hera, Athena, and Aphrodite, claimed it. So Paris, prince of Troy, was asked to settle the dispute. He chose Aphrodite because she promised him the world's most beautiful woman, Helen of Troy. Unfortunately, Helen was already married to the Greek king Menelaus. When Paris kidnapped her, a Greek army invaded Troy. This was the start of the Trojan War, the subject of Homer's *Iliad.*

8. **disparity** (noun) dĭ-spăr′ĭ-tē (plural: **disparities**)

From Latin: *dis-* (not) + *par* (equal)

inequality; difference

Despite the **disparity** in their ages, the senior citizen and his grandson ran the marathon at the same pace.

There is a great **disparity** between the lives of the very rich and the very poor.

The Economic Benefits of Finishing College

Census data released in 2005 showed a great *disparity* in the incomes of workers with a high school degree and those who have completed college. Those holding a bachelor's degree earned an average of $51,554, while those with a high school diploma earned $28,645.

▶ *Related Word*

disparate (adjective) (dĭs′pər-ĭt) U2 lead singer Bono has cited musical influences as *disparate* as punk music, the poet W.B. Yeats, and Dr. Martin Luther King Jr. (*Disparate* means "completely different and distinct.")

9. **disseminate** (verb) dĭ-sĕm′ə-nāt′

From Latin: *dis-* (apart) + *sēmin* (seed)

to scatter; to make widely known

Twitter **disseminates** opinions quickly on the Internet.

We **disseminated** news about our concert through newspapers, flyers, and our website.

▶ *Related Word*

dissemination (noun) The *dissemination* of classified government information to the press is a crime.

sym-, syn-

10. **synchronize** (verb) sĭng′krə-nīz′

From Greek: *syn-* (together) + *dramein* (to run)

to cause to occur at the same time

Dancers in a chorus line must **synchronize** their movements.

The dancers *synchronized* their movements.

Courtesy author

▶ *Related Words*

synchronization (noun) The *synchronization* of church clocks ensures that the bells throughout the city ring at the same time.

synchronous (adjective) In a *synchronous* online course, all class members must be on the computer at the same time.

11. **synopsis** (noun) sĭ-nŏp′sĭs (plural: **synopses**)

From Greek: *syn-* (together) + *opsis* (view) (In a synopsis, something is viewed "all together.")

a short summary

Movie reviews often give a **synopsis** of the film.

▶ *Related Word*

synopsize (verb) The notes *synopsized* the meeting.

12. **synthesis** (noun) sĭn′thĭ-sĭs (plural: **syntheses**)

From Greek: *syn-* (together) + *tithenai* (to put)

something made from combined parts; the making of something by combining parts

The **synthesis** of hydrocarbon fuel and oxygen produces energy.

Several movies are **syntheses** of animation and live action.

▶ *Related Words*

synthesize (verb) Plants *synthesize* carbohydrates through photosynthesis.

synthetic (adjective) (sĭn-thĕt′ĭk) Nylon and polyester are *synthetic* materials made from petroleum.

synthesizer (noun) A voice *synthesizer* uses software to convert text into speech.

NOTE: *Synthetic* refers to products such as nylon that are produced chemically or by other artificial means, in contrast to items of natural origin.

Exercises

Part 1

■ *Definitions*

Match the word and definition. Use each choice only once.

1. disseminate _______
2. collaborate _______
3. synopsis _______
4. concur _______
5. synthesis _______
6. coherent _______
7. discord _______
8. synchronize _______
9. contemporary _______
10. communal _______

a. to scatter widely
b. harmonious
c. to make occur at the same time
d. inequality
e. existing at the same time
f. logical; consistent
g. jointly owned
h. something made from combined parts
i. to agree
j. to work together
k. summary
l. strife; lack of agreement

■ *Meanings*

Match each prefix to its meaning. Use each choice only once.

1. syn- _______
2. dis- _______
3. con- _______

a. together, same
b. together
c. apart; not together

■ *Words in Context*

Complete each sentence with the best word. Use each choice only once. You may have to capitalize some words.

a. coherent	e. concur	i. disseminate
b. collaborate	f. contemporary	j. synchronize
c. communal	g. discord	k. synopsis
d. compatible	h. disparity	l. synthesis

1. The two loudly complaining committee members caused considerable ____________________ in the meeting.

2. Students who read a ____________________ of a book, rather than the book itself, miss the richness of the original language.

3. Before NASA can launch a space mission, several teams of experts must ____________________that conditions are safe.

4. Rather than producing two separate films, the two moviemakers decided to ____________________ on one project.

5. Health officials worked around the clock to ____________________ information about the flu epidemic to the public.

6. ____________________ spaces in colleges, such as cafeterias and lounges, are good places to meet people.

7. There was a ____________________ between my boss's promises and my actual working conditions.

8. The three ____________________ friends all enjoyed going to parties and dances.

9. You talked in your sleep, but since you weren't ____________________, I couldn't understand what you were talking about.

10. People who produce films must ____________________ the video and the audio so that people are appearing to speak when we actually hear the words.

■ *Using Related Words*

Complete each sentence with the correct form. Use each choice only once. You may have to capitalize some words.

1. disparities, disparity, disparate

   Statistics on how long people live are collected for several countries. Overall, there are great ____________________ among countries. The country with the longest life expectancy is Macaw (in Asia), with a life expectancy of eighty-four years. At the bottom of the list is Swaziland, with only thirty-one years. The causes of these ____________________ life spans include violence levels and access to medical care. A ____________________ also exists between rich and poor countries. The United States, which has a life expectancy of seventy-eight years, ranks 50th in a list of 225.

2. compatibility, compatible, incompatible

   As people become more sophisticated about foods, tastes that once seemed ____________________ are put together. Would it surprise you to learn that hot peppers and chocolate are considered to have enough ____________________ to be combined into a candy? Similarly, pineapples, cashew nuts, and even clams have been judged to be ____________________ enough with the flavor of dough to be used as pizza toppings.

3. contemporaries, contemporary, contemporaneously

   ____________________ scientists have discovered that approximately sixty-five million years ago, huge volcanic eruptions and meteorites hitting Earth occurred ____________________. These two events were disastrous for Earth, and probably wiped out dinosaurs. It is astonishing that geologists, and their ____________________ in biology and physics, have developed tools so sophisticated that they can determine events that happened in the Mesozoic era.

4. synthetic, synthesize, synthesized, synthetically

   Although the human body can produce many substances, vitamin C cannot be ____________________ by our bodies. Now, however, Nicholas Smirnoff has discovered how plants ____________________ this chemical and may be able to produce plants that contain more of the vitamin. Currently, people must eat foods such as oranges and grapefruits or take pills containing ____________________ vitamin C. In the future, there may well be less reliance on ____________________ produced vitamin C because smaller amounts of food will supply more of the vitamin.

■ *Reading the Headlines*

Here are some headlines that might appear in newspapers. Read each and answer the questions. (Remember that small words, such as *is, are, a,* and *the,* are often left out of headlines.)

IN QUICKLY DISSEMINATED REPORT, EXPERTS CONCUR ON DISPARITY BETWEEN MEN'S AND WOMEN'S SALARIES

1. Is the report available to many people? _______
2. Do the experts agree? _______
3. Did the report show that men and women earn the same amount? _______

PSYCHOLOGISTS REPORT THAT DISCORD OFTEN ERUPTS OVER INCOMPATIBLE USES OF COMMUNAL LIVING SPACES

4. Are conditions peaceful? _______
5. Do the different uses of the spaces conflict with each other? _______
6. Are the spaces private? _______

CONTEMPORARY FASHION A SYNTHESIS OF STYLES

7. Is new fashion being referred to? _______

8. Does the fashion reflect one style? _______

COLLABORATIVE EFFORT ON FOOD CHANNEL RESULTS IN MORE COHERENT SHOW

9. Did one person present the show? _______

10. Was the show easier to understand? _______

Word Roots

Part 2

Part 2 presents two word roots that are concerned with coming together and moving apart but that do not carry these meanings directly. These roots are *greg* and *sperse.*

This part also presents some words that were borrowed from other languages when English speakers came into contact with them.

greg (flock; herd)

Greg once referred to a flock of sheep or a herd of cattle. By extension, *greg* is now used as a word element meaning the action of **flocking** or coming together. One word you will learn, *gregarious,* describes people who like to come together with others.

sperse (scatter)

When we **scatter** things, we move them apart. Thus, the root *sperse* is concerned with being apart. *Disperse,* one of the words in this chapter, means "to **scatter** widely."

Words to Learn

Part 2

greg

13. **congregate** (verb) kŏng′grĭ-găt′

From Latin: *con-* (together) + *greg* (flock, herd)

to meet; to assemble

When the power went out, the family **congregated** in the living room and lit candles.

Ants **congregated** around the spilled sugar.

▶ *Related Word*

congregation (noun) The *congregation* listened intently to the minister's sermon.

Religious Words

Congregation is often used to refer to members of a religious organization, such as a church or synagogue. Many other religious words have interesting origins.

Catholic, meaning *universal.* When spelled with a small *c, catholic* still means "universal," rather than the religion.

Protestant, from *protest.* In the early 1500s, Martin Luther and his followers protested against certain Catholic practices. From this, we get the name of the religion Protestant.

Jewish, from the Hebrew word *Judah,* the ancient Jewish Kingdom.

Muslim, from the Arabic word *aslama,* meaning *he surrendered,* referring to people who are obedient to Allah's will.

Hindu, from the Persian word for India, *Hind.*

14. **egregious** (adjective) ĭ-grē′jəs

From Latin: *ex-* (out of) + *greg* (flock; herd) (Originally, *egregious* meant out of the ordinary.)

outstandingly and noticeably bad

Drunk driving is an **egregious** traffic violation.

In an **egregious** error, the bride referred to the groom using the name of her former boyfriend.

15. **gregarious** (adjective) grĭ-gâr′ē-əs

From Latin: *greg* (flock; herd)

sociable; fond of company

Our **gregarious** neighbor threw a block party every year.

▶ *Related Word*

gregariousness (noun) *Gregariousness* is a helpful trait if you want to run for political office.

sperse

16. **disperse** (verb) dĭ-spûrs′

From Latin: *dis-* (apart) + *sperse* (scatter)

to scatter; to distribute widely

After the fireworks ended, the crowd **dispersed.**

Refinishing furniture outdoors allows harmful chemical fumes to **disperse** into the open air.

► *Related Word*

dispersion (noun) (dĭ-spûr′zhən) The students observed the *dispersion* of light through a prism.

17. **intersperse** (verb) ĭn′tər-spûrs′

From Latin: *inter-* (between) + *sperse* (scatter)

to scatter here and there; to distribute among other things

The text in the chapter is **interspersed** with interesting photos.

Skilled speakers often **intersperse** jokes throughout their presentations.

► *Common Phrase*

intersperse with

Why We Intersperse *"Like"*

Parents and teachers become annoyed with teenagers who *intersperse* their speech with the word *like*: "It's like, did you see her?" "She's got, like, an attitude." But linguist Muffy E. A. Siegel found that this word is a powerful communicator that can mean many different things. It can be used instead of *said*: "She's like, 'I'm going.'" It can show exaggeration: "She has like a million sweaters." It can be used when the speaker is not sure: "He's like seventeen." And it can be used to emphasize: "That's so, like, last week" (or out of date).

18. **sparse** (adjective) spärs

From Latin: *sperse* (scatter)

thinly scattered or distributed; meager

Rain has been so **sparse** in western Nebraska that ruts of wagon wheels made over one hundred years ago can still be seen.

► *Related Word*

sparsely (adverb) Wyoming is America's most *sparsely* populated state.

Borrowed Words

19. **bravado** (noun) brə-vä′dō

    From French and Old Spanish, bravery, boasting

    false bravery; showy display of courage

    The bully's **bravado** disappeared as soon as he was challenged.

    In a show of **bravado,** the teenager challenged the boxing champion to a fight.

20. **charisma** (noun) kə-rĭz′mə

    From Greek, favor from the gods

    a quality of leadership that attracts other people

    Confidence and the ability to give powerful speeches are some of the ingredients of **charisma**.

▶ *Related Word*

charismatic (adjective) (kăr′ĭz-măt′ĭk) Martin Luther King Junior's *charismatic* personality drew thousands of supporters to the civil rights movement.

Martin Luther King Jr. was a *charismatic* leader.

Bettmann/CORBIS

21. **cliché** (noun) klē-shā′

From French, to stereotype

a. an overused, trite expression

The reporter's story was so full of **clichés** that his editor made him rewrite it.

A **cliché** often used in sports is "No pain, no gain."

b. a predictable and overused character or situation

The nice girl who falls in love with a rebel is a **cliché** in romance novels and movies.

You can access links to lists of clichés through the Student Companion Website at **www.cengage.com/devenglish/richek8e**.

22. **cuisine** (noun) kwĭ-zēn′

From French

a style of food or cooking

Puerto Rican **cuisine** features delicious *pasteles,* which are made of cornmeal and stuffed with meat, raisins, olives, capers, and almonds.

Worldwide Cuisine

Can you match each food item with its group of origin?

1. kushari	a. Vietnamese
2. saganaki	b. Chinese
3. sambal	c. West and Central African
4. phò tai	d. Indonesian
5. foufou	e. Egyptian
6. congee	f. Greek

Answers are on page 399.

23. **nadir** (noun) nā′dər

From Arabic: *nazīr as-samt,* the lowest point; opposite the zenith

the lowest point

At the **nadir** of his fortunes, he was broke and alone.

24. **zenith** (noun) zē′nĭth

From Arabic: *samt ar-ra's,* the path overhead; the highest point in the heavens

the highest point

Centered in present-day Iraq, the Assyrian empire reached the **zenith** of its power from 900 to 650 BCE.

Middle Eastern Roots of Astronomy

As the origin of *zenith* suggests, Middle Eastern scientists made many important contributions. The work of Abu Ma'shar, or Albumasar (born in 787 CE), who calculated the length of the year and catalogued the stars, was translated from Arabic into Latin and became one of the first books printed in Germany. The writings of Jabir ibn Hayyan, or Gerber (died in 815), who is known as the "father of chemistry," were used as textbooks in Europe for centuries.

NOTE: *Zenith* is not used to refer to physical things, such as the top of a mountain. Instead, we refer to the peak or *pinnacle* of a mountain.

Exercises

Part 2

■ *Definitions*

Match the word and definition. Use each answer choice only once.

1. intersperse ______
2. nadir ______
3. cliché ______
4. bravado ______
5. gregarious ______
6. zenith ______
7. cuisine ______
8. sparse ______
9. egregious ______
10. congregate ______

a. overused expression
b. sociable
c. outstandingly bad
d. lowest point
e. to gather together
f. a quality that attracts others
g. to distribute among other things
h. style of cooking
i. highest point
j. showy display of bravery
k. to scatter; to distribute widely
l. thinly scattered

■ *Meanings*

Match each word root to its meaning. Use each choice only once.

1. sperse _______ a. flock; herd
2. greg _______ b. scatter

■ *Words in Context*

Complete each sentence with the best word. Use each choice only once.

a. congregate	e. intersperse	i. cliché
b. egregious	f. sparse	j. cuisine
c. gregarious	g. bravado	k. nadir
d. disperse	h. charisma	l. zenith

1. The expression "easier said than done" is a(n) ____________________ that most of us have heard many times.
2. After eight days of continuous rain, everyone hoped the clouds would ____________________ and we would see the sun.
3. The famous actress sued the celebrity magazine, claiming it had printed ____________________ lies about her marriage.
4. The famous chef was a master of the ____________________ of northern China.
5. Only a few ____________________ patches of grass grew in the dirt back yard.
6. Robbing from poor people shows human nature at its ____________________.
7. Over 200,000 people will ____________________ to hear the speech of the famous leader.
8. The farmer wanted to ____________________ rows of soybeans between the rows of wheat.
9. Because of his ____________________, the rock star attracted fans and imitators.
10. With considerable ____________________, the newly elected president announced that he would quickly destroy the country's powerful enemy.

■ *Using Related Words*

Complete each sentence with the correct form. Use each choice only once.

1. congregated, congregations, congregating

   What is the largest crowd that has ever been in one place? On New Year's Eve 2009, over one million people were seen ____________________ in New York's Times Square. An even bigger gathering takes place during the Haj, when between two and three million Muslims, from ____________________ all over the world, gather each year in Mecca. The largest event, however, is the Kumbh Mela, a Hindu gathering held in India, at which an estimated 60 to 70 million people ____________________ in 2007.

2. gregariousness, gregarious

   Researchers who study mice have found that ____________________ is largely an inherited trait. Other studies show that identical twins, who share 100 percent of their genes, are also more similar in how social they are than are fraternal twins, who share only 50 percent of their genes. So how ____________________ you are probably depends, at least to some extent, upon your genetic makeup.

3. dispersion, disperse

   Small, fast-moving hummingbirds ____________________ the pollen that fertilizes flowers. The birds' long bills gather nectar, and as hummingbirds move, they carry pollen from flower to flower. This, ____________________ allows flowers to be fertilized. Hummingbirds are especially attracted to red and orange flowers. If you wear these colors, they will be attracted to you, too!

4. charisma, charismatic

   Although the special quality of ____________________ is hard to define, history records many ____________________ leaders. Emiliano Zapata, powerful leader of the 1910 Mexican Revolution, struggled for *tierra y libertad*—land and liberty—for Mexican peasants. So powerful was his *charisma* that modern-day Mexican reformers are still known as *los zapatistas*. The *charisma* of French military leader and emperor Napoleon was said to be so great that anybody who met him would be enchanted by his personality.

■ *Find the Example*

Choose the example that best describes the action or situation.

1. A cliché dealing with cuisine _______
   a. "The cooking channel will not be available tomorrow"
   b. "It's a no brainer" c. "It's as easy as pie"

2. An egregious thing to do in a place where people congregate _______
   a. stand by yourself b. socialize c. start to push and shove

3. How a very gregarious person would probably feel when the crowd disperses. _______
   a. lonely for people b. happy that he has company
   c. relieved to be alone

4. Something that would be sparse at the nadir of a career _______
   a. complaints b. family c. lots of money

5. At the zenith of a charismatic leader's career there would be _______
   a. people asking who she was b. no attention
   c. lots of blogs about her

Chapter Exercises

■ *Practicing Strategies: New Words from Word Elements*

Use your knowledge of prefixes to determine the meanings of these words and complete each sentence. Use each choice only once.

a. aggregate	e. conserve	i. discomfort
b. cofounder	f. cooperate	j. disreputable
c. compress	g. disassemble	k. lip-synch
d. conform	h. disassociate	l. sympathize

1. If you ____________________ this piece of machinery, I hope that you can put it back together.

2. Someone with a bad reputation is ____________________.

3. When a person acts and dresses like others, we say he or she is trying

   to ____________________.

4. Henry Wells, together with his ____________________ William Fargo, created the American Express company in 1852.

5. In many movies, actors ____________________ songs that are actually sung by others.

6. *Path* means "feeling," so when we feel the same as someone who

   suffers, we ____________________.

7. When all of something is herded or gathered together, the total is

   called the ____________________.

8. After the ____________________ of sitting in a small car for ten hours, I was glad to get up and stretch.

9. When we do things together, we ____________________.

10. When we press something together, we ____________________ it.

■ *Practicing Strategies: Combining Context Clues and Word Elements*

In each sentence, one word is italicized. Use the word's meaning and the context to make an intelligent guess about its meaning.

1. The pages of our handout are all separate, and we need to *collate* them.

   Collate means ____.

2. After reaching total *concordance* among the delegates, they all voted for the proposal.

   Concordance means ____.

3. All the results are bunched together, so we need to *disaggregate* them into separate categories.

   Disaggregate means ____.

The next two items are taken from newspaper sources.

4. In addition to possible prison time, he must *disgorge* most of his ill-gotten gains and could be fined as much as $350,000.

   Disgorge means ____.

5. Polish-born Roman Cieslewicz has been able to adapt and *syncretize* elements of several important twentieth-century art movements in his posters and collages.

   Syncretize means ____.

■ *Companion Words*

Complete each sentence with the best word. You may use choices more than once. Choices: with, on, of, between, to.

1. The zenith _________ her career was her service as CEO of a public company.
2. Vietnamese cuisine is a synthesis _________ Asian and French cooking.
3. The disparity _________ the brothers' incomes made exchanging gifts awkward.
4. Couldn't we all concur _________ one dress style for the bridesmaids?
5. The collaboration _________ several singers resulted in a wonderful concert.
6. Could you give me a synopsis _________ the plot in a few sentences?
7. I collaborated _________ three classmates on the project.
8. The taste of chocolate is not compatible _________ that of sardines.
9. Glue makes items cohere _________ paper.
10. It is very important that long-distance drivers intersperse traveling

    _________ periodic rests.

■ *Writing with Your Words*

To practice effective writing, complete each sentence with an interesting phrase that indicates the meaning of the italicized word.

1. If a husband and wife are *incompatible,* ______________________________

   ____ .

2. I hate the *cliché* ______________________________

   ____ .

3. I like to *intersperse* studying with ______________________________

   ____ .

4. Reading the *synopsis* ______________________________

   ____ .

5. My friends all *concur* that ______________________________

   ____ .

6. One problem with the *communal* eating arrangements is__________

   ____ .

7. I made an *egregious* error when ______________________________

   ____ .

8. There was so much *discord* that ______________________________

   ____ .

9. The secret agents *synchronized* their watches so that ______________

   ____ .

10. Because of the island's *sparse* population, ______________________

    ____ .

■ *Making Connections*

To connect new vocabulary to your life, write extended responses to these questions.

1. Describe a person you know or know about who is charismatic.
2. Describe what you imagine your life will be like at the zenith of your career.
3. Do you think you are a gregarious person? Why or why not?

Passage

Intelligence Under Fire: The Story of the Navajo Code Talkers

When Marines raised the U.S. flag on the island of Iwo Jima in 1945, a photo of Ira Hayes, a Navajo Indian, and his fellow soldiers became world famous as representing the heroes of one of the hardest-fought battles of World War II. But unlike Hayes's picture, the role of the Navajo code talkers in the battle has only recently come to wide attention. This is their story.

In many ways **(1)** the **nadir** of U.S. justice is the treatment of Native Americans. In 1863, for example, the U.S. Army destroyed crops and animals of the Navajos and forced them onto reservations. There, children attended Bureau of Indian Affairs schools, where they were forbidden to use their own language. One man remembers being chained in a basement for daring to speak his native Navajo language!

But the language that the schoolmasters disdained would prove to be a powerful weapon in World War II. When the United States entered the war in 1941, over one hundred Navajos, some as young as fifteen, volunteered to fight. **(2)** In a show of **bravado,** some even brought their own rifles, which would have been useless against the powerful weaponry of Japan and Germany. As it turned out, though, Navajos and the language they spoke proved to be one of the most precious resources of the war.

Experts **concur** that communication becomes extremely difficult during warfare. Fighting units can be miles apart, **(3)** yet they must **synchronize** their attacks. But, of course, their messages must also be kept from the enemy. Communication may be put into code, but **(4)** the enemy has "code breakers" who try to read the messages and **disseminate** them to their troops. In World War II, the conquest of the Pacific islands occupied by Japan was particularly challenging, and a good coded communication system was needed.

Rob Crandall/The Image Works

Ira Hayes, a Navajo, helps to plant a flag celebrating victory at Iwo Jima.

Philip Johnston, an army engineer, came up with an idea. Because he had lived on a Navajo reservation, he understood some Navajo and recognized what a complex, sophisticated, and precise language it was. With no written symbols, Navajo was almost impossible for the Japanese enemy to study. He asked the armed forces to gather Navajo enlistees and have them create a code for their native language.

In response, twenty-nine Navajos gathered in San Diego and began a **collaborative** effort to create the code. Messages could not simply be given in Navajo, for then a captured Navajo soldier might be forced to translate them for an enemy. **(5)** So, the coders **synthesized** symbols into a coded language. Some words got symbols, such as *bird* for *airplane* and *fish* for *ship*. In addition, each letter of the English alphabet was given a Navajo word, so that other words could be spelled. *A*, for example, was given the Navajo word for *ant,* which is *wol-la-chee*. **(6)** Since symbols for words were **interspersed** with symbols for letters, the code could not be understood, even by those who spoke Navajo. One had to speak Navajo, speak English, and know the code for a message to be **coherent**.

(7) After composing, the code writers were **dispersed** into Marine battalions fighting the Japanese in the Pacific. Within a few weeks, they had proven their worth. At one point, one American force accidentally attacked another. When the soldiers under attack radioed their fellow Americans, the attackers refused to stop unless they heard the message in code. A code talker was located and, within minutes, the firing was over.

But the value of code talking reached its **zenith** during the attack on Iwo Jima, one of the most dangerous missions of the war. U.S. Marines had to land on the Japanese island and then cross loose volcanic ash. With their movements slowed and **(8)** only **sparse** tree growth to hide them, Americans became easy targets. In contrast, the Japanese were hidden in deep trenches. Under terrible fire, the Marines painfully made their way up the important target of Mount Suribachi, the highest point on the island. As they climbed, the code talkers sent more than eight hundred error-free messages. Six men worked without sleep for forty-eight hours. One official referred to the Navajos as "walking, talking weapons."

When the Marines got to the peak of Suribachi, Ira Hayes planted the U.S. flag. Another Navajo sent the message of victory: "Sheep-Uncle-Ram-Ice-Bear-Ant-Cat-Horse-Itch." The first letters of each word spell "Suribachi." The mountain had been conquered!

Unfortunately, when World War II ended **(9)** the U.S. government continued its **egregious** treatment of Navajo Native Americans. The code talkers were released without honors or awards. In fact, the armed forces cautioned them not to talk about their experiences, in case the code had to be used again. There was a shameful **disparity** between the priceless service the men had given and their lack of recognition. Even worse, the men who had served their country so well went back to states where they were not permitted to vote! Today, most of the Navajo code talkers and **(10)** their **contemporaries** are gone, but their story is becoming widely known. Their intelligence under fire serves as a reminder of a nation's shameful past, a war's most heroic moments, and the enduring value of diversity.

■ *Exercise*

Each numbered sentence corresponds to a sentence in the passage. Fill in the letter of the choice that makes the sentence mean the same thing as its corresponding sentence in the passage.

1. The _______ of U.S. justice is the treatment of Native Americans.
   a. worst point b. strangest example c. test d. defining example

2. In a show of _______, some even brought their own rifles.
   a. youth b. fashion c. innocence d. bravery

3. Yet they must _______ their attacks.
   a. separate b. coordinate in time c. assure the success of
   d. make sophisticated plans for

4. The enemy has "code breakers" who try to read the messages and _______ them to their troops.
   a. manage b. sell c. distribute d. reveal

5. So the soldiers _______ symbols into a coded language.
   a. translated b. greatly changed c. separated d. put together

6. Symbols for words were _______ symbols for letters.
   a. necessary to b. combined with c. used instead of d. placed among

7. After composing, the code writers were _______ into Marine battalions.
   a. forced b. scattered c. trapped d. shipped

8. They had only _______ tree growth to hide them.
   a. thinly scattered b. one type of c. short, stubby d. lots of

9. The U.S. government continued its _______ treatment of Navajos.
   a. terrible b. prejudiced c. strange d. hoped for

10. Today, most of their _______ are gone.
    a. people who lived at the same time b. witnesses c. fellow soldiers d. people in the same war

■ *Discussion Questions*

1. Give at least two pieces of evidence showing that Navajo code talkers worked hard.
2. In what way was the Navajo code a synthesis?
3. Would you have been a code talker if given the opportunity? Why or why not?

INSIGHT INTO IDIOMS

Agreement and Anger

When you are angry with people you might *read them the riot act,* which means to give them a warning that if they don't stop misbehaving, they will be punished. This idiom has its origins in England. The original riot act was passed in 1774 to stop protests against King George III. When more than twelve people gathered, a riot act could be read that ordered them to disperse. If they did not, they could be arrested or shot. Here are some other idioms that, like *read the riot act,* deal with agreement and anger.

a. People who become angry are said to be *blowing their tops,* (or *losing their cool).*

b. Such individuals *let off steam,* or show their anger, through harsh words or actions.

c. *To speak one's piece* is to speak frankly, stating exactly what you are thinking.

d. Something or someone that annoys or irritates you is said to *set your teeth on edge.*

e. When people want to end disagreements, they *mend fences,* perhaps by apologizing.

f. People who are in agreement or have interests in common are said to have *common ground.*

Practice chapter words one more time by filling in the letter of the correct idiom into the blank before each sentence.

_______ 1. You shouldn't work collaboratively with that person because his manner and suggestions always seem to _________.

_______ 2. When the charismatic minister talked to his congregation about making peace, many former enemies started to _________.

_______ 3. There was a lot of discord at that meeting and people started _________.

_______ 4. Even though ones views may not be compatible with those of other people, it is important _________.

_______ 5. When we talked over our opinions, we concurred that we had a lot of _________ on the issue.

Links to more lists of English idioms and their meanings can be found at the Student Companion Website for this book: **www.cengage.com/devenglish/richek8e.**

REVIEW

Chapters 5–8

■ *Reviewing Words in Context*

Complete each sentence with the word or term that fits best. You may have to capitalize some words. Use each choice only once.

A JOURNEY FROM VIETNAM TO THE UNITED STATES

a. antipathy	e. interminable	i. resilient	m. transcend
b. circumventing	f. induced	j. status quo	n. transitory
c. communal	g. jettison	k. subverted	o. traverse
d. congregated	h. odyssey	l. tenacity	p. vital

Background: Viem, a student in one of the author's classes, was born in Vietnam. This is the story of his life there and his escape to the United States.

1. I was born in Saigon, Vietnam. My father had fought for the U.S. allies against the Communists. The Communists felt considerable ____________________ for people like him. They even put him in jail for six months.

2. I too felt some discrimination and had to ____________________ many difficulties. To get into college, I needed a higher exam score than children of people who had fought for the Communists.

3. I knew that unless the ____________________ changed, I would have a hard time in Vietnam.

4. Feeling that my efforts to make a good life for myself would be ____________________ by the government, I decided to escape.

5. ____________________ was very important because ten of my efforts failed.

6. But I was a(n) ____________________ person and recovered from the disappointment of each unsuccessful attempt.

7. The prospect of living a free life ____________________ me to try again and again; in 1982, I finally succeeded.

8. In my last, successful effort, I made my way to the seacoast, carefully ____________________ the police, who would have arrested me.

9. Forty-three people ____________________ on a beach to board the small, open fishing boat that would take us from Vietnam to Malaysia.

10. The sea grew so rough that at times we had to bail water out of the boat and even ____________________ some of our belongings.

11. We ran short of food, water, and other ____________________ supplies.

12. Although the trip seemed ____________________, it was actually only four days.

13. In fact, we were very lucky. The boat before us that tried to ____________________ the ocean was lost at sea for fifty-two days, and many died. The boat after us was captured by the Vietnamese police.

14. Once I arrived in Malaysia, I was put in a refugee camp with ____________________ living quarters that I shared with several men.

15. My ____________________ to the United States included transfers to two other refugee camps. Finally, though, I arrived in Chicago, where I have lived for over twenty years. I have finished the college education I dreamed of and am now working in the field of computer science.

■ *Passage for Word Review*

Complete each sentence with the word or term that fits best. Use each choice only once.

RUNNING TRACK

a. abstained	e. dejected	i. renowned	m. synopsis
b. compatible	f. gregarious	j. spartan	n. tenaciously
c. conducive	g. inadvertently	k. stature	o. traversed
d. degenerated	h. psyche	l. subdue	p. viable

Background: William, a student in one of the author's classes, describes what competitive running did for him—and to him. Later, he went on to serve his country in Afghanistan.

When I started high school, I was only five feet two inches in **(1)** ____________________ and I weighed ninety-five pounds.

As you can imagine, I was very small. I wanted to play a sport, and I didn't have much of a choice of which one. I didn't have the size for football, the height for basketball, or an interest in baseball. But I could run fast, so joining the track team seemed to be my only **(2)** ____________________ option. I was afraid of the coach, but I decided to go ahead. After a week of tryouts, I finally made it.

I was so enthusiastic that I worked out every day, including weekends. After a boring job, I remember going home to do yet another workout. I also trained **(3)** ____________________, practicing my running whenever I could. I was so tired that I would sometimes fall asleep while eating my dinner. I **(4)** ____________________ from anything unhealthy, like smoking. I lived a(n) **(5)** ____________________ existence, concentrating on school, work, and running.

My **(6)** ____________________ teammates liked to socialize. I found their interests to be **(7)** ____________________ with my own, and so I really enjoyed spending time with them. This atmosphere was **(8)** ____________________ to developing a winning team spirit.

By my senior year, I became captain of a(n) **(9)** ____________________ track team that had set records throughout the state. Supporters gathered to see our races. I even had a personal fan or two!

Then, during the indoor track season of my senior year, a terrible thing happened. I **(10)** ____________________ pulled both my hamstrings! I went through two months of physical therapy before I could walk normally. You can probably imagine that I felt extremely **(11)** ____________________ when I heard I would never be able compete again.

But I could not **(12)** ____________________ my desire to run. I knew that I would be at a disadvantage in competition, yet I was determined to try. I went through therapy, began working out again, and told my coach I wanted to run in the city meets. He let me run, despite the pain I experienced. I was thrilled when I qualified for the city meet.

The situation **(13)** ____________________, though. The following week, I had to quit running in the middle of my race—the race I was favored to win. I had to walk the rest of the way. As I **(14)** ____________________ the finish line, I heard the crowd cheer! You can imagine that this soothed my **(15)** ____________________.

I have not given up on my dream of competing. Perhaps some day I can run, not walk, across that line.

■ *Reviewing Learning Strategies*

New Words from Word Elements The listed words, which are not presented in preceding chapters, are formed from ancient Greek and Latin word elements. Use your knowledge of these elements and write in the word that best completes each sentence. You may have to capitalize some words. Use each choice only once.

a. anthropogenesis	e. pan-global	i. symphony
b. convivial	f. regenerates	j. symposium
c. inequity	g. restart	k. traction
d. introvert	h. subbasement	l. vivid

1. The effects of the economic downturn were ______________________, and felt in every country.
2. When we ______________________ something, we begin again.
3. People who are generally social are sometimes referred to as ______________________ or liking to "live together."
4. The force of ______________________ pulls at objects, so that they stop moving.
5. In a(n) ______________________, many different instruments play sounds at the same time.
6. A(n) ______________________ is a person turned in upon herself, or not sociable.
7. When two things are lacking in fairness or equality, there is a(n) ______________________.
8. ______________________ refers to the origins of human beings.
9. When a plant grows new leaves or is "born again" after appearing to be dead, it ______________________.
10. The ______________________ is under the basement.

CHAPTER 9

Word Elements: Numbers and Measures

In the ancient world, much of life was organized around growing and harvesting food. Our ancestors needed words to tell them when to plant crops, how much food their soil yielded, and how much money they would spend or receive. The modern words we use for numbers, sizes, and quantities were developed from these necessities. This chapter presents number and measurement word elements taken from ancient Greek and Latin. Thousands of English words are based upon these roots and prefixes.

Chapter Strategy: Word Elements: Numbers and Measures

Chapter Words:

Part 1

uni-	unanimity	*di-, du-*	dilemma
	unilateral		duplicity
mono-	monarchy	*tri-*	trilogy
	monopoly		trivial
bi-	bilingual	*dec-*	decade
	bipartisan		decimate

Part 2

cent-	centennial	*integer*	disintegrate
	centigrade		integrity
ambi-, amphi-	ambiguous	*magn-, mega-*	magnanimous
	ambivalent		magnitude
ann, enn	annals	*meter, -meter*	metric
	perennial		symmetrical

Visit the Student Companion Website at **www.cengage.com/devenglish/richek8e** to test your knowledge of these words before you study, hear each word pronounced, find additional practice exercises, and access more information on words and topics.

Did You Know?

How Were the Months of the Year Named?

Setting up the calendar we now use was not an easy task. Ancient calendars were so inaccurate that people sometimes found themselves planting crops when the calendar claimed that winter was approaching. For this reason, the Roman leader Julius Caesar ordered a calendar reform about two thousand years ago. That is why our months have Latin names. There have been other changes, but even now the calendar is not perfect. We must adjust the length of our years by adding an extra day (February 29) in every fourth, or leap, year. Here's how the months were named:

January gets its name from the Roman god Janus, the god of doors and gates. Since doors are used to enter, Janus represented beginnings, and the first month of the year is dedicated to him. Janus is usually pictured with two faces; one might be said to look back to the past year, and one looks forward to the next.

February comes from Februa, the Roman festival of purification. *March* is named for Mars, the Roman god of war. *April* has an uncertain origin. It may be from *apero,* which means "second," for at one time it was the second month of the year, or from *aperīre* (to open) since it is the month when flowers and trees open out in bloom. *May* comes from the goddess of fertility, Maia. It was natural to name a spring month for the goddess who was thought to control the crops.

June was named either for the Junius family of Roman nobles or for the goddess Juno, wife of Jupiter. Julius Caesar named the month of *July* after himself. *August* is named for Augustus Caesar, the nephew of Julius and the first emperor of Rome. His actual name was Octavian, but he took the title of *Augustus* because it meant "distinguished." The word *august* still means "distinguished" when the second syllable of the word is stressed.

The last four months all contain number prefixes: *September, sept-* (seven); *October, oct-* (eight); *November, nov-* (nine); *December, dec-* (ten). As you can see, prefixes are wrong!

How did the ninth, tenth, eleventh, and twelfth months get the elements of seven, eight, nine, and ten? Until 153 BCE the new year was celebrated in March, so the months corresponded to the correct numbers. Then a change in the calendar left these months with misleading meanings.

Links to the a history of the calendar can be found through the Student Companion Website at **www.cengage.com/devenglish/richek8e**.

Learning Strategy

Word Elements: Numbers and Measures

The word elements in this chapter carry meanings of number and measurement. A list of the prefixes for the first ten numbers follows. Although you won't be studying all of them in this chapter, you will find that this list is a handy reference for textbooks and other reading. English uses these number prefixes frequently; in fact, we are still making new words from them.

Prefix	*Meaning*	*Example Word*
**uni-*	one	unidirectional (in one direction)
**mono-*	one	monologue (speech by one person)
**bi-*	two	bidirectional (in two directions)
**di-, du-*	two	diatomic (made up of two atoms)
**tri-*	three	trio (a group of three)
quad-, quar-	four	quarter (a coin that is one-fourth of a dollar)
quint-, quin-	five	quintuplets (five babies born together)
sex-	six	sextet (a musical group of six)
sept-	seven	septuagenarian (a person in his or her seventies)
oct-	eight	octopus (a sea creature with eight arms)
nov-	nine	novena (a prayer offered for nine days)
**dec-*	ten	decade (ten years)

*You will study these word elements intensively in this chapter.

To test your understanding of these prefixes, fill in the blanks with the correct numbers.

a. A duplex is an apartment with __________ floors.

b. A trilingual person speaks __________ languages.

c. A quadruped is an animal that walks on __________ feet.

d. When a mother has quintuplets, __________ children are born.

e. Sextuple means to multiply by __________.

f. A septennial occurs once every __________ years.

Answers are on page 399.

All the word elements you will study in this chapter are either number prefixes *(uni-, mono-, bi-, di-, tri-, dec-, cent-)* or measurement roots and prefixes *(ambi-, ann, integer, magn-, meter)*.

Element	*Meaning*	*Origin*	*Function*	*Chapter Words*
Part 1				
uni-	one	Latin	prefix	unanimity, unilateral
mono-	one; single	Greek	prefix	monarchy, monopoly
bi-	two	Latin	prefix	bilingual, bipartisan
di-, du-	two	Greek; Latin	prefix	dilemma, duplicity
tri-	three	Greek; Latin	prefix	trilogy, trivial
dec-	ten	Greek; Latin	prefix	decade, decimate
Part 2				
cent-, centi-	hundred	Latin	prefix	centennial, centigrade
ambi-, amphi-	both; around	Latin Greek	prefix	ambiguous, ambivalent
ann, enn	year	Latin	root	annals, perennial
integer	whole; complete	Latin	root	disintegrate, integrity
magn-, mega-	large	Latin Greek	prefix	magnanimous, magnitude
meter, -meter	measure	Greek Latin	root; suffix	metric, symmetrical

This chapter presents a large number of word elements for study, twelve in all. However, the number prefixes follow a clear pattern. They are arranged in order of the numbers they represent rather than in alphabetical order. The first six are discussed next.

Prefixes

Part 1

uni- (one)

The Latin prefix for one, *uni-*, is used in many English words. To *unite*, for example, is to make several things into **one.** A *uniform* is **one** style of clothing that is worn by many people.

mono- (one, single)

The Greek prefix for one, *mono-,* is usually joined to Greek combining roots. For example, *monogamy* is marriage to **one** person. A *monologue* is a speech given by **one** person. *Mono-* is also used to form many technical words in scientific fields.

bi- (two)

The Latin prefix for two, *bi-,* forms words such as *bifocals,* glasses that contain **two** visual corrections. The *bicycle* was named for its **two** wheels.

di-, du- (two)

This Greek prefix for **two** is often used in scientific and technical words, so you will find it useful in your college courses. For example, the word *dichromatic* refers to animals that change their colors in different seasons and therefore have **two** colors.

tri- (three)

A *triangle* is a **three**-sided figure. A *tricornered* hat has a brim turned up on **three** sides. A *tricycle* has **three** wheels.

dec- (ten)

The *decimal* system uses the base **ten.** The common word *dime,* a **tenth** part of a dollar, is also taken from the prefix *dec-*.

Words to Learn

Part 1

uni-

1. **unanimity** (noun) yo͞o′nə-nĭm′ĭ-tē

From Latin: *uni-* (one) + *animus* (soul) (When people agree, they seem to have one soul.)

complete agreement

If jurors in a criminal trial cannot reach **unanimity**, the case must be tried again.

The nation demonstrated **unanimity** in facing the aggressor's threat.

▶ *Related Word*

unanimous (adjective) The Canadian ice skater was the judges' *unanimous* choice for the Olympic gold medal.

The decision was *unanimous*.

Courtesy author

2. **unilateral** (adjective) yo͞oʹnə-lătʹər-əl

   From Latin: *uni-* (one) + *latus* (side)

   arbitrary; one-sided; relating to only one side or part

   Students and faculty became angry when the dean made a **unilateral** decision to ban cell-phone use on campus.

   Unilateral contracts require that only one side take action.

mono-

3. **monarchy** (noun) mŏnʹər-kē (plural: **monarchies**)

   From Greek: *mono-* (one) + *arkein* (rule)

   a state ruled by a king, queen, or emperor

   The Japanese **monarchy**, founded more than 2,600 years ago, is the oldest continuous one in the world.

   ► *Related Word*

   monarch (noun) The state of Georgia was named for British *monarch* George II.

Sons and Monarchies

Through much of history, the inheritance of a kingship through an eldest son had been an orderly way to deal with the death of a king. For this reason, kings wanted to have sons. In the 1500s, Henry VIII of England actually married six times, and executed two of his wives, mainly in the pursuit of a male heir. Still, he did not succeed. His only surviving son died in childhood, and eventually a daughter, Elizabeth I, inherited the crown, becoming a great *monarch*. Today, Queen Elizabeth II rules England and there has been increasing acceptance of female rulers in Europe. From 1980 to 2010, five monarchies (Sweden, the Netherlands, Norway, Belgium, and Denmark) changed their policies to allow women rulers.

4. **monopoly** (noun) mə-nŏp′ə-lē

From Greek: *mono-* (single) + *pōlein* (to sell) (When only one company or person can sell something, a monopoly exists.)

exclusive possession or control

In Norway, all liquor is sold by a government-owned **monopoly.**

No nation has a **monopoly** on world power.

▶ *Related Words*

monopolistic (adjective) *Monopolistic* control of an industry generally leads to high prices for the consumer.

monopolize (verb) Sakeena's friend always seemed to *monopolize* their conversations.

bi-

5. **bilingual** (adjective) bī-lĭng′gwəl

From Latin: *bi-* (two) + *lingua* (tongue, language)

having or speaking two languages

Children can easily become **bilingual,** but adults have more difficulty learning a second language.

The **bilingual** prayer book was printed in Hebrew and English.

▶ *Related Word*

bilingualism (noun) The growing numbers of Hispanics in the United States make *bilingualism* essential in many professions.

Words that describe speakers of different languages demonstrate the use of number prefixes.

A *monolingual* person speaks one language.
A *bilingual* person speaks two languages.
A *trilingual* person speaks three languages.
In terms of official languages, one U.S. state, Hawaii, is bilingual in English and Hawaiian. Three U.S. territories are bilingual and one is trilingual. (The Northern Marianas Islands have the official languages of English, Chamorro, and Carolinian.) The country of Canada is officially bilingual in English and French.

Many people in the United States are bilingual. A summary of languages spoken in the United States can be found through the Student Companion Website at **www.cengage.com/devenglish/richek8e.**

6. **bipartisan** (adjective) bī-pär′tĭ-zən

   From Latin: *bi-* (two) + *pars* (part)

   supported by members of two parties

   The **bipartisan** bill on auto fuel mileage was sponsored by Democrats and Republicans.

   ▶ *Related Word*
   bipartisanship (noun) In a rare display of *bipartisanship,* the Canadian Liberal and Conservative parties proposed a joint bill for immigration reform.

di-, du-

7. **dilemma** (noun) dĭ-lĕm′ə

   From Greek: *di-* (two) + *lēmma* (proposition) (A choice between two propositions, or alternatives, puts us in a *dilemma.*)

   difficult choice between equally bad things

   Trung faced the **dilemma** of living in poverty or moving to an unfamiliar country.

   NOTE: *Dilemma* is also used to mean "problem."

8. **duplicity** (noun) do͞o -plĭs′ĭ-tē

   From Latin: *du-* (two) + *plicāre* (to fold or complicate) (A person who is involved in duplicity is not straightforward but is "folded in two ways.")

   betrayal; deceit; double-dealing

   The spy's **duplicity** was revealed to a shocked nation.

   In an act of **duplicity,** the celebrity's personal driver taped his phone calls and sold them to reporters.

► *Related Word*

duplicitous (adjective) Duplicitous Benedict Arnold was an American general who sold secrets to the British during the American Revolution.

tri-

9. **trilogy** (noun) trĭl′ə-jē (plural: **trilogies**)

From Greek: *tri-* (three) + *log* (word; to speak)

a group of three works, such as books, plays, movies, or stories

Lord of the Rings is a book **trilogy** that was made into films.

10. **trivial** (adjective) trĭv′ē-əl

From Latin: *tri-* (three) + *via* (road) (In Latin, *trivium* meant "where three roads meet," the public square where people would gossip.)

a. unimportant; silly

Pain or numbness in one's feet can be due to **trivial** problems, such as tight shoes, or may be an early warning of diabetes.

b. ordinary; commonplace

Changing a car's oil is a **trivial** task for professional auto mechanics.

After almost dying in the accident, Fred started to enjoy **trivial** things in life, such as cleaning the house or filling the car with gas.

► *Related Words*

trivia (noun) The fan seemed to know endless amounts of *trivia* about basketball. (*Trivia* is unimportant information.)

trivialize (verb) A focus on gifts and parties can *trivialize* the meaning of religious holidays.

NOTE: *Trivial* often also connotes "easy." (Mentally adding two numbers is a *trivial* task for a person with a Ph.D. in math.)

dec-

11. **decade** (noun) dĕk′ād′

From Greek: *dec-* (ten) (*Dekas* meant "group of ten.")

a ten-year period

The **decade** of the 1960s was marked by political protest.

Because he had to support a family, it took Mr. Markman almost a **decade** to complete his college degree.

Number Bases

As you may know, our number system is constructed using the base ten, as seen in such words as *decade* and *decimal*. The use of ten as a base is thought to come from our ten fingers, which the ancients, like us, used for counting. But other bases have been employed. There is evidence for a *duodecimal* system, or base twelve. The word is constructed from *duo* (two) and *dec* (ten). Note that there are twelve months in a year. The Sumerians used base sixty, and perhaps this influenced the sixty minutes in our hour. Most computer systems are programmed with a base two *binary* system, with its two values of "on" and "off."

12. **decimate** (verb) dĕs′ə-māt′

From Latin: *dec-* (ten) (*Decimāre* meant "to take the tenth." This was the severe practice of killing every tenth soldier, chosen by lot, in order to punish a mutiny.)

to destroy or kill a large part of

Hailstones **decimated** the farmer's crop.

Severe governmental budget cuts will **decimate** support programs for disabled adults.

▶ *Related Word*

decimation (noun) Loss of land for grazing and overhunting resulted in the *decimation* of the American bison population.

Exercises

Part 1

■ *Definitions*

Match the word and definition. Use each choice only once.

1. decade _______	a. deceit
2. unilateral _______	b. three books, plays, or movies
3. trivial _______	c. ten-year period
4. duplicity _______	d. speaking two languages
5. decimate _______	e. supported by both sides
6. monarchy _______	f. a state ruled by a king or queen
7. bilingual _______	g. complete agreement
8. dilemma _______	h. arbitrary

9. bipartisan ______
10. trilogy ______

i. to destroy most of something
j. control by one company
k. choice of two bad alternatives
l. unimportant

■ *Meanings*

Match each word element to its meaning. You may use choices more than once.

1. uni- ______
2. bi- ______
3. mono ______
4. dec- ______
5. tri- ______
6. di- ______

a. ten
b. two
c. one
d. three

■ *Words in Context*

Complete each sentence with the best word. Use each choice only once.

a. unanimity	e. bilingual	i. trilogy
b. unilateral	f. bipartisan	j. trivial
c. monarchy	g. dilemma	k. decade
d. monopoly	h. duplicity	l. decimate

1. The job required that Jerzy be ______________ in Polish and English.
2. *Back to the Future I, II,* and *III* form a well known film ______________.
3. Jake faced the ______________ of dropping the course or flunking it.
4. Betraying a good friend is an act of ______________.
5. By their 9–0 vote, the U.S. Supreme Court members showed ______________ in declaring school segregation unconstitutional in the 1954 case *Brown* v. *Board of Education*.

6. In a constitutional ____________________, a king or queen shares power with elected lawmakers.

7. In 1984 the U.S. Supreme Court ended the NCAA's ____________________ on college football telecasts and allowed others to broadcast them.

8. The Great Depression lasted about a(n) ____________________, from 1930 to 1940.

9. Seven Labour Party members and six Conservative Party members served on the ____________________ committee of the British Parliament.

10. Without asking the opinion of his wife or daughters, my grandfather made a(n) ____________________ decision to move the family to the United States.

■ *Using Related Words*

Complete each sentence with the correct form. Use each choice only once.

THE LIFE OF JULIUS CAESAR

1. unanimity, unanimous

Historians are ____________________ in considering Julius Caesar one of the towering figures of history. His conquests, reforms in government, and famous writings all contribute to this ____________________ of opinion.

2. decimation, decimated

Born in about 100 BCE, Caesar came from a poor but noble family. As he rose in leadership, he conquered other lands. He attacked and ____________________ forces in Gaul (now Belgium and France). He also invaded England, and although his forces did not inflict the same ____________________ there, they established a Roman base that lasted for hundreds of years.

3. monopolize, monopoly

A decade of conquest gained Caesar considerable political importance. He formed a ruling triumvirate with Crassus and Pompey. Crassus died, and despite the fact that Pompey had married Caesar's daughter, Caesar and Pompey became rivals. It seemed that one of

them was destined to ____________________ power. After some hesitation, Caesar crossed the Rubicon River and attacked Pompey. To this day, the phrase "crossing the Rubicon" means to do something that cannot be undone. Caesar's victory gave him a

____________________ on power.

4. trivialize, trivial

Caesar extended Roman citizenship to everyone in Italy and improved the conditions of Roman farmers. He replaced an inaccurate calendar with the "Julian" calendar, which forms the basis of our

modern dates. In a somewhat more ____________________ action, he named the month of July after himself. However, his romance with the Egyptian queen Cleopatra angered Romans. While this

may seem unimportant, we should not ____________________ Cleopatra's influence on historical events.

5. duplicitous, duplicity

As Caesar became ever more powerful, Romans came to resent

him. Led by Cassius, several ____________________ senators plotted to murder Caesar on the Ides of March. When Caesar entered the Senate, they attacked. Caesar resisted until he realized the

____________________ of his friend, Brutus, who had turned against him. "Et tu, Brute?" (You too, Brutus?), he exclaimed as he collapsed and died.

6. monarch, monarchy

Caesar never became a ____________________, but after his

death, Rome became a ____________________. A few years after Caesar's death, his nephew, Octavian, became the first Roman emperor.

■ *Reading the Headlines*

Here are some headlines that might appear in newspapers. Read each and answer the questions. (Remember that small words, such as *is*, *are*, *a*, and *the*, are often left out of headlines.)

MONARCH ENDS DECADE-LONG MONOPOLY OF OIL COMPANY

1. Did the monopoly last ten years? _______
2. Is the person who acted elected democratically? _______
3. Was oil in the hands of one company? _______

DESPITE BIPARTISAN SUPPORT FOR BILINGUAL EDUCATION, PRESIDENT MAKES UNILATERAL DECISION TO VETO BILL

4. Did two parties support the bill? _______
5. Did the bill deal with education in one language? _______
6. Did the president act alone in vetoing the bill? _______

BOOK TRILOGY GETS UNANIMOUS VOTE FOR BOOKER PRIZE

7. Were there three books? _______
8. Were the judges divided? _______

FLOWER GROWERS ARE OUTRAGED WHEN DECIMATION OF HONEYBEE POPULATION IS LABELED A TRIVIAL PROBLEM

9. Is the honeybee population increasing? _______
10. Has the problem been labeled as important? _______

Word Elements

Part 2

Part 2 presents the last number prefix, *cent-,* as well as five roots and prefixes that refer to quantities.

cent- (hundred)

The prefix *cent-* is used in many common words. A *century* is a period of **one hundred** years. A *cent* is a coin worth **one-hundredth** of a dollar.

ambi-, amphi- (both; around)

These prefixes have two meanings. The meaning of "both" occurs in the word *ambidextrous,* meaning "able to use **both** hands." The meaning of "around" is found in *amphitheater,* a theater with seats on all sides of, or **around,** the stage. This prefix comes from ancient Greek and Latin: *amphi-* is the Greek form; *ambi-* is the Latin form.

The common word *ambitious* is derived from the Latin verb *ambīre* (to go around). In ancient Rome, an ambitious person was a political candidate who "went around" asking people to vote for him. Now, of course, an ambitious person is one who desires achievement.

ann, enn (year)

An *annual* event occurs every **year.** At times, *ann* is spelled *enn,* as in the word *perennial.*

integer (whole; complete)

This root can refer to numbers, as in the English word *integer,* which means a **whole** number without a fraction value. Thus, 3 is an integer, but 3.5 is not. This root can also describe a "**whole**" person who does not have serious character flaws. Such a person is said to have *integrity.*

magn-, mega- (large)

To *magnify* something is to make it **larger.** Books have been written about *megatrends,* meaning **large** trends in society. A *megalopolis* is a region including several **large** cities. *Magn-* is the Latin spelling; *mega-* is the Greek spelling.

meter, -meter (measure)

This element often appears as a root, but can also be used as a suffix. One word using *meter* as a root is *metronome,* an instrument for **measuring** musical time. The element *-meter* is used as a suffix in the words *thermometer,* an instrument for **measuring** heat, and *speedometer,* an instrument for **measuring** speed.

Words to Learn

Part 2

cent-

13. **centennial** (noun) sĕn-tĕn′ē-əl

From Latin: *cent-* (hundred) + *ann* (year)

one-hundred-year anniversary; a period of one hundred years

The year 2008 marked the **centennial** of the first use of numbers on football jerseys.

The Roman numeral C meant one hundred. Today, the cent sign—¢—and the abbreviation for century—C—remind us that the root *cent* means one hundred.

14. **centigrade** (adjective) sĕn′tĭ-grād′

From Latin: *cent-* (hundred) + *gradus* (step)

referring to a temperature scale based on 100 degrees

In the **centigrade** scale, 0 degrees marks the freezing point of water and 100 degrees marks its boiling point.

The *centigrade* scale is also referred to as *Celsius* in honor of its originator, Anders Celsius. The Fahrenheit scale was named for its inventor, Daniel Fahrenheit. The *centigrade* scale is part of the metric system; the Fahrenheit scale is not.

ambi-, amphi-

15. **ambiguous** (adjective) ăm-bĭg′yōō-əs

From Latin: *ambi-* (around) + *agere* (to lead) (When something is ambiguous, two meanings are equally possible, and a person is led around rather than "straight toward" the meaning.)

not clear; having two or more meanings

Because of the **ambiguous** instructions, we could not tell exactly how to install the software.

▶ *Related Word*

ambiguity (noun) (ăm′bĭ-gyōō′ĭ-tē) (plural: **ambiguities**)

When writing multiple-choice test items, try to avoid *ambiguities*.

This deliberately *ambiguous* figure can be either a vase or two faces. Which do you see?

Creacion/iStockphoto.com

16. **ambivalent** (adjective) ăm-bĭv′ə-lənt

From Latin: *ambi-* (both) + *valēre* (to be strong) (A person who is *ambivalent* about something has two equally strong feelings about it.)

having mixed or conflicting feelings

Steve felt **ambivalent** about the difficult but worthwhile course.

▶ *Common Phrases*
ambivalent toward; ambivalent about

▶ *Related Word*
ambivalence (noun) Jose's *ambivalence* toward marriage led to a long engagement.

ann, enn

17. **annals** (noun, plural) ăn′əlz

From Latin: *ann* (year) (*Annālis* meant "yearly." Written *annals* are often divided by years.)

a. a written record of events, especially those kept on a yearly basis

The **annals** of the association's meetings were so detailed that they included the dinner menus!

b. historical records

Italian explorers famous in the **annals** of American history include Christopher Columbus and Giovanni Caboto (known as John Cabot).

NOTE: *Annals* can also refer to a journal in an academic field that is published on a periodic basis, such as the *Annals of Surgery*.

18. **perennial** (adjective) pə-rĕn′ē-əl

From Latin: *per-* (through) + *ann* (year)

occurring again and again; constant; lasting for a long time

Traffic is a **perennial** problem in large urban areas.

Candy is a **perennial** favorite gift for Valentine's Day.

Perennial flowers bloom for several years without having to be replanted.

integer

19. **disintegrate** (verb) dĭs-ĭn′tĭ-grāt′

From Latin: *dis-* (apart) + *integer* (whole) (When something disintegrates, it becomes "not whole," or falls apart.)

a. to separate into small parts

In a terrible 2003 tragedy, the space shuttle *Columbia* **disintegrated**, with astronauts on board, when it reentered Earth's atmosphere.

An aspirin left in water will soon **disintegrate**.

b. to become worse; to go wrong; decay

The family dinner party **disintegrated** into a fight.

▶ *Common Phrase*
disintegrate into

▶ *Related Word*
disintegration (noun) My great-grandmother blames the TV and computer for the *disintegration* of family life.

20. **integrity** (noun) ĭn-tĕg′rĭ-tē

From Latin: *integer* (whole)

a. honesty; good moral character

Keeping one's promises is a measure of **integrity.**

b. wholeness; completeness

Earthquakes can cause cracks in foundations, affecting a building's **integrity.**

A Man of Integrity

A passenger left a bag in the trunk of Mohammed Hussain's taxi. A few days later, Hussain found the bag while cleaning the car. To his amazement, it contained a collection of precious jewels. As a man of *integrity,* Hussain notified the police. The police returned the jewels to their owner, who rewarded Hussain with a check and a pair of earrings for his mother.

magn-, mega-

21. **magnanimous** (adjective) măg-năn′ə-məs

From Latin: *magn-* (great) + *animus* (soul)

noble; above revenge or resentment; forgiving of insults

Magnanimous five-year-old Kai Leigh Harriott publicly forgave the man who shot and paralyzed her in 2003.

Try to be **magnanimous** toward your defeated rival.

▶ *Common Phrase*
magnanimous toward

▶ *Related Word*
magnanimity (noun) (măg′nə-nĭm′ ĭ-tē) In 1994, Nelson Mandela demonstrated *magnanimity* when he formed a government that included some white South Africans who had imprisoned him.

22. **magnitude** (noun) măg′nĭ-to͞od′

From Latin: *magn-* (great) (*Magnitūdō* meant "greatness.")

greatness of size or importance

It is impossible to imagine the **magnitude** of the universe.

Residents were stunned by the **magnitude** of the flood's damage.

▶ *Common Phrase*
magnitude of

NOTE: *Magnitude* can also refer to the brightness of stars.

meter, -meter

23. **metric** (adjective, noun) mĕt′rĭk

From Greek: *meter* (measure)

a. referring to a measurement system based on grams and meters (adjective)

The **metric** system measures distance in kilometers, rather than in miles.

b. a standard of judgment (noun)

The number of hits (or visits) is the **metric** used to measure the popularity of a website.

Typically, a professional baseball player's batting average is the **metric** used to evaluate how well he hits.

A Convenient System

The *metric* system is easier to use than the U.S. system of pounds and feet. Whereas the U.S. system is based on numbers such as 16 (number of ounces in a pound) and 5,280 (number of feet in a mile), the metric system is a decimal system based on multiples of 10. Common metric measures include centimeters, meters, liters, kilometers, grams, kilograms. (*Kilo* means 1,000.) There are also *metric* tons. Most countries use the metric system, but the United States has delayed conversion several times.

24. **symmetrical** (adjective) sĭ-mĕt′rĭ-kəl

From Greek: *sym-* (same) + *meter* (measure) (Things that "measure the same" are balanced, or symmetrical.)

balanced in physical size or form

Because there are slight differences between the left and right sides of the human body, it is not perfectly **symmetrical.**

▶ *Related Word*

symmetry (noun) (sĭm′ə-trē) (plural: symmetries) The Japanese breed the koi fish for the *symmetry* of patterns decorating their bodies.

Exercises

Part 2

■ *Definitions*

Match the word and definition. Use each choice only once.

1. ambiguous _______	a. written records
2. ambivalent _______	b. having conflicting feelings
3. magnitude _______	c. hundred-year anniversary
4. annals _______	d. greatness of size or importance
5. perennial _______	e. honesty

6. magnanimous _______ f. referring to a temperature scale
7. centigrade _______ g. standard of measurement
8. metric _______ h. balanced
9. integrity _______ i. not clear
10. centennial _______ j. lasting a long time
k. to fall apart
l. noble; forgiving

■ *Meanings*

Match each word element to its meaning. Use each choice only once.

1. meter, -meter _______ a. whole
2. magn-, mega- _______ b. both; around
3. cent- _______ c. hundred
4. ann, enn _______ d. large
5. ambi-, amphi _______ e. year
6. integer _______ f. measure

■ *Words in Context*

Complete each sentence with the best word. Use each choice only once.

a. centennial	e. annals	i. magnanimous
b. centigrade	f. perennial	j. magnitude
c. ambiguous	g. disintegrate	k. metric
d. ambivalent	h. integrity	l. symmetrical

1. Taking bribes indicates a lack of _____________________.
2. The Civil War is an important event in the _____________________ of U.S. history.
3. The metric system uses the _____________________ scale to measure temperature.
4. Since the lengths of the table's legs were not _____________________, it rocked from side to side.
5. Because of its great _____________________, the earthquake's tremors were felt hundreds of miles away.

6. Since weeds are a(n) ____________________ problem, people must constantly care for their gardens.

7. The old piece of iron will soon ____________________ into a rusty powder.

8. We got lost when we tried to follow my uncle's ____________________ directions.

9. Oklahoma, admitted to the United States in 1907, celebrated its ____________________ in 2007.

10. Grades are a common ____________________ for measuring students' success.

■ *Using Related Words*

Complete each sentence with the correct form. Use each choice only once.

1. symmetry, symmetrically, symmetries, symmetrical

   Scientists have determined that many birds look for ____________________ of physical features when they are choosing a mate. Female swallows, for example, prefer mates with long, ____________________ tails. Female zebra finches look for males with the same ____________________ formed decorations in their leg bands. It is thought that these ____________________ are signs of health.

2. ambivalent, ambivalence

   The U.S. public remains ____________________ about the use of human stem cells in medical research. On one hand, these cells show promise in developing medical treatments for heart problems, Parkinson's disease, and spinal injuries. On the other hand, the use of human material makes many people uncomfortable. This ____________________ has been reflected in polls on this subject.

3. ambiguity, ambiguous, ambiguities

It is easy to find different ____________________ in sentences. The sentence "I saw her duck" is an example. The ____________________ of this sentence results from the meaning of "duck." Does it mean to crouch down, or is it an animal? Another ____________________ sentence is "They are flying planes." Does it mean "The people are flying planes?" Or does it mean "Those things are planes that fly?"

4. disintegration, disintegrate, disintegrates

Would you like to protect your great-great-great-grandmother's precious letters from ____________________? If they were written after 1850, it may be difficult. Before 1850, paper was made of strong rags. After that time it was made of wood pulp, which ____________________ much more rapidly. The acidity of modern paper causes it to ____________________, but an alkaline spray can slow the damage.

5. magnanimous, magnanimity

The great baseball player Lou Gehrig remained ____________________ even when illness forced him to retire at age thirty-five. In a farewell speech at Yankee Stadium, he displayed ____________________, rather than bitterness, when he said, "Today I am the luckiest man in the world." He died two years later of ALS, now also called Lou Gehrig's disease.

■ *Find the Example*

Choose the example that best describes the action or situation.

1. Symmetrical disintegration _______
   a. iron repairs on both sides of a building b. water damage to the left of the door of a building c. crumbling brickwork on all sides of a building

2. A centigrade metric _______
   a. kilometer b. 20 degrees c. 40 oxen

3. A statement that illustrates perennial ambivalence ______
   a. I can never decide if I like my work. b. I will always love my job. c. I have some doubts about my job today.

4. Integrity of great magnitude ______
   a. making sure that you never repeat gossip b. betraying your friends when you are threatened with death c. not revealing secrets under torture

5. Annals of a magnanimous act ______
   a. tennis club record of a loser congratulating a winner b. video recordings of a great golf competitive win c. written records of a loser claiming that the winner had cheated.

Chapter Exercises

■ *Practicing Strategies: New Words from Word Elements*

Use your knowledge of prefixes to determine the meanings of these words and complete each sentence. You may need to capitalize some words. Use each choice only once.

a. amphibious	e. duet	i. monorail
b. bicentennial	f. integrate	j. photometer
c. centimeter	g. magnify	k. triannual
d. decagram	h. monocular	l. unisex

1. If you ________________ one thing with another, you form them into a whole.

2. The ________________ meetings take place in February, July, and November.

3. Two people sing in a(n) ________________.

4. Since "ocular" means eye, a(n) ________________ provides correction for one eye.

5. If you ________________ something, you make it bigger.

6. A(n) ________________ is a measure equal to one-hundredth of a meter.

7. A(n) ________________ aircraft can land on both land and water.

8. Admitted to the United States in 1790, Tennessee celebrated its

    ____________________ in 1990.

9. Ten grams may be called a(n) ____________________.

10. ____________________ clothing refers to one style suitable for men and women.

■ *Practicing Strategies: Combining Context Clues and Word Elements*

In each sentence, one word is italicized. Use the meaning of the word element and the context to make an intelligent guess about its meaning.

1. The gracious room, beautiful furniture, and pleasant music all contributed to the wonderful *ambience* of the restaurant.

    Ambience means ____.

2. The *megahit* movie was in first place for six months.

    Megahit means ____.

3. The words "yes," "it," and "tea" are *monosyllabic*.

    Monosyllabic means ____.

The next two items are from newspaper sources.

4. Italy's *bicameral* Parlamento, or Parliament, includes the Senato della Republica and the Camera dei Deputati.

    Bicameral means ____.

5. The creatures, only 347 *micrometers* (about one-hundredth of an inch) long, have a complex reproductive cycle, producing babies both sexually and asexually.

    Micrometer means ____

    ____.

■ *Practicing Strategies: Using the Dictionary*

The following entry is taken from an online source. Read it and then answer the questions.

crunch (krunȼh)

intransitive verb, transitive verb

1. to bite or chew with a noisy, crackling sound
2. to press, grind, tread, fall, etc. with a noisy, crushing sound
3. INFORMAL to process (a vast quantity of numbers or other data) rapidly using a computer to *crunch* population statistics

noun

1. the act or sound of crunching
2. an exercise much like a sit-up, in which the upper body is raised only slightly off the floor rather than to an upright position
3. ☆ INFORMAL a tight situation; specif., an economic squeeze
4. ☆ SLANG, a showdown

Etymology: earlier *craunch*, of echoic orig.

1. What is an earlier form of the word *crunch*? ____________________

What part of speech and definition number best fit each of the following sentences?

2. When I work out, I do ten *crunches* and ten sit-ups. ____________________

3. Because our state has a deficit, we have a *crunch* in finances. ____________________

4. When it came to the *crunch*, our team pulled together and won the game. ____________________

5. We *crunched* lots of numbers and came up with the statistics. ____________________.

■ *Companion Words*

Complete each sentence with the best word. You may use choices more than once, and some items may have more than one correct answer. Choices: of, toward, into, about.

1. Jose felt ambivalent ____________ his loyal, but dull friend.

2. Julius Caesar was magnanimous ____________ his defeated enemies.

3. We were amazed by the magnitude ____________ the state of Alaska.

4. The paper mâché mask disintegrated ____________ dust.

5. The centennial ____________ great-grandma's birth was a momentous occasion for the family.

■ *Writing with Your Words*

To practice effective writing, complete each sentence with an interesting phrase that indicates the meaning of the italicized word.

1. One *perennial* concern of society is ______________________________

   ____.

2. An example of a *trivial* problem is ______________________________

   ____.

3. We marked the *centennial* of our village by ______________________

   ____.

4. He showed his *duplicity* by ___________________________________

   ____.

5. When a person makes a *unilateral* decision, ______________________

   ____.

6. The *magnanimous* champion ____________________________________

   ____.

7. An event of great *magnitude* ______________________________

____.

8. My family demonstrates *unanimity* of opinion in ______________

____.

9. If we *decimate* the forests in the area, ____________________

____.

10. Since he was a person of *integrity*, ______________________

____.

■ *Making Connections*

To connect new vocabulary to your life, write extended responses to these questions.

1. What are your hopes and dreams for the next decade?
2. Describe a dilemma you have faced.
3. Describe an issue you feel ambivalent about.

Passage

Tattoos—So Modern and Yet So Ancient

The tattoo you may, or may not, wear has a long and honorable history. It has inspired rebels, fascinated artists, and even kept copyright lawyers busy.

(1) Parents' and elders' disapproval of the styles of the young are a **perennial** issue. Yet, tattoos seem to have sparked special debate. Perhaps this is because of the permanence of the tattooing process: Once a tattoo has been placed on the skin, it does not wear off. And tastes change with age. A person who loves her beautifully tattooed hands or face at seventeen **(2)** may develop some **ambivalence** toward them when she is applying for an executive position at the age of forty. **(3)** Beautiful tattoos on one's hands place a conservative businesswoman in something of a **dilemma.**

Still, tattoos have grown dramatically in popularity in the past few **decades.** Their beauty and cultural significance have also received attention.

The tattoo on this woman's arm shows pictures of her two pug dogs.

Kathy Willens/AP Photo

Critics are almost **unanimous** in recognizing them as an important art form. Historians and anthropologists have studied their cultural significance.

Although we may think of tattoos as a symbol of the young, they are far from new. **(4)** The **annals** of history reveal that tattooing has been around for thousands of years. The oldest known tattoos have been found on the body of "Otzi," a man who froze in the Alps 5,200 years ago. **(5)** Because it was frozen, his body did not **disintegrate**. In recent years, though, the ice around the body melted due to global warming, and Otzi was revealed. Now stored in Italy, Otzi's body has fifty-seven small dots and crosses. Many are placed over joints. Scientists feel that the tattoos were meant to relieve the pain of arthritis, a **perennial** problem of adults who live in cold, wet climates. Otzi did not die of arthritis, though. Analysis of his mummy reveals that, **(6)** perhaps in an act of **duplicity,** he was shot by an arrow in the back.

Ancient Egyptian women also wore tattoos. Female figures found in the tombs of **monarchs** (called pharaohs) show patterns of tattooing that were probably meant to protect them from the dangers of childbirth. No tattoos are found on the bodies of men, or on male statues.

(7) Other tattoos served as a **metric** of status. Over 2,500 years ago, Sythian and Thracian noblemen wore tattoos on their faces to show their high social standing. The Romans found a wild tribe in Scotland whose leaders and warriors were so heavily tattooed with pictures that they named them the Picts, for "pictures." The **magnitude** of the tattooing increased with the importance of the person.

Tattoos became popular in modern Europe when Captain James Cook, an Englishman, explored the south Pacific Islands of Polynesia, Australia, and New Zealand in 1770. He found tribes covered with "tatataus." This word gave "tattoo" its name in English. In New Zealand, Maori warriors etched their battle careers in tattoos. One tattoo might show a triumph; **(8)** another might give a picture of how a warrior had displayed **magnanimity** toward a conquered enemy.

Tattoos soon spread around Europe, becoming popular ways for people to ward off the dangers of their trades. Miners often tattooed lamps on their arms. Sailors etched their bodies with roosters and pigs, which were thought to protect against drowning. Other tattoos were individually designed. Macy's department stores carry the symbol of a red star. It is taken from a tattoo on the arm of founder Roland Macy, who started to work on a whaling ship, in 1837, at the age of fifteen. Unique tattoos served an important function: if a sailor drowned, his body could be identified through a personal design.

In today's world, tattoos are influenced by many cultures. **Bilingual** parlors offer their services to a multicultural trade, with representations from different languages and locations. Some tattoos describe one's character. For example, many people display the Japanese Kanji that stands for **integrity**. The ladybug is a symbol of luck in Italy and Turkey.

Scarification, which is closely related to tattooing, is a type of marking used by traditional Nigerians, as well as in other countries. **(9)** Small, **symmetrical** marks (once done with the shell of a cashew nut) may be made in the cheeks of babies. These identify a person's tribe and village. Austin Okocha, who now lives in Illinois, has half-inch vertical lines in his face that mark him as a member of the Ibo tribe, from Ibusa, in the state of Delta, Nigeria.

Tattoos can also show personal achievements. Marco Parra was proud of his organizational efforts within the Hispanic community, so he had the Aztec calendar tattooed on his arm. Later, when he had the honor of tending the fire in a Native American sweat lodge, he added a ring of smoke around his first tattoo.

Tattoos are also works of art. Collectors Lawrence and Evelyn Aronson own many historic tattoo flash, or designs, and decorated tattooing equipment. This includes objects from New Zealand and Myanmar. In the United States, many of the artists worked in circuses and carnivals. One tattoo artist the Aronsons collect, Stoney St. Clair, suffered from crippling arthritis and had to use a wheelchair from the age of four. Joining the circus as a sword swallower, he learned the art of tattooing and became world-renowned for his stunning designs.

Art belongs to its creators or purchasers, and thus tattoos can be trademarked and copyrighted. **(10)** This ensures that the owner has a **monopoly** on a tattoo, and it cannot be used without permission. In 2002, Elayne Angel received a copyright on her back from the U.S. Patents Office.

Are you thinking of getting a tattoo? It should be done under sanitary conditions. Otherwise, infections can result. The decision is not **trivial**, for your tattoo will probably be with you for the rest of your life.

■ *Exercises*

Each numbered sentence corresponds to a sentence in the passage. Fill in the letter of the choice that makes the sentence mean the same thing as its corresponding sentence in the passage.

1. Parents' and elders' disapproval of the styles of the young are a(n) _______ issue.
   a. honorable b. rare c. long-lasting d. unimportant
2. A person may develop _______ them.
   a. hatred of b. regret for c. strong feelings about d. mixed feelings toward
3. Beautiful tattoos may place a businesswoman in something of _______.
   a. a position of being envied b. the situation of communicating two messages c. a position of distrust d. a problem
4. The _______ of history reveal that tattooing has been around for thousands of years.
   a. trends b. records c. investigations d. legends
5. Because it was frozen, his body did not _______.
   a. decay b. decrease in size c. harden d. melt
6. Perhaps in an act of _______, he was shot in the back by an arrow.
   a. deterioration b. betrayal c. widespread killing d. war
7. Other tattoos served as a(n) _______ status.
   a. art form of b. symbol for c. rebellion against d. measure of
8. Another might give a picture of how a warrior had displayed _______.
   a. symbols b. generosity c. triumphs d. power
9. Small, _______ marks may be made in the cheeks of babies.
   a. difficult to interpret b. one-sided c. unimportant d. balanced

10. This ensures that the owner has _______ the tattoo.
 a. one opinion of b. control by one person of c. conflicted feelings about d. continuous use of

■ *Discussion Questions*

1. Identify three purposes that tattooing has served, and explain your answers.
2. Identify historic differences between women's and men's use of tattoos.
3. Do you think the government should allow tattoo designs to be copyrighted? Why or why not?

INSIGHT INTO IDIOMS

Money

The idioms in this chapter deal with money. In addition to idioms, there are several common symbols for money, including our dollar sign ($). The $ first described the Spanish-Mexican peso. The symbol for English money, the pound sign (£), also did not originate in the country that uses it. The sign £ comes from the word *librae* or "pound" in Latin, the ancient language of Italy.

Some common idioms for money are as follows:

a. To lose all your money is to *lose your shirt* or to be *broke.*

b. Not to have enough money to pay for something is to be *caught short.*

c. People who have been cheated out of money have been *taken to the cleaners* or *ripped off.*

d. People who have very little money may be forced to *live from hand to mouth,* with just enough to cover their immediate needs.

e. When people go from poverty to wealth, they are said to go *from rags to riches.*

f. A rich person might *live high on the hog,* spending money freely and buying the best of everything.

g. A rich man or woman who refuses to spend money is often called a *cheapskate.*

Practice chapter words one more time by filling in the letter of the correct idiom into the blank before each sentence.

_____ 1. Because of the magnitude of her wealth, she was able to _________, and she owned five homes and a yacht.

_____ 2. After his duplicitous partner cheated my father out money, my dad had to _________.

_____ 3. Keeping cash in my wallet is a perennial problem and often when I must pay for something, I am _________.

_____ 4. Despite the fact that her family had a monopoly on the department stores in town, the _________ wore second-hand clothes and drove a ten-year-old car.

_____ 5. When the poor man became monarch of the wealthy country, he went _________.

Links to more lists of English idioms and their meanings can be found at the Student Companion Website for this book: **www.cengage.com/devenglish/richek8e.**

CHAPTER 10

Word Elements: Thought and Belief

Our ability to think and our system of beliefs help to define us as human beings. Not surprisingly, English has many words for these mental activities. Part 1 of this chapter presents word elements related to thought and belief. Part 2 presents prefixes of negation, which we use when we do *not* believe something. Finally, several idioms are discussed in this chapter. Idioms involve our thoughts and beliefs, as well as the influences of the cultures we live in.

Chapter Strategy: Word Elements: Thought and Belief

Chapter Words:

Part 1

cred	credibility	*ver*	veracity
	creed		verify
	discredit		veritable
fid	confidant	*-phobia*	acrophobia
	defiant		claustrophobia
	fidelity		xenophobia

Part 2

de-	delude	*Idioms*	bury your head in the sand
	destitute		give carte blanche
	deviate		leave no stone unturned
non-	nonchalant		olive branch
	noncommittal		star-crossed
	nondescript		tongue-in-cheek

Visit the Student Companion Website at **www.cengage.com/devenglish/richek8e** to test your knowledge of these words before you study, hear each word pronounced, find additional practice exercises, and access more information on words and topics.

Did You Know?

Animal Words of Thought and Belief

Animals have played an important part in human beliefs for thousands of years. Primitive humans tried to give themselves the powers they observed in these creatures. To acquire the speed of a jaguar or the power of a lion, people dressed in the skins of these animals and imitated their cries and movements. Such customs have contributed words to modern English. The feared ancient warriors of what is now Norway covered themselves in bear *(ber)* skin shirts *(serkr)* and rushed into mad attack. From this custom, we derive the phrase *to go berserk,* or to act violent in a crazy, uncontrolled way.

Many great civilizations represented their gods using animals. In ancient Egypt, the god of the dead had the head of a jackal; the protectress goddess had a cat's head. Quetzalcoatl, an important god throughout the ancient Americas, was a feathered serpent. His twin brother, Xolotl, is often portrayed as a skeleton with the head of a dog. To demonstrate their regard for animals, ancient peoples often preserved them. Mummies of parrots, foxes, hawks, dogs, cats, bulls, and crocodiles have been found in Egypt and Peru.

Some animals retain important positions in modern religions, and these are honored in words and idioms. The Hindu religion holds cows in high esteem, and traditional Hindus will not kill cows or eat beef. One type of cow, the East Indian humped zebu, is particularly revered. These practices have resulted in the English expression *sacred cow,* meaning a belief that is so well established that it cannot be challenged.

More than two thousand years ago, the ancient Jews had a custom in which they chose one goat to symbolize people's sins against God. This goat was released into the desert wilderness, symbolically carrying sins away with it. Although this custom vanished long ago, the English word *scapegoat* still means someone who takes the blame for another.

The creation of animal idioms remains a strong trend in modern English. Many modern expressions use animal actions to symbolize human behavior. For example, to *parrot* means "to repeat," as a parrot repeats familiar words. To *horse around* means "to play," as horses do in a field. A man who is nagged by his wife is called *henpecked,* recalling the actions of female chickens. When we do something wonderful, we may *crow* about it. We may *eat like pigs* (greedily) or disappoint our host by *eating like birds* (eating little). The generally bad reputation of the rat has given us the phrase *to rat on,* meaning "to turn someone in," or "squeal" on someone.

Can you identify the human meanings given to these common animal expressions?

1. in the dog house
2. a can of worms
3. lion's share
4. a dinosaur
5. lame duck
6. puppy love

Answers are on page 399.

Learning Strategy

Word Elements: Thought and Belief

The first part of this chapter concentrates on word elements relating to thought and belief. Three roots are presented: *cred* (believe), *fid* (faith), and *ver* (truth). Part 1 also introduces the suffix *-phobia* (fear of). Part 2 of this chapter presents two prefixes with negative meanings. We use them when we do *not* believe in something. *Non-* means "not." *De-* also has a negative sense, indicating "to remove from" or "down."

Element	*Meaning*	*Origin*	*Function*	*Chapter Words*
Part 1				
cred	believe	Latin	root	credibility, creed, discredit
fid	faith	Latin	root	confidant, defiant, fidelity
ver	truth	Latin	root	veracity, verify, veritable
-phobia	fear of	Greek	suffix	acrophobia, claustrophobia, xenophobia
Part 2				
de-	remove from; down; negative	Latin	prefix	delude, destitute, deviate
non-	not	Latin	prefix	nonchalant, noncommittal, nondescript

Word Elements

Part 1

More information on the roots and suffix for Part 1 is presented in the following discussion.

cred (believe)

The root *cred* is used in many English words. When we do not **believe** something, we may call it *incredible. Credit* is granted to a customer because merchants **believe** that they will be paid. The concept of a *credit card* is also based upon **belief** that something charged now will be paid later.

fid (faith)

The English word *faith* is taken from this root. When you are *confident* about something, you have **faith** that you can do it.

ver (truth)

The root *ver* means "truth." A *verdict,* the judgment of a jury, is made up from the root *ver* **(truth)** and the root *dict* (say). Even the common word *very,* meaning "**truly**" or "really," comes from *ver.*

-phobia (fear of)

As a suffix, *-phobia* describes a strong or illogical **fear** of something and often forms words that are used in psychology. For example, *zoophobia* is a **fear** of animals. The base word *phobia* also means "**fear.**" In Greek mythology, Phobos was the son of Ares (or Mars), the god of war. Greek warriors sometimes painted the likeness of Phobos on their shields to frighten their enemies.

Words to Learn

Part 1

cred

1. **credibility** (noun) krĕd′ə-bĭl′ĭ-tē

From Latin: *cred* (believe)

believability; ability to be trusted

Errors on the blog undermined its **credibility**.

The consultant's Ph.D. and extensive experience established his **credibility**.

NOTE: Undermine is often used with a possessive pronoun, as in "She undermined *her* credibility," "Don't undermine *your* credibility," "I'll try not to undermine *my* credibility."

▶ *Related Word*

credible (adjective) (krĕd′ə-bəl) Rodney's handsomeness and sex appeal made him a *credible* Romeo in the play.

2. **creed** (noun) krēd

From Latin: *cred* (believe)

set of beliefs or principles

The **creed** of journalists is to provide accurate and fair news that is in the public interest.

The **creed** of the Muslim religion includes five central duties: reciting the words of witness, prayer, charity, fasting, and pilgrimage.

NOTE: *Creed* often refers to a formal system of religious or moral beliefs.

▶ *Common Phrase*

creed of

3. **discredit** (verb, noun) dĭs-krĕd′ĭt

From Latin: *dis-* (not) + *cred* (believe)

a. to damage in reputation; disgrace; prove untrue (verb)

The witness was **discredited** when he admitted that he had not been at the scene of the crime.

The theory that the sun revolves around the Earth has been **discredited**.

b. damage; disgrace (noun)

One corrupt judge can cast **discredit** on the whole court system.

▶ *Common Phrase*

cast discredit on

fid

4. **confidant** (noun) kŏn′fĭ-dănt′; kŏn′fĭ-dänt′

From Latin: *con-* (together) + *fid* (faith)

a person who is trusted with the secrets of another

Rosemary told her **confidant** about her plans to elope.

▶ *Related Word*

confide (verb) Don't *confide* in people who gossip.

NOTE: (1) Don't confuse *confidant* with *confident*. *Confid**e**nt* means sure of oneself. (2) The word *confidante* (with an *e*) refers specifically to a woman who is trusted with secrets. However, *confidant* is now generally used as both the male and female form.

Courtesy author

Rosemary told her *confidant* about her plans to elope.

5. **defiant** (adjective) dĭ-fī′ənt

From Latin: *dis-* (not) + *fid* (faith) (This word underwent a spelling change from *dis-* to *de-* as it came through French.)

refusing to follow orders or rules; resisting boldly

The **defiant** player refused to follow the coach's training rules.

▶ *Related Words*

defiance (noun) The lung cancer patient continued to smoke in *defiance* of his doctor's orders.

defy (verb) (dĭ-fī′) Ashanti *defied* her landlord's rules on pets by keeping a cat in her apartment.

6. **fidelity** (noun) fĭ-dĕl′ĭ-tē

From Latin: *fid* (faith)

a. faithfulness to obligation or duty

Mamed showed his **fidelity** to his mother by caring for her in her old age.

Sexual **fidelity** is important to a marriage.

b. exactness, accuracy

Headphones provide better musical **fidelity** than speakers do.

The actress reproduced a British accent with such **fidelity** that we were amazed to find out she was an American.

▶ *Common Phrase*
fidelity to

ver

7. **veracity** (noun) və-răs′ĭ-tē

From Latin: *ver* (truth)

truth or accuracy of a statement or story

It is difficult to determine the **veracity** of young children's testimony.

Many experts question the **veracity** of information that has been gotten through torture.

▶ *Common Phrase*
veracity of

8. **verify** (verb) vĕr′ə-fī′

From Latin: *ver* (truth) + *facere* (to make)

to determine the truth or accuracy of; to confirm

Websites often ask people to **verify** their passwords by typing them twice.

People often use a dictionary to **verify** a word's meaning.

▶ *Related Word*
verification (noun) The company obtained *verification* of the job candidate's experience by calling previous employers.

9. **veritable** (adjective) vĕr′ĭ-tə-bəl

From Latin: *ver* (truth)

a. unquestionable; being truly so

The paintings in Cora's attic proved to be a **veritable** treasure of old family portraits.

b. almost; nearly; very similar to

The low gas prices caused a **veritable** traffic jam at the station.

-phobia

10. **acrophobia** (noun) ăk′rə-fō′bē-ə

From Greek: *acros* (highest) + *-phobia* (fear)

fear of heights

Yuiry's **acrophobia** prevented him from riding on the Ferris wheel.

► *Related Words*

acrophobic (adjective) *Acrophobic* people often have difficulty looking out the windows of high-rises.

acrophobe (noun) *Acrophobes* are not good at climbing mountains.

Phobic *Word Patterns*

Note these word patterns:

*acro**phobia**, claustro**phobia**, xeno**phobia***—nouns naming the fear
*acro**phobic**, claustro**phobic**, xeno**phobic***—adjectives
*acro**phobe**, claustro**phobe**, xeno**phobe***—nouns naming the person who suffers from the fear

11. **claustrophobia** (noun) klô′strə-fō′bē-ə

From Latin: *claustrum* (enclosed space) + Greek: *-phobia* (fear)

fear of closed or small spaces

Mr. Kim's **claustrophobia** made him panic when traffic stopped in the tunnel.

► *Related Word*

claustrophobic (adjective) I felt *claustrophobic* in the cramped elevator.

12. **xenophobia** (noun) zĕn′ə-fōb′ē-ə

From Greek: *xenos* (stranger) + *-phobia* (fear)

fear or hatred of strangers, foreigners, or things that are strange or foreign

Because of his **xenophobia,** the senator sponsored bills to prohibit all immigration into the country.

► *Related Word*

xenophobic (adjective) *Xenophobic* people usually avoid foreign travel.

Do You Know These Fears?

Match these phobias to their meanings.

1. gatophobia	a. fear of poison
2. ablutophobia	b. fear of being alone
3. toxiphobia	c. fear of cats
4. monophobia	d. fear of washing or bathing

Answers are on page 399.

Links to lists of phobias can be accessed through the Student Companion Website at **www.cengage.com/devenglish/richek8e.**

Exercises

Part 1

■ *Definitions*

Match the word and definition. Use each choice only once.

1. xenophobia _______	a. fear of heights
2. veritable _______	b. fear of small spaces
3. confidant _______	c. faithfulness
4. acrophobia _______	d. truth
5. claustrophobia _______	e. resisting boldly
6. creed _______	f. damage reputation; disgrace
7. defiant _______	g. fear, hatred of foreigners
8. fidelity _______	h. to determine truth or accuracy
9. credibility _______	i. unquestionable; being truly so
10. verify _______	j. set of beliefs
	k. a person trusted with secrets
	l. ability to be believed

■ *Meanings*

Match each word element to its meaning. Use each choice only once.

1. fid ______ a. fear
2. ver ______ b. faith
3. -phobia ______ c. believe
4. cred ______ d. truth

■ *Words in Context*

Complete each sentence with the best word. Use each choice only once.

a. credible	e. fidelity	i. veritable
b. creed	f. discredit	j. acrophobia
c. confidant	g. veracity	k. claustrophobia
d. defiant	h. verify	l. xenophobia

1. Marisa showed her ________________ to her employer by turning down a higher-paying job.

2. The ________________ of the news report was confirmed by several eyewitnesses.

3. The ________________ of almost all religions includes charity and kindness toward others.

4. Because of his ________________, the camper refused to enter in the small cave.

5. I was furious when my ________________ told my boss that I was looking for a new job.

6. War often increases ________________ within a nation as people begin to distrust foreigners.

7. The food convention was a(n) ________________ gold mine of ideas for the student chef.

8. The ________________ workers went on strike when they were ordered to add an hour to their work day.

9. The badly done, error-filled report written by one worker should cast no

   ________________ upon her many honest coworkers.

10. We need to ________________ your age by inspecting your driver's license before we can serve you a beer.

■ *Using Related Words*

Complete each sentence with the correct form. Use each choice only once.

1. discredited, discredit, discrediting

   For thousands of years, physicians used leeches, or "blood suckers," to cure the sick. It was thought that the slimy creature could cure everything from fevers to pneumonia. But, in fact, loss of blood actually caused many deaths, finally ______________ the use of the leech. This ______________ therapy was discontinued. Today, however, leech therapy is back. Modern physicians find that it can prevent blood clotting. So, despite the ______________ cast upon leeches for two hundred years, modern physicians have found ways to use the blood sucker.

2. verified, verification, verify

   In the high-stakes world of art, it is important to ______________ that a painting is authentic. No museum or art dealer wants to be caught with a phony Picasso! As the production of fakes has become more sophisticated, so have methods of ______________. Dr. Hany Farid of Dartmouth College can digitally analyze art to determine an artist's individual pattern of strokes. He recently ______________ that a drawing attributed to Perugino, an Italian painter who lived from 1446 to 1524, was actually done by several of his students.

3. acrophobia, acrophobic, acrophobe

   The two-hundred-foot-high Mackinac Bridge, in Michigan, evokes ______________ in many people who cannot bear to look down into the water. Some burst into tears or have attacks of dizziness. Fortunately, officials are available to drive the cars of ______________ people, who usually shut their eyes during the journey. So an ______________ can now cross the bridge in comfort.

4. credibility, credible

   Are you concerned about your weight? Perhaps you should eat in Brookline, Massachusetts, for this city is considering requiring every restaurant to post calorie counts. Of course, there are some problems. Getting ______________ calorie counts is expensive. While restaurant chains like McDonalds can afford laboratories, small restaurants, with menus that change often, would find this law very costly. Another problem is the ______________ of the counts. A restaurant that specializes in rich desserts might be tempted to lower calories, so as not to ruin its sales.

5. defied, defiance

A man of great conscience who ______________ his government, Sempo Sugihara is credited with saving more than two thousand Jews from murder during the Holocaust. Because he was the Japanese diplomat to Lithuania, people begged him for visas that would protect them from Nazi persecution. In ____________ of government orders and at risk to his own life, Sugihara signed the visas as fast as he could write. His memory is revered by humanitarians.

Links to the story of Sugihara and others who aided the persecuted during the Holocaust can be accessed through the Student Companion Website at **www.cengage.com/devenglish/richek8e.**

■ *Reading the Headlines*

Here are some headlines that might appear in newspapers. Read each and answer the questions. (Remember that small words, such as *is*, *are*, *a*, and *the*, are often left out of headlines.)

SHOCK TREATMENT DISCREDITED AS METHOD OF CURING CLAUSTROPHOBIA

1. Is shock treatment an effective cure? _______
2. Are sufferers afraid of small spaces? _______

PROFESSORS DOUBT THE VERACITY OF IMMIGRATION STATISTICS PRESENTED AT WEBSITE OF XENOPHOBE

3. Do the professors think the statistics are false? _______
4. Does the person who writes the website like foreigners? _______

CREDIBILITY OF EXPERT WITNESS DESTROYED WHEN INVESTIGATION FAILS TO VERIFY HIS M.D.

5. Do people now believe what the witness will say? _______
6. Did people confirm that the witness had an M.D.? _______

CONFIDANT DEFIES GOVERNMENT'S ORDERS TO RELEASE INFORMATION

7. Has the person been told secrets? _______

8. Is the person following government orders? _______

DESPITE WISH TO SHOW FIDELITY TO CREED BY CLIMBING MOUNTAIN, ACROPHOBIC MAN HELD BACK BY FEARS

9. Does the acrophobic wish to be faithful? _______

10. Is the person afraid of basements? _______

Prefixes

Part 2

Part 2 of this chapter presents two very common prefixes with negative meanings. *De-* means "to remove from" or "down"; *non-* means "not." Both prefixes are used in thousands of English words.

This *Words to Learn* section also presents several idioms. These phrases involve our thoughts, beliefs, and cultural understandings. Many idioms are the result of common experiences or well-known stories. The individual words do not carry their usual meanings, but together they form one generally understood meaning.

de- (removal from, down, worse)

The common prefix *de-* can mean **remove from, down,** or **negative.** When we *decontaminate* something, we **remove** the contamination or impurities **from** it. When people *deforest* land, they **remove** trees **from** it. In another meaning, when we *depress* a button, we push it **down.** When something *declines,* it goes **down,** or becomes more **negative.** When a currency is *devalued,* its value goes **down**, or becomes more **negative**.

non- (not)

The prefix *non-* simply means "not." *Nonsense* is something that does **not** make sense. A *nonsmoker* person is one who does **not** smoke. *Non-* often combines with base words (roots that can stand alone as English words). Many root words, like *smoker,* join with *non* by using a hyphen.

Words to Learn

Part 2

de-

13. **delude** (verb) dĭ-lo͞od′

From Latin: *de-* (down, negative) + *lūdere* (to play) (*Delūdere* meant "to deceive, to mock.")

to cause someone to think something that is false; to mislead

The man **deluded** himself into thinking that he would make a fortune by gambling.

If prosecutors know that a man is innocent of a crime, they are not allowed to **delude** a jury into thinking he committed it.

▶ *Related Words*

delusion (noun) (dĭ-lo͞o′zhən) Some parents seem to be under the *delusion* that their children are perfect!

delusional (adjective) The *delusional* man thought police officers were constantly following him.

▶ *Common Phrases*

delude oneself (Delude often uses a reflexive prououn such as myself, yourself, or herself.); suffer from the delusion; under the delusion

NOTE: *Delusion* and *delusional* often refer to mental illness.

14. **destitute** (adjective) dĕs′tĭ-to͞ot′

From Latin: *de-* (down, negative) + *stat* (placed)

completely without money; poor

The **destitute** family moved into a homeless shelter.

▶ *Related Word*

destitution (noun) The establishment of the Social Security system in 1935 saved many of America's elderly from a life of *destitution*.

NOTE: At times *destitute* can be used as a noun, as in the box that follows.

Working with the Destitute

The saintly Mother Teresa, a nun who died in 1998, opened the Nirmal Hriday (Pure Heart) home for the dying and *destitute* in Calcutta, India. Treating the very poorest, those who had been abandoned because they were dying of AIDS or leprosy, Mother Teresa provided help to those who needed it most. She founded an order of nuns who continue her wonderful work.

Keystone Features/on Archive/Getty Images

15. **deviate** (verb) dē′vē-āt′

From Latin: *de-* (remove from) + *via* (road) (*Dēviāre* meant "to go away from the road.")

to vary from a path, course, or norm

We **deviated** from the path because we wanted to explore the forest.

Ayba **deviated** from tradition when she refused to enter into an arranged marriage.

▶ *Common Phrases*
deviate from

▶ *Related Words*
deviant (adjective) (dē′vē-ənt) Wearing a winter coat on a 90-degree day is *deviant* behavior. (*Deviant* means "odd in a negative way.")
deviation (noun) Any *deviations* from safety procedures at a nuclear power plant may result in a terrible disaster.

non-

16. **nonchalant** (adjective) nŏn′shə-länt′

From Latin: *non-* (not) + *calēre* (to be warm) (Many people feel physically warm when they get angry. Therefore, someone who is nonchalant, "not warm," does not feel angry or concerned.)

unconcerned; carefree

We were surprised at the **nonchalant** attitude of the mother as her four-year-old wandered onto the street.

With a **nonchalant** toss of the covers, John declared that he had made the bed.

▶ *Related Word*

nonchalance (noun) The resistance fighter displayed *nonchalance* in the face of danger.

NOTE: *Nonchalant* can be a somewhat negative word, indicating that someone should care, but does not.

17. **noncommittal** (adjective) nŏn′kə-mĭt′l

From Latin: *non* (not) + *com-* (together) + *mittere* (to send)

a. not expressing opinions or information

When asked whether he would put more troops in Iraq, the general was **noncommittal.**

b. refusing to choose an opinion or action

It upset Perry that after two years of dating, Peggy was **noncommittal** about getting married.

18. **nondescript** (adjective) nŏn′dĭ-skrĭpt′

From Latin: *non-* (not) + *de-* (down) + *script* (write) (Something nondescript is hard to describe in writing because it is plain and lacks specific distinguishing features.)

not distinct; difficult to describe because it lacks individuality

Amazingly, the **nondescript** mall was home to a world-famous restaurant.

The valuable documents were hidden in a **nondescript** brown briefcase that looked like hundreds of others.

Idioms

19. **bury your head in the sand**

ignore unpleasant or threatening news

When you get behind in payments, you should call your creditors, rather than **burying your head in the sand** by ignoring the situation.

The Ostrich Doesn't Do It

Many people believe that ostriches *bury their heads in the sand* when they are attacked by their enemies. However, this is only a legend: ostriches run away from attackers just like any other animal. Nonetheless, the ostrich has given us the idiom *bury your head in the sand.* Ostriches do swallow pebbles to help them digest food, and perhaps this gave them the appearance of burying their heads.

NOTE: This idiom is used with a possessive pronoun, as in "I won't bury *my* head in the sand" and "He is burying *his* head in the sand."

20. **give carte blanche** kärt blänsh′

From French: a blank document

to give full, unrestricted power

Dave was so busy that he **gave** his friend **carte blanche** to plan their vacation.

After Damaris **gave** the art student **carte blanche** to decorate her apartment, she was shocked to find that the walls had been painted purple.

A Way to Surrender

A *carte blanche* was originally a piece of paper with nothing but a signature on it, used when an army surrendered. The defeated leader would sign his name, and the victor could then write in the terms of surrender. In French, the words *carte blanche* mean "blank card." It should be noted that French was, for centuries, the international language of diplomacy.

21. **leave no stone unturned**

to search thoroughly; to investigate thoroughly

The security guard **left no stone unturned** in his search for the lost child.

The Peace After the Flood

According to the Bible, God punished the wicked world by sending a flood. However, God chose to save one good man, Noah, along with his family and one pair of each type of animal on Earth. Noah floated in an ark for the forty days of the flood. When the waters at last went down a dove flew from the boat and brought back an *olive branch* as a symbol of the fact that God's anger was over, and a new peace had begun. Today, both the dove and the *olive branch* symbolize an offer of peace.

▶ *Common Phrases*

hold out an olive branch; offer an olive branch; extend an olive branch

22. **olive branch**

to make an offer of peace

The government held out an **olive branch** to rebels when it offered to negotiate.

If I offer an **olive branch** to my rival, will he accept it? (The term *offer an olive branch* is acceptable.)

A Thorough Search

In 477 BC, a Greek commander of the city of Thebes won a victory. However, he failed to locate a treasure that he was seeking in the defeated enemy's camp. So the commander consulted the Delphic Oracle (sort of a mythical question-and-answer service). The oracle advised him to *"leave no stone unturned,"* and he finally found the treasure.

23. **star-crossed**

doomed to a bad fate; unlucky

Shakespeare described the tragic lovers Romeo and Juliet as **star-crossed.**

Signs of the Stars

For centuries, people of many cultures have believed that the astrological position, or placement, of the stars at a person's birth determined the person's future. A *star-crossed* person was born under unfavorable astrological influences.

24. **tongue-in-cheek**

joking; insincere; without really meaning something

When mom made a **tongue-in-cheek** comment that she planned to get a nose ring, her kids burst out laughing.

A popular series of manuals carries such **tongue-in-cheek** titles as *Windows for Dummies* and *eBay for Dummies.*

A Joking Gesture

At one time, people indicated that they didn't mean what they said by pushing one of their cheeks out with their tongue.

Exercises

Part 2

■ *Definitions*

Match the word and definition. Use each choice only once.

1. head in the sand ______	a. joking; insincere
2. leave no stone unturned ______	b. not distinct
3. olive branch ______	c. not giving opinions
4. nondescript ______	d. to search thoroughly
5. tongue-in-cheek ______	e. ignoring threats
6. give carte blanche ______	f. to give full power
7. star-crossed ______	g. to vary from a path
8. noncommittal ______	h. a peace offer
9. deviate ______	i. without money
10. nonchalant ______	j. to mislead
	k. unconcerned
	l. unlucky

■ *Meanings*

Match each prefix to its meaning. Use each choice only once.

1. non- ______	a. to remove from; down
2. de- ______	b. not

■ *Words in Context*

Complete each sentence with the best word. Use each choice only once.

a. delude	g. bury your head in the sand	j. hold out an olive branch
b. destitute	h. give carte blanche	k. star-crossed
c. deviate	i. leave no stone unturned	l. tongue-in-cheek
d. nonchalant		
e. noncommittal		
f. nondescript		

1. Don't ______________________ yourself into thinking you can get through college without studying.

2. If you are having problems with a course, you should not ______________________, but talk to the professor and ask for help.

3. After being robbed five times in one year, Alexis decided he was ______________________.

4. It was hard to tell one ______________________ gray-walled office from another.

5. When I realized my brother was ______________________, I invited him to live with me.

6. "Maybe," was her ______________________ answer when we asked if she would go.

7. The police will ______________________ in their search for the dangerous criminal.

8. The rich father is expected to ______________________ to his daughter to plan a fancy wedding.

9. "I can't catch you," was dad's ______________________ remark as he chased the three-year-old.

10. To make peace, the parents will ______________________ to the son they have not spoken to in years.

■ *Using Related Words*

Complete each sentence with the correct form. Use each choice only once.

1. destitute, destitution

   Homeless and ______________, Joe Long was spending a day alone when he spied a car on fire. Rushing to the scene, he heroically pulled two people from the flames, saving their lives.

   A grateful public has now saved Joe from ______________ by gifts of money and the offer of a job.

2. nonchalance, nonchalant

   What was all the fuss about the discovery of the H1N1 virus a few years ago? The ________________ of the public contrasted sharply with the fearful reactions of health officials. Flu epidemics can, however, kill millions of people. It is estimated that the 1918 "Spanish Flu" caused fifty million deaths. So rather than being ________________, health officials prefer to take extra precautions to prevent a new flu from spreading.

3. delusions, delude, delusional

   Schizophrenia is a form of mental illness, often linked to certain genes, in which people suffer from ________________. Typically, the medications used to treat the illness have considerable side effects, so physicians don't prescribe them until they are badly needed. However, a study by Dr. McGlashan found that prescribing medicine at the first sign of mental illness can sometimes prevent patients from becoming ________________. Thus, rather than letting families simply hope for the best or ________________ themselves into believing that their loved one will not worsen, some doctors are willing to try earlier intervention.

4. deviant, deviates

   Cultures have different customs. In the Middle East, people stand close together when they talk. In North America and Europe, people stand farther apart. If someone ________________ from this distance and stands too close, the other speaker becomes uncomfortable. In Japan, one speaker does not look directly at the other. To look directly at someone is considered ________________ and offensive.

■ *Find the Example*

Choose the example that best describes the action or situation

1. Most nondescript way to hold out an olive branch ______
   a. shake your enemy's hand b. hug your rival
   c. refuse to talk to a friend

2. Nonchalant way to bury your head in the sand _______
   a. don't cash in a winning lottery ticket
   b. bawl out policeman who gave you a warning
   c. toss a parking ticket in the garbage

3. Delusion of a destitute person _______
   a. homelessness b. bench to sit on c. great riches

4. Noncommittal response to being given carte blanche to shop _______
   a. I'm not sure I can accept your offer. b. I am very disappointed.
   c. I gladly accept your offer.

5. A tongue-in-cheek response to someone who deviated from directions _______
   a. You should have done it like you were told.
   b. Wow! You really followed those directions well.
   c. That is so funny!

Chapter Exercises

■ *Practicing Strategies: New Words from Word Elements*

Use your knowledge of word elements to determine the meanings of these words and complete each sentence. Use each choice only once. You may need to capitalize some words.

a. anthrophobia	e. deplane	i. nonprofit
b. bona fide	f. Fido	j. phobic
c. deforestation	g. incredulous	k. verisimilitude
d. demote	h. infidel	l. very

1. When you cannot believe something, you are ___________________.

2. *Bona* means "good," so something presented in good faith is ___________________.

3. ___________________ is causing loss of trees all over the world.

4. Fear of other human beings is ___________________.

5. After the aircraft lands, passengers ___________________ and enter the airport terminal.

6. Those people who are fearful of many things are often called ________________.

7. A(n) ________________ organization is not expected to make money.

8. As a tribute to their great faithfulness, dogs have often been named ________________.

9. A person who does not believe is called a(n) ________________.

10. Something that is similar to the truth has ________________.

■ *Practicing Strategies: Combining Context Clues and Word Elements*

In each sentence, one word is italicized. Use the meaning of the word element and the context to make an intelligent guess about its meaning.

1. After ascending the hill, we *descended* and went to our campsite.

   Descended means ________________________________.

2. I suffer from *cynophobia*, so please keep that dog on a leash.

   Cynophobia means ________________________________.

3. The knight swore *fealty* to his lord.

   Fealty means ________________________________.

The next two items are from newspaper sources.

4. Oddly, some journalists give little *credence* to such official, attributable reports. In today's upside-down world, official government reports don't carry the same weight as whispered, unattributed reports.

   Credence means ________________________________.

5. According to Mothers Without Custody, a 9-year-old national organization with 35 chapters, including one in northern Illinois, more than 2.5 million mothers live apart from their children as *noncustodial* parents.

   Noncustodial means ________________________________.

■ *Companion Words*

Complete each sentence with the best word or words. You may use choices more than once. Choices: from, undermine, into, of, in, cast, hold out, his.

1-2. The athlete violated curfew ____________ defiance ____________ the coach's orders.

3. The musician deluded herself ____________ thinking she could perform successfully without practicing.

4. These directions are so complicated that the slightest deviation ____________ them will probably get you lost.

5. Check the veracity ____________ your statements.

6. Try to ____________ an olive branch and make peace with your in-laws.

7. His cheating ____________ discredit on his character.

8. The creed ____________ a U.S. juror states, "I am a seeker of truth."

9. He should face the truth rather than burying ____________ head in the sand!

10. Errors in your resume will ____________ your credibility.

■ *Writing with Your Words*

To practice effective writing, complete each sentence with an interesting phrase that indicates the meaning of the italicized word.

1. I felt I was *star-crossed* when ____ ____.

2. I was surprised that he remained *nonchalant* when ______________ ____.

3. I gave a *noncommittal* answer to the party invitation because _____ ____.

4. Despite her *nondescript* appearance, ______________________________

____.

5. I feel like *burying my head in the sand* when ______________________

____.

6. My day became a *veritable* disaster when _________________________

____.

7. I would like to have *carte blanche* to ____________________________

____.

8. One way to *hold out an olive branch* is to _________________________

____.

9. A person who was both *acrophobic* and *claustrophobic* would fear ___

____.

10. Despite her *nondescript* appearance, ______________________________

____.

■ *Making Connections*

To connect new vocabulary to your life, write extended responses to these questions.

1. Describe a time you left no stone unturned to find or accomplish something.
2. Describe a time when you deviated from what everyone else was doing.
3. Report on a time you, or someone you know or have heard about, had a veritable disaster on a trip.

Passage

The Origins of Superstitions

Just about everyone holds one superstition or another. Read this passage to find out about the origins of your favorites—or should we say your least favorites?

Is the number thirteen unlucky? Why do people who spill salt throw some over their shoulder? Are black cats evil? Can a mirror steal your soul? **(1)** No scientist has **verified** these superstitions, yet people once believed them without question. How did they originate?

The number thirteen has long been considered unlucky. **(2)** Thirteen was believed to be a central number in the **creed** of witches. **(3)** These supposedly evil souls were thought to **defy** religion by swearing **fidelity** to the devil. Thirteen was also the ideal number for a witches' coven, or meeting. As a result of the evil reputation of the number thirteen, some tall buildings do not have a thirteenth floor; the floor numbers skip from twelve to fourteen.

Many people considered Friday unlucky because it was the day of the week on which Christ was crucified. When Friday coincides with the thirteenth of the month, we get a particularly unlucky day. However, other Fridays have also been known to bring misfortune. On Friday, May 10, 1886, a financial panic in London, known as Black Friday, left many people **destitute.**

Yann Arthus-Bertrand/Encyclopedia/CORBIS

Unlike the number thirteen and Friday, salt was considered lucky. Because salt was used to preserve food, people believed that it would drive away bad spirits. However, spilling salt was thought to invite evil. In fact, **(4)** dropping a salt container could make **nonchalant** diners suddenly frantic. To avoid disaster, they had to take the salt into their right hands (the side for one's lucky spirit) and throw it over their left shoulders. **(5)** Any **deviation** from this procedure would invite the invasion of the evil spirit, who was always lurking on the left.

Cats have held a special place in our superstitions. While ancient Egyptians worshiped cats, **(6)** these creatures have had a **star-crossed** fate in Europe. The fact that cats' eyes reflect light in the dark caused Europeans of the Middle Ages to think that the animals were evil spirits. Cats were often pictured as witches' companions and **confidants.** Some people believed that, after seven years' service, a cat might even become a witch! Since black was the color of the devil, black cats inspired especially intense fear. God-fearing people walking at night might see a black cat cross their path. Certain that they had met the devil, **(7)** they would break into a **veritable** panic. A cat that crossed from left to right was particularly frightening.

People often made ridiculous claims about cats. For example, in 1718 a man named William Montgomery claimed that two elderly women had been found dead in their beds on the morning after he had killed two noisy cats. **(8)** Montgomery **deluded** himself into thinking that the cats had been these women in disguise.

A less harmful, though no less silly, superstition revolved around mirrors. The ancients believed that breaking a mirror would bring seven years of bad luck, avoidable only if the pieces were quickly buried. The length of the bad luck stemmed from the Roman tradition that the human body renewed itself every seven years. Throughout history, people have feared that a mirror would steal the weak soul of a sick person or a newborn. Of course, this had no **veracity**, yet some people would not allow infants to see a mirror until their first birthdays.

(9) Such superstitions have been **discredited;** still, an occasional modern high-rise lacks a thirteenth floor. **(10)** Some people throw spilled salt over their left shoulders, even if it is a **tongue-in-cheek** gesture or they no longer know why they are doing it. Perhaps you know people who shiver with fright when a black cat crosses their paths at night and flashes its fiery eyes. Whatever the origin of superstitions, it's clear that some haunt us even today. Do you think they have any **credibility?**

■ *Exercise*

Each numbered sentence corresponds to a sentence in the passage. Fill in the letter of the choice that makes the sentence mean the same thing as its corresponding sentence in the passage.

1. No scientist has ______ these superstitions.
   a. determined the truth of b. experimented with
   c. shown the silliness of d. criticized people for

2. Thirteen was believed to be a central number in the _______ of witches.
   a. beliefs b. faithfulness c. poverty d. truths

3. These supposedly evil souls were thought to _______ religion.
   a. resist b. hate c. ignore d. lie about

4. Dropping a salt container could make _______ diners suddenly frantic.
   a. unhappy b. calm c. unbelieving d. strange

5. Any _______ from this procedure would invite the invasion of the evil spirit.
   a. change b. noise c. benefit d. risk

6. These creatures have had a rather _______ fate in Europe.
   a. fortunate b. unlucky c. religious d. unusual

7. They would break out into a _______ panic.
   a. sudden b. faithful c. unquestionable d. dangerous

8. Montgomery _______ himself into thinking that the cats had been these women in disguise.
   a. fooled b. frightened c. advised d. helped

9. Such superstitions have been _______.
   a. widely accepted b. unfashionable c. feared
   d. proven untrue

10. People throw salt over their left shoulders, even if it is a _______ gesture.
    a. joking b. foolish c. believing d. frightened

■ *Discussion Questions*

1. Why were infants not allowed to see mirrors?
2. Why do you think so many people feel cats have supernatural powers?
3. Would you be comfortable living on a thirteenth floor? Why or why not?

INSIGHT INTO IDIOMS

Animals

Many animal idioms originate in folk tales and fairy tales. Hans Christian Anderson, the famous Danish writer, composed the story of an *ugly duckling* that grew into a beautiful swan. In another example, an Aesop's fable features a wolf that dressed as a sheep, in order to appear harmless. That way, he could kill and eat a member of the flock. The story gives us the term *wolf in sheep's clothing*. These idioms and others are featured here.

a. An *ugly duckling* is a physically unappealing child who has the potential to be attractive or successful.

b. When we tell people to *hold your horses,* we want them to slow down.

c. A political candidate who is not favored to win is a *dark horse.*

d. When a situation has gotten very bad it has *gone to the dogs*.

e. When we complain about the brutality and competition in life we say *"It's a dog-eat-dog world."*

f. A *wolf in sheep's clothing* is an evil person who pretends to be well intentioned.

g. A *fat cat* is a very rich and privileged person.

Practice chapter words one more time by filling in the letter of the correct idiom into the blank before each sentence.

_____ 1. Do you think most people display fairness and fidelity, or do you think __________?

_____ 2. Only a(n) __________ could give all of the members of his family carte blanche to spend as much money as they wanted to.

_____ 3. The kindly looking man appeared to be harmless, but in fact he had a long history of crime and was a veritable __________.

_____ 4. If you bury your head in the sand you may not understand what is wrong until the situation has __________ and it is too late to fix the problem.

_____ 5. We were incredulous when we found out that the __________ had actually been elected governor.

Links to more lists of English idioms and their meanings can be found at the Student Companion Website for this book: **www.cengage.com/devenglish/richek8e.**

CHAPTER 11

Word Elements: The Body and Health

Since 1900, life expectancy in the United States has risen from forty-seven to almost eighty years. Some researchers even feel that the human body can last up to 150 years. Medical science has learned to prevent or cure scores of diseases. Polio, measles, chicken pox, smallpox, and tetanus have almost been eliminated. Such inventions as refrigeration and plumbing have also contributed to healthier lives. The word elements in this chapter are related to the human body and health. Part 1 presents four roots; Part 2 presents four prefixes. These word elements are common in the sciences and health professions and also form words you will meet in general reading.

Chapter Strategy: Word Elements: The Body and Health

Chapter Words:

Part 1

audi	audit auditory inaudible	*ped*	expedite impede pedigree
patho, -pathy	empathy pathetic pathology	*spec, spic*	auspicious conspicuous despise

Part 2

a-, an-	anarchy anomaly apathy	*bio-, bio*	biodegradable biopsy symbiotic
bene-	benefactor beneficial benign	*mal-*	malady malice malpractice

Visit the Student Companion Website at **www.cengage.com/devenglish/richek8e** to test your knowledge of these words before you study, hear each word pronounced, find additional practice exercises, and access more information on words and topics.

Did You Know?

How Did Snacks Originate?

If you are like most people, you are far more likely to snack on a package of potato chips than on a raw carrot. Modern life is filled with "junk food" that is perhaps not healthy, but is tasty and readily available in packaged form. The names of these treats are part of our history.

Erperlstrom, 2009/Used under license from Shutterstock.com

It is not entirely clear how the potato chip, which originated in the 1860s, got its name. According to one story, Chef George Crum had an annoying customer who kept complaining that his french fries were too thick. Mr. Crum cut the potatoes into thinner and thinner slices until the potato chip was born. However, others say that California settlers of Spanish descent invented the potato chip. In any event, the first potato chip factory opened in 1925.

In 1896 Leo Hirschfield, an Austrian immigrant, invented a chewy candy and gave it the nickname of his childhood sweetheart, Tootsie. Today we still enjoy Tootsie Rolls. In the 1940s, the daughter of Charles Lubin gave her name, Sara Lee, to cakes and desserts.

According to the International Association of Ice Cream Manufacturers, the ice cream cone was invented in 1904 at the St. Louis World's Fair. Ernest A. Hamwi, a Syrian immigrant, was selling *zalabias*, or soft wafers. When a person at the ice cream booth next to him ran out of plates, Hamwi rolled up his wafers to hold the ice cream, and the cone was born.

In the early 1900s, eleven-year-old Frank Epperson accidentally invented a snack food by leaving a sweet drink out overnight in the cold. The liquid froze around a stick. Epperson originally called his invention the "epsicle," but the name later changed to the more appealing "popsicle."

Enjoyed by children and adults throughout the world, the Twinkie was named for the Twinkle Toe shoe. In 1930, inventor Jimmy Dewar passed a billboard advertising the shoe and decided it would be a fitting name for a snack. How do they get the filling into the Twinkie? The manufacturers bake the surrounding cake and then inject the cream.

M&M's got their name from the initial letters of the last names of inventors Forrest Mars and Bruce Murrie. The candies first became popular during World War II because soldiers could eat them without making their trigger fingers sticky.

Food Origins

Match the food to the origin of its name.

1. ketchup
2. cookie
3. Cracker Jack
4. Pez

a. Dutch word for little cake
b. the Chinese word for pickled fish
c. the first, middle, and last letters of the word for *peppermint* in German
d. slang, in the 1890s, for something very pleasing

Answers are on page 399.

Learning Strategy

Word Elements: The Body and Health

With the many advances in medicine and the life sciences during the past century, more and more scientific words have been made from the word elements in this chapter. Part 1 presents four common roots; Part 2 presents four common prefixes.

Element	*Meaning*	*Origin*	*Function*	*Chapter Words*
Part 1				
audi	hear	Latin	root	audit, auditory, inaudible
patho, -pathy	feeling, suffering; disease	Greek	root; suffix	empathy, pathetic, pathology
ped	foot	Latin	root	expedite, impede, pedigree
spec, spic	look	Latin	root	auspicious, conspicuous, despise
Part 2				
a-, an-	without	Greek	prefix	anarchy, anomaly, apathy
bene-	good, well	Latin	prefix	benefactor, beneficial, benign
bio-, bio	life	Greek	prefix; root	biodegradable, biopsy, symbiotic
mal-	bad, harmful	Latin	prefix	malady, malice, malpractice

Word Elements

Part 1

The four roots in Part 1 are explained in more detail here.

audi (hear)

Our *auditory* nerves enable us to **hear**. The word root *audi* is used also in such words as *audience*, a group of people who **hear** a performance, and *auditorium*, a place where crowds gather to **hear** something.

patho, -pathy (feeling, suffering; disease)

The root *patho* has two meanings, both stemming from ancient Greek. First, *patho* can mean "feeling, suffering," as in the word *pathos*, meaning "a **feeling** of pity." A second meaning of *patho* is "disease," as in *pathologist*, a doctor who diagnoses **disease**, and *psychopath*, a person with a **diseased** mind. The spelling *-pathy* is used for the suffix form. For example, *sympathy* means "**suffering** along with the sorrows of another."

ped (foot)

Ped is found in such words as *pedal*, a control operated by the **foot**, and *quadruped*, an animal with four **feet**. Some words made from *ped* reflect society's scorn for the lowly

foot. *Pedestrian*, which refers to people who travel by **foot**, is also used to describe something that is dull or ordinary.

spec, spic (look)

The root *spec* is used in such words as *inspect*, "to **look** at carefully." *Spectators* **look** at movies and sports events. Finally, the word *spy*, a person who secretly **looks** at the actions of others, may also be derived from *spec*.

Words to Learn

Part 1

audi

1. **audit** (noun, verb) ô′dĭt

From Latin: *audit* (hear) (At one time, examinations of finances were held in public so that all could hear.)

a. examination of financial accounts or records to determine accuracy (noun)

The Internal Revenue Service conducted an **audit** of our tax returns for last year.

b. a methodical investigation of a situation (noun)

An **audit** of university records revealed that many people had overpaid tuition.

c. to examine accounts (verb)

When the accountant **audited** the financial records, she found evidence of theft.

d. to attend a class without receiving credit (verb)

To prepare for nursing school, I **audited** organic chemistry.

► *Related Word*
auditor (noun) The *auditor* found the company's finances to be in order.

2. **auditory** (adjective) ô′dĭ-tôr′ē

From Latin: *audi* (hear)
referring to hearing

Exposure to loud blasts in combat zones can damage the **auditory** nerve and cause deafness.

Lectures require students to process **auditory** information.

Auditory *Stress: A Controversial Device*

As people age, they lose their ability to hear high sounds. A device called the Mosquito emits an unpleasant sound, almost painful to the ears, that is *audible* to most people under twenty-five, but not to their elders. Young people move away, but older ones are not annoyed. The Mosquito has been used to prevent "hanging out" in commercial areas. However, many people feel it should be banned because it discriminates against the young.

3. **inaudible** (adjective) ĭn-ô′də-bəl

From Latin: *in-* (not) + *audi* (hear)

impossible to hear

Dogs and gerbils can hear sounds that are **inaudible** to the human ear.

► *Related Word*

audible (adjective) Although she tried to whisper, her voice was *audible* all the way across the room. (*Audible* is the opposite of *inaudible.*)

patho, -pathy

4. **empathy** (noun) ĕm′pə-thē (plural: **empathies**)

From Greek: *em-* (in) + *-pathy* (feeling, suffering)

understanding of or identification with another person's feelings

Because I fought in the Vietnam war, I have **empathy** for the soldiers who are returning from Iraq and Afghanistan.

► *Common Phrase*

empathy for

► *Related Words*

empathic/empathetic (adjective) (ĕm-păth′ĭk); (ĕm′pə-thĕt′ĭc) Alcoholics Anonymous offers support groups in which *empathic* (or *empathetic*) members, who have all struggled against drinking problems, address their addictions.

empathize (verb) To help clinic staff *empathize* with the disabled, each employee spent one day in a wheelchair.

NOTE: How do *empathy* and *sympathy* differ? *Sympathy* means feeling sorry for another person. However, if we have *empathy*, we identify with, or experience, the feelings of another human being.

5. **pathetic** (adjective) pə-thĕt′ĭk

From Greek: *patho* (feeling, suffering)

pitiful; arousing pity

The injured cat made a **pathetic** attempt to jump.

NOTE: In an informal usage, *pathetic* can be used in a scornful way, to mean "bad": "What a *pathetic* excuse for a dinner!" he remarked, as he looked at the two celery stalks on the plate.

6. **pathology** (noun) pă-thŏl′ə-jē (plural: **pathologies**)

From Greek: *patho* (disease) + *-logy* (study of)

a. the study of disease

The science of **pathology** advanced greatly after the microscope was invented.

b. signs of disease; something that is not normal

Lack of the gene ERK1 contributes to the **pathology** of autism, a condition that makes it difficult to communicate with others.

Long-term unemployment can lead to neglect, violence, and other forms of family **pathology**.

▶ *Related Words*

pathological (adjective) (păth′ə-lŏj′ĭ-kəl) He was a *pathological* liar. (*Pathological* can mean mentally ill.)

pathologist (noun) Forensic *pathologists* investigate tissue samples for clues to crimes. (A *pathologist* is a physician.)

ped

7. **expedite** (verb) ĕk′spĭ-dīt′

From Latin: *ex-* (out) + *ped* (foot) (*Expedīre* meant "to free a person's feet from fetters or chains.")

to speed up; to accomplish quickly

Filing your taxes online, rather than through the mail, **expedites** your refund.

To **expedite** the sale of the house, we reduced the price.

NOTE: Don't confuse *expedite* with *expedient*, which means "convenient."

► *Related Words*

expeditious (adjective) (ĕk′spĭ-dĭsh′əs) Emergency rooms give *expeditious* service to the very ill.

expedition (noun) (ĕk′spĭ-dĭsh′ən) Karl Bushy is attempting a 36,000-mile walking *expedition* around the Earth. (*Expedition* means "journey.")

expediter/expeditor (noun) The shipping company's *expediter* coordinated truck routes to ensure fast delivery.

8. **impede** (verb) ĭm-pēd′

From Latin: *im-* (in) + *ped* (foot) (*Impedīre* meant "to entangle," as one's foot becomes caught.)

to delay; to block

Carrying a heavy load will **impede** your ability to run.

My view of the stage was **impeded** by the pole in front of my seat.

► *Related Word*

impediment (noun) (ĭm-pĕd′ə-mənt) Not finishing college can be an *impediment* to getting the job you want.

9. **pedigree** (noun) pĕd′ĭ-grē′

From Latin (*ped*) through Old French: *pie* (foot) + *de* (of) + *grue* (crane) (In a pedigree, or family tree, the visual form used to show generations is shaped like the foot of a crane.)

a. ancestry; certificate of ancestry

The **pedigree** of Queen Elizabeth II includes many German ancestors.

My cat may not have a distinguished **pedigree**, but I love her.

b. personal or professional history (informal usage)

Many appointments of President Obama had a Clinton White House **pedigree**.

Our Pedigrees

The word *pedigree* can be used to refer to noble or royal ancestry, or simply to all of a person's ancestry. Recent genetic research has shown that people's pedigrees include diverse ancestry, and we are more related than we think. Dick Cheney, Republican vice president under George W. Bush, shares ancestors with Democratic political rival Barack Obama. Obama's *pedigree* is quite diverse, as he had an African father and an American mother of European descent. Although he was the first elected African-American president, one of his mother's ancestors probably owned slaves!

spec, spic

10. **auspicious** (adjective) ô-spĭsh′əs

From Latin: *avis* (bird) + *spic* (look, watch)

favorable; promising success

Rising employment is an **auspicious** sign for our economy.

The beautiful, sunny day was an **auspicious** one for a wedding.

The Auspex

The ancient Romans believed that since the flight of birds was close to the heavens, it could easily be guided by the gods. Thus, birds were watched as signs or omens. A religious official trained to observe flight patterns was an *auspex*. When an important matter was being considered, the *auspex* decided whether the signs given by birds were *auspicious*.

11. **conspicuous** (adjective) kən-spĭk′yoo-əs

From Latin: *con-* (closely) + *spec* (look)

easy to notice; attracting attention

The **conspicuous** presence of police helped lower the crime rate in the low-income neighborhood.

To make his tattoos less **conspicuous**, Albert wore long-sleeved shirts at work.

► *Related Words*

conspicuousness (noun) The *conspicuousness* of Anna's outfit made her easy to spot in a crowd.

inconspicuous (adjective) The banquet servers were trained to be *inconspicuous* at events. (*Inconspicuous* is the opposite of *conspicuous*.)

Courtesy author

The *conspicuousness* of Anna's outfit made her easy to spot in a crowd.

12. **despise** (verb) dĭ-spīz′

    From Latin: *de-* (down) + *spec* (look)

    to look down upon with intense dislike

    I **despise** those who are cruel to animals.

    ▶ *Related Word*
    despicable (adjective) Selling a toy that you know is dangerous is *despicable*.

Exercises

Part 1

■ *Definitions*

Match the word and definition. Use each choice only once.

1. impede ______	a. record of ancestry
2. audit ______	b. to hinder
3. empathy ______	c. pitiful
4. inaudible ______	d. not able to be heard
5. auditory ______	e. examination of financial accounts
6. expedite ______	f. study of disease
7. conspicuous ______	g. to speed up

8. pathetic _______
9. pedigree _______
10. auspicious _______

h. referring to hearing
i. favorable
j. to scorn with feelings of hate
k. noticeable
l. identification with the feelings of another person

■ *Meanings*

Match each word element to its meaning. Use each choice only once.

1. ped _______
2. patho, -pathy _______
3. audi _______
4. spec, spic _______

a. foot
b. look
c. feeling, suffering; illness
d. hear

■ *Words in Context*

Complete each sentence with the best word. Use each choice only once.

a. audit	e. pathetic	i. pedigree
b. auditory	f. pathology	j. auspicious
c. inaudible	g. expedite	k. conspicuous
d. empathy	h. impede	l. despise

1. I would like to ____________________ the course rather than take it for credit.
2. We were shocked to see ____________________ children begging in city streets.
3. The shy child spoke so softly that her voice was ____________________.
4. To ____________________ answers to consumer questions, the company has installed a hot line that operates twenty-four hours a day.
5. The public has come to ____________________ corporation presidents who cheat their employees.
6. The racehorse had a distinguished ____________________, and was descended from many champions.
7. The spilled grape juice left a(n) ____________________ stain on Louie's white shirt.

8. The wonderful reviews for the movie were ________________ for ticket sales.

9. Researchers are still struggling to understand the ________________ of autism, a condition that makes it difficult to communicate with others.

10. Many people wear hearing aids to improve their ________________ functioning.

■ *Using Related Words*

Complete each sentence with the correct form. Use each choice only once. You may have to capitalize some words.

1. empathy, empathic, empathize

   Do men and women differ in their management skills? One study found that women managers were ________________ to employees. They served as role models and fostered creativity. Women would ________________ with their subordinates and encourage them. In contrast to the ________________ shown by women, male managers tended to appeal to the self-interest of the subordinate, explaining, for example, how taking on an extra project could lead to a promotion.

2. impede, impediment

   World-famous golfer Tiger Woods seems to have a life we would all envy. Yet as a child, he suffered from the speech ________________ of stuttering. After years of hard work, he was able to overcome his problem, but his speech disability continues to ________________ his ability to learn foreign languages

3. despise, despicable

   ________________ acts of violence and kidnapping are committed each year against aid workers who provide food and medical services to people in poor countries. In the African country of Somalia, for example, over thirty workers have been kidnapped and held for ransom, or shot dead. People of goodwill can only ________________ those who would kill the innocent and deprive the needy of services.

4. pathological, pathologist

Physicians can freeze some cancerous tumors that cannot be removed by surgery. After a ______________ determines that a tumor is malignant, the surgeon locates it through ultrasound techniques. The tumor is then injected with liquid nitrogen, which freezes it. This destroys the ______________ tissue without harming healthy organs.

■ *Reading the Headlines*

Here are some headlines that might appear in newspapers. Read each and answer the questions. (Remember that small words, such as *is, are, a,* and *the,* are often left out of headlines.)

AUSPICIOUS DEVELOPMENT ANNOUNCED FOR AUDITORY DEVICES

1. Is the development positive? ______
2. Do the devices help vision? ______

AUDIT OF COMPANY FINANCES REVEALS CONSPICUOUS ABSENCE OF FUNDS DUE TO DESPICABLE ACTIONS OF OWNER

3. Were financial accounts inspected? ______
4. Was the absence noticeable? ______
5. Were the owner's actions honorable? ______

ATTEMPTS TO EXPEDITE INTERNET SERVICE IMPEDED BY PATHETIC WIRELESS SYSTEM

6. Do people want to speed up Internet service? ______
7. Are people able to speed up Internet service? ______
8. Is the wireless system a good one? ______

PEDIGREE CAUSES PATHOLOGY IN HEART FUNCTIONING

9. Is the condition hereditary? _______

10. Does the condition involve illness? _______

Word Elements

Part 2

Part 2 concentrates on four prefixes that are often used in words about the body and in the health sciences.

a-, an- (without)

The words *amoral* and *immoral* help demonstrate the prefix *a-, an-* by contrasting it with *im-* (meaning "not"). An *immoral* person is *not* moral: this person has a sense of right and wrong yet chooses to do wrong. An *amoral* person is **without** morals: such a person has no sense of right and wrong. The prefix *a-* is used in many medical words, such as *aphasia* (**without** speech) and *anesthetic* ("**without** feeling," referring to chemicals that make patients unable to experience pain during a medical procedure).

bene- (good; well; helpful)

Bene- is used in such words as *benefit* (something that is **helpful**) and *beneficiary* (one who receives **help** or money from another).

bio-, bio (life)

The prefix *bio-* is used in the word *biology*, "the study of **living** things." You may have taken a biology course in school. *Biochemistry* deals with the chemistry of **living** things.

mal- (bad; badly; harmful)

The prefixes *mal-* and *bene-* are opposites. *Mal-* is used in the adjective *maladapted*, or "**badly** adapted." In 1775, the playwright Richard Sheridan coined the word *malaprop* as a name for his character Mrs. Malaprop, who used words that were not appropriate (or **badly** appropriate). One of her malapropisms is "He's the very *pineapple* of politeness." (She should have used the word *pinnacle*.)

For more about *malapropisms*, access sites on them through the Student Companion Website at **www.cengage.com/devenglish/richek8e.**

Words to Learn

Part 2

a-, an-

13. **anarchy** (noun) ăn′ər-kē

From Greek: *an-* (without) + *arkhos* (ruler)

total disorder; lawless political confusion

When the police could not control the rioting and looting, the city plunged into **anarchy**.

Without an adult present, **anarchy** soon broke loose in the high-school classroom.

► *Related Words*

anarchist (noun) The *anarchist* hoped to bring about the fall of the government.

anarchic (adjective) (ăn-är′kĭk) The streets of Baghdad were *anarchic* following the U.S. invasion of Iraq in 2003.

14. **anomaly** (noun) ə-nŏm′ə-lē (plural: **anomalies**)

From Greek: *an-* (without) + *homalos* (even, same)

something abnormal; something very unusual

A four-leaf clover is an **anomaly** of nature.

At five foot three inches in height, player Tyrone (Muggsy) Bogues was an **anomaly** in the National Basketball League.

► *Related Word*

anomalous (adjective) On one *anomalous* February day, the temperature in Chicago hit 72 degrees Fahrenheit.

15. **apathy** (noun) ăp′ə-thē (plural: **apathies**)

From Greek: *a-* (without) + *-pathy* (feeling)

lack of emotion, feeling, or interest

The city's **apathy** toward soccer turned to enthusiasm when the hometown team started winning.

An Observation on Apathy

The great physicist Albert Einstein said of *apathy*, "The world is a dangerous place to live, not because of the people who are evil but because of the people who don't do anything about it."

▶ *Related Word*

apathetic (adjective) (ăp′ə-thĕt′ĭk) At first, public response to the rapes and massacres in Darfur was *apathetic*, but then people worldwide rose up in protest.

bene-

16. **benefactor** (noun) bĕn′ə-făk′tər

From Latin: *bene-* (well) + *facere* (to do)

a person who gives financial or other aid; a donor

An unknown **benefactor** has agreed to pay college tuition for students enrolled in the public schools of Kalamazoo, Michigan.

Pope Julius II was the **benefactor** who commissioned Michelangelo to paint the ceiling of the Sistine Chapel.

A Humble Benefactor

Ms. Oseola McCarthy was an unlikely *benefactor*. Born in Mississippi, she quit school in the sixth grade and worked most of her life doing laundry. She never earned more than $9,000 a year. But her frugal nature allowed her to save money. In 1995, she donated $150,000 to fund scholarships for needy African Americans. Her gift was the largest endowment the University of Southern Mississippi had ever received.

17. **beneficial** (adjective) bĕn′ə-fĭsh′əl

From Latin: *bene-* (well) + *facere* (to do)

helpful; producing benefits

The 2009 financial stimulus package was **beneficial** to the economy.

Omega-3 fatty acids, found in certain fish, are **beneficial** to health.

▶ *Related Word*

benefit (noun) May's job provided her with health insurance *benefits*.

18. **benign** (adjective) bĭ-nīn′

From Latin: *bene-* (well) + *genus* (birth) (*Benignus* meant "well-born, gentle.")

a. kind, gentle; not harmful

Santa Claus is a **benign**, fatherly figure.

Scientists continue to search for compounds that kill insects, but are **benign** for humans and the environment.

b. not containing cancer cells

A pathology report revealed that the mole on my arm was **benign**.

NOTE: The antonym, or opposite, of *benign* is *malignant*.

bio-, bio

19. **biodegradable** (adjective) bī′ō-dĭ-grā′də-bəl

From Greek: *bio-* (life) + Latin: *de-* (down) + *gradus* (step)

capable of being chemically broken down by natural biological processes

We avoid using Styrofoam cups because they are not **biodegradable**.

NOTE: *Biodegradable* substances break down into natural elements.

► *Related Words*

biodegrade (verb) In airless landfills, trash does not *biodegrade* and one can still read newspapers buried there forty years ago.

biodegradation (noun) (bī′ō-dĕg-rə-dā′-shən) Sodium bicarbonate (or baking soda) can aid the *biodegradation* of sewage.

20. **biopsy** (noun, verb) bī′ŏp′sē (plural: **biopsies**)

From Greek: *bio-* (life) + *opsis* (sight)

a. the removal and study of living tissue to diagnose disease (noun)

A needle **biopsy** of breast tissue showed she did not have cancer.

b. removing and studying living tissue in order to study disease (verb)

The skin doctor decided that the mole needed to be **biopsied**.

NOTE: The *y* of the verb *biopsy* changes to *i* in the third-person singular (He *biopsies*) and past tense (I *biopsied*).

Biopsy, Benign, *and* Pathology

The words *biopsy, benign*, and *pathology* are often used together. A physician who suspects cancer will take a small sample of cell tissue for a *biopsy*. A *pathologist* will then examine it, usually under a microscope, for *pathology*, or disease. If the tumor is *benign*, it is usually harmless. If the tumor is *malignant* (note the *mal-* prefix), it must be treated.

21. **symbiotic** (adjective) sĭm′bē-ŏt′ĭk

From Greek: *sym-* (together) + *bio* (life)

living together dependently; referring to a relationship where two organisms live in a dependent state and each one benefits

Peanut plants have a **symbiotic** relationship with the nitrogen-fixing bacteria that live on their roots.

The sisters' **symbiotic** relationship was so strong that when one died, the other soon followed.

NOTE: Symbiotic relationships can be either biological or social. If they are social, *symbiotic* can be a negative word.

▶ *Related Word*

symbiosis (noun) (sĭm′bē-ō′sĭs) Sea anemones live in *symbiosis* with some types of algae.

Redbilled oxpeckers and impalas have a *symbiotic* relationship.

Carol Hughes; Gallo Images/Encyclopedia/Corbis

mal-

22. **malady** (noun) măl′ə-dē (plural: **maladies**)

From Latin: *mal-* (bad) + *habēre* (to keep) (*Mal habitus* meant "ill-kept, in bad condition.")

disease; bad condition

The **malady** of severe depression can often be helped with medication.

Poverty is a social **malady** that affects the entire world

23. **malice** (noun) măl′-ĭs

From Latin: *mal-* (bad) + *volens* (wishing)

a desire to harm others or to see them suffer

In an act of **malice**, the man kicked the puppy.

► *Related Words*

malicious (adjective) After a *malicious* individual poisoned Tylenol tablets in 1982, safety seals were added to the packaging of medications.

maliciousness (noun) In an act of terrible *maliciousness*, the bomber targeted a preschool.

24. **malpractice** (noun) măl-prăk′tĭs

From Latin: *mal-* (bad) + *practice*

failure of a licensed professional to give proper services

A patient who received the wrong medicine accused the nurse of **malpractice**.

A client sued the lawyer for **malpractice** because she missed an important court date.

Who Can Commit Malpractice?

To commit *malpractice*, one must be licensed or regulated by the government. Lawyers, accountants, attorneys, actuaries, dentists, physicians, nurses, psychologists, and chiropractors are professionals who can be sued for *malpractice*. In contrast, nonprofessionals can only be accused of negligence.

Exercises

Part 2

■ *Definitions*

Match the word and definition. Use each choice only once.

1. anarchy ______
2. benefactor ______
3. symbiotic ______
4. apathy ______
5. beneficial ______
6. biodegradable ______
7. malady ______
8. malpractice ______
9. biopsy ______
10. malice ______

a. living together dependently
b. capable of being broken down by natural processes
c. not containing cancer cells
d. donor
e. study of living tissue
f. lack of feeling
g. helpful
h. a deviation from normal
i. lawlessness
j. illness
k. desire to harm others
l. failure to give proper professional services

■ *Meanings*

Match each word element to its meaning. Use each choice only once.

1. a-, an- ______
2. mal- ______
3. bio-, bio ______
4. bene- ______

a. good
b. bad
c. life
d. without

■ *Words in Context*

Complete each sentence with the best word. Use each choice only once.

a. anarchy	e. beneficial	i. symbiotic
b. anomaly	f. benign	j. malady
c. apathy	g. biodegradable	k. malice
d. benefactor	h. biopsy	l. malpractice

1. Warren Buffet, a well-known financial expert and ________________, gave billions of dollars to medical research.

2. Manta rays have a(n) ____________________ relationship with remora fish, which eat parasites from the rays' skin while feeding on their leftover food.

3. Owning a pet can be ____________________ to the mental health of a lonely person.

4. Attacking a helpless person is an act of ____________________.

5. Vaccination protects us against small pox, a(n) ____________________ that, in the past, killed millions of people.

6. Although leather shoes are ____________________, it takes over fifty years for them to break into natural elements.

7. Even adults who look ____________________ may wish to kidnap or harm children.

8. Physicians often carry insurance to protect them if they are sued for ____________________.

9. The rising sales of one department store were a(n) ________________ in the industry, for all the other stores experienced declines.

10. The pathologist examined tissue from the ____________________ to determine if it contained any cancer cells.

■ *Using Related Words*

Complete each sentence with the correct form. Use each choice only once.

1. anomaly, anomalously, anomalies

Severe obesity has been linked to "binge eating." People with this condition eat ____________________. They are unable to stop themselves from eating things like several gallons of ice cream. Recently, studies have demonstrated that these eating ____________________ may be a result of genetic makeup. An

____________________ in the melanocortin 4 receptor (*MC4R*) gene shows up in many people who demonstrate this eating condition.

2. apathy, apathetic

The U.S. presidential election of 2008, in which Barak Obama ran against John McCain, reversed the trend of American voting ____________________. In fact, voter turnout was the highest in forty-four years. Still, at 56.8 percent, U.S. turnout still indicated a somewhat ____________________ response.

3. malice, malicious

Computer hackers can break into bank or credit card files, steal financial information, and enrich themselves. Or, in acts of pure ____________________, they can simply destroy a system for the fun of it. Now, though, companies are hiring "ethical" or "white-hat" hackers to protect their systems. These hackers are equally skilled but lack the ____________________ intentions of their criminal counterparts.

4. symbiotic, symbiosis

A few short years ago, the tiny Miami blue butterfly was one of the world's rarest species. With only eight adults left, the Florida Wildlife Conservatory Commission declared it an endangered species. When it is a caterpillar, the butterfly lives in ____________________ with ants. In this ____________________ relationship, ants care for the caterpillar and in return the caterpillar's body gives off a sweet substance that the ants eat. Fortunately, a breeding program has been successful, and the butterfly is being reintroduced into the wild.

5. anarchy, anarchists, anarchic

In a famous case, Nicola Sacco and Bartolomeo Vanzetti, who were self-proclaimed ____________________, were found guilty of murder. Their supporters charged that the two men were convicted only because of their ____________________ beliefs that all forms of government oppress people. Sacco and Vanzetti felt that

_____________________ was, therefore, desirable. Even though evidence surfaced that other people had committed the murder, the two were executed in 1927.

■ *Find the Example*

Choose the example that best describes the action or situation.

1. An anomalous malady _______
   a. cure for common cold b. eye infection that is uncomfortable
   c. flu that gives you energy

2. Benign biodegradable objects _______
   a. cups that dissolve in soil b. plastic plates
   c. splinters of glass on a floor

3. What a benefactor who received an apathetic response most probably

   would do _______
   a. get another opinion b. double the amount c. not give again

4. A malicious act that would cause anarchy _______
   a. setting off a bomb b. telling people to flee a storm
   c. lining people up at the exit of a theater

5. Physician accused of malpractice did this with biopsy _______
   a. read it wrong b. ordered treatment c. helped the patient

Chapter Exercises

■ *Practicing Strategies: New Words from Word Elements*

Use your knowledge of prefixes to determine the meanings of these words and complete each sentence. Use each choice only once.

a. atonal	e. benevolent	i. pathogen
b. atypical	f. biosphere	j. peddler
c. audiometer	g. introspection	k. pedometer
d. audition	h. malfunction	l. spectator

1. A(n) __________________ travels on foot selling things.

2. A(n) __________________ act is done with good intentions.

3. A person who looks at something is called a(n) __________________.

4. The variola virus is the __________________ of smallpox.

5. Our globe, which houses plants and animals, may be called a(n) __________________.

6. A(n) __________________ measures one's ability to hear.

7. The __________________ in the equipment was due to a faulty part.

8. The __________________ measured the number of miles I walked on foot.

9. At a(n) __________________, people listen to you in order to determine if you should be hired for a performance.

10. When we "look into ourselves" to think about our own thoughts and feelings, we engage in __________________.

■ *Practicing Strategies: Combining Context Clues and Word Elements*

In each sentence, one word is italicized. Use the meaning of the word element and the context to make an intelligent guess about its meaning.

1. Crews of people trained in cleaning up poisons were able to remove all traces of the *biohazard*.

   Biohazard means ______________________________.

2. When I think of my life in *retrospect*, I wish I had finished college.

   Retrospect means ______________________________.

3. A *sociopath* may be capable of terrible crimes.

   Sociopath means ______________________________

   ______________________________.

The next two items are from newspaper sources.

4. At the depth at which it was sunk, it was *anaerobic*—there was no oxygen—so there were no barnacles or seaweed to engulf it.

   Anaerobic means ______________________________.

5. The state constitution says the governor can remove a commissioner "for incompetence, neglect of duty, or *malfeasance* in office."

   Malfeasance means ______________________________.

■ *Practicing Strategies: Using the Dictionary*

The following entry is taken from online print source. Read it and then answer the questions.

pearl[1] (pûrl) *n.* **1.** A smooth, lustrous, variously colored deposit, chiefly calcium carbonate, formed around a grain of sand or other foreign matter in the shells of certain mollusks and valued as a gem. **2.** Mother-of-pearl; nacre. **3.** One that is prized for beauty or value. **4.** *Printing* A type size measuring approximately five points. **5.** A yellowish white. ❖ *v.* **pearled, pearl•ing, pearls** —*tr.* **1.** To decorate or cover with or as if with pearls. **2.** To make into the shape or color of pearls. —*intr.* **1.** To dive or fish for pearls or pearl-bearing mollusks. **2.** To form beads resembling pearls. [ME *perle* < OFr. < Lat. **pernula*, dim. of *perna*, ham, sea shell.]

1. List all the parts of speech for *pearl.* ______________________________

____

2. The *ear* in *pearl* is pronounced like the vowel in what common words?

____

3. In which language did *pearl* originate? ______________________________

What is the part of speech and definition number of the definition that best fits these sentences?

4. This famous stamp is the *pearl* of my collection. ____________________

5. We watched people dive in the sea and *pearl.* ____________________

■ *Companion Words*

Complete each sentence with the best word. You may use choices more than once, and some items may have more than one correct answer. Choices: of, toward, by, to, for.

1. The pathology __________ cancer often includes malignancies that spread throughout the body.

2. Unfortunately, the teenager showed only apathy ____________ school.

3. The malady __________ discontent lay heavily on the land.

4. The pedigree __________ the racehorse included many famous champions.

5. The man's "I do" was so soft that it was inaudible ________ the guests at his wedding.

6. The patient falsely accused the cardiologist ________ malpractice.

7. A birthday is an auspicious day ________ starting a new job.

8. My progress in college is impeded ________ the long hours I must work.

9. Vegetables are beneficial ________ one's health.

10. Because of the poverty of his childhood, the famous rap artist felt empathy ________ poor young people.

■ *Writing with Your Words*

To practice effective writing, complete each sentence with an interesting phrase that indicates the meaning of the italicized word.

1. The *pathetic* people ____
____.

2. Things that are *beneficial* to a person's mental state include________
____.

3. In a *conspicuous* display of wealth, ________________________________
____.

4. The *benefactor* ____
____.

5. The *anarchic* crowd ____
____.

6. I *despise* ____
____.

7. The lecture was *inaudible*, so ________________________________
____.

8. He had *empathy* for the disabled because ________________________

____.

9. We knew he was *apathetic* about work because ____________________

____.

10. My dog's *pedigree* ____

____.

■ *Making Connections*

To connect new vocabulary to your life, write extended responses to these questions.

1. What kind of person would you feel empathy for? Why?
2. Describe the most memorable malady you have ever had.
3. On which issue do you think the public is too apathetic? Why?

Passage

A New Language—of Silence

After generations of isolation, the deaf children of Nicaragua finally came together in a school—and created an entirely new language! Nicaraguan Sign Language shows us that communication does not depend on the ability to speak or hear.

Deafness has many causes. Some people are simply born with ears that are not formed properly; others suffer damage to the **auditory** nerve; **(1)** still others lose hearing from damage caused by tumors, even **benign** ones. The effects of **maladies** such as meningitis can cause a person to lose hearing. But whatever the cause, the deaf are condemned to live in a world of silence.

In addition to the **pathology** of deafness itself, **(2)** living in an **inaudible** world has negative effects on human beings. Without the ability to hear, deaf people struggle to develop the reasoning powers that depend so heavily on the give and take of human communication.

In some countries, schools for the deaf have taught the students to communicate through sign languages and lip reading. But deaf children do not always have access to this education. In Nicaragua, for example, generations of deaf children were kept at home, isolated and unschooled.

They typically developed only primitive signs to communicate. But in 1977 all that changed. Deaf children finally came together and, in an amazing feat of human intelligence, created the world's newest language!

How did this happen? The newly installed Sandinista government decided to establish the first Nicaraguan schools for the deaf. Several hundred children were enrolled, but **(3)** the instruction was **pathetically** ineffective. Based largely on finger spelling, the methods required knowledge of the alphabet, which deaf children did not possess. The teachers had terrible problems communicating with the children.

After a few months, though, the teachers began to notice that, in the halls and at recess, **(4)** the children were making **conspicuous** gestures to each other. These appeared to be a form of communication, but only the children understood them. **(5)** Was this an **anomaly** or a new language? Faculty invited linguist Judy Kegl in to study what was happening.

Kegl's work with the children showed that, despite the unsuitable instruction in the school, **(6)** simply bringing the children together had enormously **beneficial** effects. Beginning with a simple system of signs, the children had created their own communication system!

Most amazing, **(7)** the children's inability to hear or speak did not **impede** language creation. Children communicated with one another using their own, silent language. This language, which Kegl labeled Nicaraguan Sign Language (NSL), became more and more complex. **(8)** Its development was **expedited** as additional, younger children came into the community. Using the language taught to them by older children, the new users added layers of complexity. The language started to use advanced features such as subject-verb agreement and verb tenses.

The students are able to communicate complex ideas. Nine-year-old Yuri Maujia asks, "When are the alligators going to wake up? Every time I come to the park they are asleep." Twenty-year-old Anselmo Aleman comments on chess, "It's like war. You must concentrate or you lose." In contrast, a boy who has stayed at home and has not mastered NSL makes only personal signs for "catch," "tree," "river," and a gestured "whack."

Most linguists think that young children have the inborn capability to create language. **(9)** The development of NSL is **auspicious** evidence for this theory. The younger the children, the more of this language ability they have. In fact, everyday experience indicates that young children learn new languages easily, whereas adults struggle.

Unfortunately, the unique opportunity to study a newborn language has resulted in some controversy. In an effort to protect the new language of NSL, linguists like Judy Kegl have not tried to teach American Sign Language (ASL) to these children. ASL is used around the world for deaf children, and many argue that Nicaraguan children should learn it, too. Failure to teach the Nicaraguan children ASL is, in the opinion of some, **(10)** an almost **malicious** attempt to isolate them.

Others defend Kegl and her coworkers. In fact, Kegl has been a **benefactor** to the Nicaraguan deaf community. Her organization helped to establish a school where the children are taught entirely by deaf teachers, the very people who can best **empathize** with them.

Whatever the fate of NSL, the world has witnessed something miraculous. A small group of disabled children got together and, without any apparent effort, developed the world's newest language. It was the invention of our most creative language users—children.

■ *Exercise*

Each numbered sentence corresponds to a sentence in the passage. Fill in the letter of the choice that makes the sentence mean the same thing as its corresponding sentence in the passage.

1. Others lose hearing from damage caused by tumors, even _______ ones.
   a. badly treated b. noncancerous c. diseased d. helpful

2. Living in a(n) _______ world has negative effects on human beings.
   a. evil b. sick c. silent d. suffering

3. The instruction was _______ ineffective.
   a. hurriedly b. noticeably c. uncaringly d. pitifully

4. The children were making _______ gestures to each other.
   a. uncaring b. good c. silent d. noticeable

5. Was this a(n) _______ or a new language?
   a. abnormality b. feeling c. sickness d. uncaring attitude

6. Simply bringing the children together had enormously _______ effects.
   a. sympathetic b. harmful c. noticeable d. helpful

7. The children's inability to hear or speak did not _______ language.
   a. block b. help c. speed d. silence

8. Its development was _______.
   a. speeded up b. slowed down c. harmed d. examined

9. The development of NSL is _______ evidence for this theory.
   a. pitiful b. silent c. noticeable d. promising

10. It is an almost _______ attempt.
    a. uncaring b. unusual c. sick d. vicious

■ *Discussion Questions*

1. If you were a deaf child, would you prefer to live in the NSL community or with a family that could hear?
2. How did school affect the development of NSL? Give evidence for your answer.
3. Do you think that Nicaraguan children should be taught ASL? Why or why not?

INSIGHT INTO IDIOMS

Food

Eating is a necessary and frequent human activity, so it is not surprising that many idioms are associated with food. The potato, for example, has given us two idioms that are cited here. Another idiom, the *couch potato*, was coined by Tom Iacino in 1976 as a nickname for people so lazy that they just wanted to lie around and watch television. Following the invention of the term, a book entitled *The Official Couch Potato Handbook* was published, offering a humorous guide to pursuing this lazy life.

a. A *hot potato* is a sensitive and difficult issue that is hard to talk about.

b. A *half-baked* idea is not fully thought out.

c. When we are in difficulty, we are *in hot water*.

d. People who are strong and energetic are *feeling their oats*.

e. When we are disgusted with something, we are *fed up* with it.

f. To *go bananas* or to *go nuts* means to go crazy.

g. One's *salad days* are the days of one's youth.

h. To *take with a grain of salt* means not to take something seriously.

i. To *butter up* means to flatter somebody in an effort to make that person feel good.

Practice chapter words one more time by filling in the letter of the correct idiom into the blank before each sentence.

_____ 1. Road rage can cause drivers whose right-of-way is impeded to _________.

_____ 2. When he was elderly and suffering from many maladies, he thought back fondly to the _________ of his early twenties.

_____ 3. I despise your malicious actions and am thoroughly _________ with your behavior.

_____ 4. That dietary supplement is really beneficial to their energy level, and they are _________.

_____ 5. I caused lots of trouble when I was in school, so I have empathy for students who are frequently _________.

Links to more lists of English idioms and their meanings can be found at the Student Companion Website for this book: **www.cengage.com/devenglish/richek8e.**

CHAPTER 12

Word Elements: Speech and Writing

College students and professionals speak and write every day. Not surprisingly, English has many words to describe communication. The first part of this chapter covers three word elements related to the concept of speech. The second part focuses on two word elements connected to writing. Part 2 also presents three pairs of words that people often confuse and helps you learn to use these words correctly.

Chapter Strategy: Word Elements: Speech and Writing

Chapter Words:

Part 1

dict	contradict dictator edict	*voc, vok*	advocate invoke revoke vouch
log, loq, -logy	colloquial ecology loquacious monologue prologue		

Part 2

-gram, -graph, -graphy, graph	demographic epigram graphic	*Confusable Words*	affect effect conscience conscious imply infer
scrib, script	ascribe inscription manuscript		

Visit the Student Companion Website at **www.cengage.com/devenglish/richek8e** to test your knowledge of these words before you study, hear each word pronounced, find additional practice exercises, and access more information on words and topics.

Did You Know?

Shortening English

English speakers seem to prefer short words. The most widely used English words all have four or fewer letters. Listed from number one to ten, they are *the, of, and, a, to, in, is, you, that,* and *it.*

In fact, when an English word is used frequently, it is often shortened, or *clipped.* Many people now refer to *television* as *TV, telephone* as *phone,* and *Internet* as *net.* Most students use the word *exam* to refer to an *examination. Fax,* as in *fax machine,* has been shortened from *facsimile.*

Some words were clipped so long ago that people may not remember their original form. The word for a common malady, the *flu,* was clipped from *influenza.* A *bus* was once called an *omnibus,* and signs for *omnibuses* can still be seen in Scotland. The word *caravan* has been replaced by *van.* In the 1500s, Italian comedies featured a foolish character named *Pantaloon* who wore an unfashionable, loose-fitting garment to cover his legs. This piece of clothing became known as *pantaloons,* a word shortened to *pants* in the 1800s. For centuries, when people parted, they said, "God be with you" to each other. Four hundred years ago, this was shortened to "good-bye."

A relatively modern way to shorten expressions is to form an *acronym,* a series of words that are replaced by their initial letters. *Laser* stands for *l*ight *a*mplification by *s*imulated *e*mission of *r*adiation. *Radar* was created from the initials of *ra*dio *d*etection *a*nd *r*anging.

In business, an IPO is an *i*nitial *p*ublic *o*ffering of stock. In sports, a *scuba* diver uses a *s*elf-*c*ontained *u*nderwater *b*reathing *a*pparatus. If an athlete sprains a muscle, *"rice,"* meaning *r*est, *i*ce, *c*ompression, and *e*levation, is often prescribed.

Acronyms have also been devised for lifestyles. *Dinks* are *d*ouble *i*ncomes, *n*o *k*ids—that is, childless couples who both work outside the home. The U.S. census now counts the number of *POSSLQ*s, or unmarried *p*ersons of the *o*pposite *s*ex *s*haring *l*iving *q*uarters. Even political views have acronyms. People who favor reforms until they are personally affected are referred to as *NIMBY*s, or *n*ot *i*n *m*y *b*ack *y*ard.

Texting (short for *text messaging*) has dramatically increased the use of acronyms, as well as shortenings of all forms. These include such acronyms, often used by teens, as *AITR* for *adults in the room.*

Find the *longest* words in English and text message abbreviations at websites you can access through the Student Companion Website at **www.cengage.com/devenglish/richek8e.**

Learning Strategy

Word Elements: Speech and Writing

English has many word elements that are related to communication in oral and written form. Part 1 of this chapter concentrates on speech, and Part 2 addresses writing.

Element	*Meaning*	*Origin*	*Function*	*Chapter Words*
Part 1				
dict	speak	Latin	root	contradict, dictator, edict
log, loq, -logy	word; speak; study of	Greek; Latin	root; suffix	colloquial, ecology, loquacious, monologue, prologue
voc, vok	voice; call	Latin	root	advocate, invoke, revoke, vouch
Part 2				
-gram, -graph, -graphy, graph	write	Latin; Greek	suffix; root	demographic, epigram, graphic
scrib, script	write	Latin	root	ascribe, inscription, manuscript

Word Elements

Part 1

The word roots for Part 1 are explained in more detail here.

dict (speak)

This root appears in several common words. *Dictation* is something **spoken** by one person and written by another. *Diction* is the clearness and quality of one's **speech.**

log, loq, -logy (word; speak; study of)

The roots *log* and *loq* mean "word" or "speak." To be *eloquent* is to **speak** well. A *dialogue* is a conversation between two people. The suffix *-logy* means "study of." You may have taken courses in *biology* (the **study of** living things), *psychology* (the **study of** the mind), or *anthropology* (the **study of** human beings).

voc, vok (voice; call)

A record that contains the human **voice** speaking or singing is called a *vocal* recording. *Vocabulary,* meaning "things spoken by the **voice,**" or "words," also comes from *voc.* You will not confuse this root with the others if you remember to associate it with the word *voice.*

Words to Learn

Part 1

dict

1. **contradict** (verb) kŏn′trə-dĭkt′

   From Latin: *contra-* (against) + *dict* (speak)

   a. to say or put forth the opposite of something

   In court, the defendant **contradicted** the statement he had given police.

   Mike's excuse of being sick was **contradicted** by his mother, who said he was out playing football.

   It is not wise to **contradict** your boss in front of coworkers.

   b. to be contrary or inconsistent

   DNA samples from five-hundred-year-old bones in Spain **contradict** the Dominican Republic's claim that Christopher Columbus was buried there.

► *Related Words*

contradiction (noun) A tough boxer, yet a gentle caretaker of his children, he was a man of many *contradictions*.

contradictory (adjective) The children's *contradictory* stories made us suspect that neither was telling the truth.

Contradictory *Oxymorons*

Oxymorons are *contradictions* of language, or statements in which one word seems to *contradict* another. Examples are *definite maybe, sweet sorrow, exact estimate, jumbo shrimp, killing with kindness, tough love, dull shine, whole half, awfully good, devout atheist,* and *plastic silverware*.

Find other *oxymorons* through the Student Companion Website at **www.cengage.com/devenglish/richek8e.**

2. **dictator** (noun) dĭk′tā-tər

   From Latin: *dict* (speak) (A dictator is a ruler who speaks with power; whatever the ruler says is done.)

   a ruler with total authority

   Francisco Franco, the **dictator** of Spain from 1936 to 1975, established a government in which all cultural activities had to be approved.

▶ *Related Words*

dictatorial (adjective) (dĭk′tə-tôr′ē-əl) The project leader's *dictatorial* style alienated the students who worked with her.

dictatorship (noun) Josef Stalin established a *dictatorship* in the Soviet Union from 1928 to 1953.

dictate (verb) The conquering general *dictated* the terms of surrender.

dictates (noun, plural) "You don't always have to follow the latest fashion *dictates*," mom told her teenager.

3. **edict** (noun) ē′dĭkt′

From Latin: *e-* (out) + *dict* (speak)

an official order or command

In 1996, the Taliban government of Afghanistan issued an **edict** forbidding females from working or going to school.

The football player was suspended when he violated the league's safety **edict** against head butting.

An Edict *of Great Effect*

Edicts can have long-lasting effects. On May 4, 1493, Pope Alexander VI issued an edict dividing the "New World," or the Americas, between Spain and Portugal. Today these countries rule not one square inch of land in the Americas. However, their legacy remains. Most countries south of the United States are Spanish speaking. In Brazil, though, Portuguese is spoken.

log, loq, -logy

4. **colloquial** (adjective) kə-lō′kwē-əl

From Latin: *com-* (together) + *loq* (speak) (When we "speak together" with friends, our speech is colloquial.)

informal in speech or expression

Text messages typically are written in **colloquial** language.

▶ *Related Word*

colloquialism (noun) "Hang a right" is a *colloquialism* that means "turn right."

5. **ecology** (noun) ĭ-kŏl′ə-jē (plural: **ecologies**)

From Greek: *oikos* (house) + *-logy* (study of) (Ecology is concerned with the environment, the "home" or "house" in which we all live.)

the relationship of living things and their environment; the study of this relationship

Naturally occurring fires play a key role in the **ecology** of forests.

In 2006, when the **ecology** of Siberian Lake Baikal was threatened by a pipeline, Marina Rikhvanova campaigned successfully to have it moved.

► *Related Words*

ecological (adjective) (ĕk′ə-lŏj′ĭ-kəl) Rain containing a high level of acid has ruined the *ecological* balance of many lakes and ponds.

ecologist (noun) *Ecologists* have established that alewives, fish once considered a nuisance, play an essential role in Lake Michigan's food chain.

Coltan and Ecology

A search for columbite-tantalite, or "coltan," is dramatically affecting the *ecology* of Central Africa. This metallic ore is used in cell phones. Searching for coltan, laborers dig up land, destroying soil and trees, as well as polluting streams. Farmers are driven from their homes when competing military factions battle for control of coltan reserves. In response, a campaign of "No blood on my cell phone" has been launched to prevent the use of coltan. However, there are conflicting *ecological* and economic interests. Coltan mining harms the land but provides badly needed work for people.

6. **loquacious** (adjective) lō-kwā′shəs

From Greek: *loq-* (speak)

very talkative

The talk show host silenced the **loquacious** guest by calling for a commercial.

► *Related Word*

loquaciousness (noun) The *loquaciousness* of the two teenagers annoyed the man who was trying to read in the airplane.

7. **monologue** (noun) mŏn′ə-lôg′

From Greek: *mono* (one) + *log* (speak)

a speech or performance by one person

At the club meeting, the president unexpectedly started the meeting with a twenty-minute **monologue** about the need to change the rules.

In Hamlet's **monologue** "To be or not to be," Shakespeare examines the mind of a person who cannot make a decision.

Aaron was skilled at delivering funny and expressive *monologues*.

Courtesy author

8. **prologue** (noun) prō′lôg′

    From Greek: *pro-* (before) + *log* (speak)

    a. the introduction to a literary or artistic work

        If you skip the **prologue**, you won't understand the reasons the author wrote the novel.

    b. an introductory event

        The qualifying race is a **prologue** to the actual competition.

    ▶ *Common Phrase*
    prologue to

voc, vok

9. **advocate** (verb) ăd′və-kāt′; (noun) ăd′və-kĭt

    From Latin: *ad-* (toward) + *voc* (to voice, call)

    a. to urge publicly; to argue for (verb)

        The senator **advocated** for improved veteran's benefits.

        Several public interest groups **advocate** increased funding for education.

    b. a person who urges a cause (noun)

        Food safety **advocates** worked for increased inspections of the meat and produce sold in supermarkets.

        I am an **advocate** of free speech.

▶ *Common Phrases*
advocate for (verb); an advocate of (noun)

NOTE: An *advocate* can also mean a lawyer who pleads a case.

10. **invoke** (verb) ĭn-vōk′

From Latin: *in-* (in) + *voc* (to call) (*Invocāre* means "to call upon.")

to call in assistance; to call upon

The manager **invoked** the aid of the security guards to remove the violent man from the store.

Martin Luther King's "I Have a Dream" speech powerfully **invoked** the core values of the United States.

▶ *Related Word*
invocation (noun) (ĭn′və-kā′shən) The priest gave an *invocation*. (*Invocation* means "to call on a higher power," as in prayer.)

Invoking *the Fifth Amendment*

The Fifth Amendment to the U.S. Constitution states that those accused of a crime cannot be forced to testify against themselves. Thus, when asked a question whose answer may injure their case or make them appear guilty, accused people may "*invoke* the Fifth Amendment" and refuse to answer.

11. **revoke** (verb) rĭ-vōk′

From Latin: *re-* (back) + *vok* (to call)

to cancel or withdraw

Olympic Games officials **revoke** the medals of athletes who test positive for illegal drugs.

▶ *Related Word*
revocation (noun) (rĕv′ə-kā′shən) Using foul language in an online forum can lead to the *revocation* of membership.

12. **vouch** (verb) vouch

From Latin: *voc* (call)

a. to give personal assurances

I can **vouch** for my friend's honesty.

When an employer **vouched** for me, I was admitted into the United States on an H1B visa that permitted me to work.

b. to support with evidence

Online reviewers **vouch** for the excellent service at the hotel.

► *Related Word*
voucher (noun) Food stamps are issued as *vouchers*. (A *voucher* is a promise or a proof of payment.)

► *Common Phrase*
vouch for

Exercises

Part 1

■ *Definitions*

Match the word and definition. Use each choice only once.

1. ecology _______
2. revoke _______
3. loquacious _______
4. dictator _______
5. prologue _______
6. edict _______
7. monologue _______
8. colloquial _______
9. advocate _______
10. invoke _______

a. to call in assistance
b. speech by one person
c. to give personal assurances
d. informal
e. the relationship of living things and their environment
f. to say something opposite
g. ruler with total authority
h. very talkative
i. introduction to book or play
j. to recommend; to plead for
k. official order
l. to cancel

■ *Meanings*

Match each word element to its definition. Use each choice only once.

1. dict _______
2. log, loq, -logy _______
3. voc, vok _______

a. voice; call
b. speak
c. word; speak; study of

■ *Words in Context*

Complete each sentence with the best word. Use each choice only once.

a. contradict	e. ecology	i. advocate
b. dictator	f. loquacious	j. invoke
c. edict	g. monologue	k. revoke
d. colloquial	h. prologue	l. vouch

1. State officials may ____________________ the assistance of the federal government during hurricanes, floods, tornados, and other natural disasters.

2. Since the results of the two experiments ____________________ each other, we had better investigate further.

3. I am a(n) ____________________ of rights for children and adults with disabilities.

4. Since the gambling casino owners were involved in illegal activities, officials moved to ____________________ their license.

5. I can ____________________ that the suspect was with me on the night of the crime.

6. I thought we were both going to talk, but instead you seem to be delivering a(n) ____________________.

7. The city government of Guanajuato, Mexico, issued a(n) ____________ forbidding people to kiss romantically in public.

8. The ____________________ beautician talked nonstop as she cut my hair.

9. The 1929 stock market crash was the ____________________ to the Great Depression of the 1930s.

10. Students should use formal rather than ____________________ English when they write term papers.

■ *Using Related Words*

Complete each sentence with the correct form. Use each choice only once. You may have to capitalize some words.

1. ecology, ecological, ecologists

Changes in ______________ have negatively affected Minnesota moose. Over the last twenty years, summers have cooled four degrees, and winters twelve degrees. ______________ find that this weather change has been a disaster for the moose, whose population has decreased from four thousand to fewer than one hundred. These ______________ changes also affect the water supply, and the amount of shade. When the weather gets too warm for them, the moose do not move north, but rather stop reproducing.

2. revoked, revocation

Tom and Elizabeth Preston went through all the right steps to get a permit for their tattoo studio. After the approval, they invested over $25,000. To their shock, the city of Tempe, Arizona, suddenly ______________ their permit! So they went to court. Two years later, a judge decided that the ______________ was illegal and arbitrary. The studio is expected to open soon after this writing.

3. colloquial, colloquialisms

Farmers have invented many ______________ for weather. "White plague," a play on words for the disease known as the "black plague," is a ______________ expression for "hail," which causes much destruction of crops. Residents of Wisconsin and Michigan call rain that falls after March 31 "time-release rain" because it is well timed for crop growth.

4. dictators, dictatorial, dictatorship

Cuba has been governed by what many consider to be two ______________. Fulgencio Batista ruled the country from 1933 to 1944 and, after a coup, again from 1952 to 1959. Under his

_______________ rule, U.S. interests were served, but the Cuban population was mired in poverty. Overthrowing Batista in 1959, Fidel Castro established a Communist state. Many consider his rule

also to be a _______________.

5. vouched, vouch, voucher

   Anyone who has driven an older SUV or minivan can

   _______________ for how often the gas tank needs filling. In 2009, the U.S. Congress offered an incentive to buy fuel-efficient cars.

   The bill gave people a _______________ if they bought a car that gets more than twenty-seven miles per gallon. Many people have

   _______________ that a monetary gift of several thousand dollars provided an incentive to save gas.

6. contradicted, contradictory, contradiction

   The great, well-known architect Frank Lloyd Wright is a study in

   _______________. His masterful artistic achievements often were

   _______________ by his disturbing private behavior. He left his family for the wife of a client. He accumulated debts and did not fulfill his contracts. Wright's example shows that public

   achievements and private behavior may be _______________.

■ *Reading the Headlines*

Here are some headlines that might appear in newspapers. Read each and answer the questions. (Remember that small words, such as *is*, *are*, *a*, and *the*, are often left out of headlines.)

INDUSTRY ADVOCATE VOUCHES THAT NEW FACTORY WILL NOT AFFECT ECOLOGICAL CONDITIONS

1. Does the person work to harm the industry? _______
2. Is the advocate giving assurances? _______
3. Do conditions deal with the environment? _______

DICTATOR ISSUES EDICT BANNING COLLOQUIALISMS

4. Does the dictator lack power? _______

5. Did the dictator issue a suggestion? _______

6. Is informal language allowed? _______

LONG MONOLOGUE IS PROLOGUE TO PLAY'S ACTION

7. Does the monologue come before the play's action? _______

8. Is the prologue delivered by many different people? _______

INVOKING A NEW LAW, SUPREME COURT CONTRADICTS PREVIOUS RULING

9. Did the Supreme Court change its ruling? _______

10. Does the Supreme Court use the justification of a law? _______

Word Elements

Part 2

The second part of this chapter presents two word elements relating to the concept of writing. Then it introduces three pairs of easily confused words that college students often have trouble distinguishing.

-gram, -graph, -graphy, graph (write)

This suffix has three spellings. It is spelled *-gram,* as in *telegram,* a **written** message sent by wires. (*Tele-* means "far.") The spelling *-graph* is used in *autograph,* a person's signature, or "self-**writing.**" (*Auto* means "self.") Finally, the suffix can be spelled *-graphy,* as in *photography* (literally, "**writing** in light"). *Graph* can also function as a root.

Graffiti, that often illegal writing that appears in elevators, on overpasses and walls, and, of course, in bathrooms, has plagued us throughout history. The word *graffiti* comes, through Italian, from the word element *graph.* Archaeologists have discovered the name of Padihorpakhered, who, identifying himself as a powerful Egyptian priest, carved on the sandstone sides of a monument in Thebes 2,700 years ago. Thus, like *graffiti* writers of today, he assured himself notice.

scrib, script (write)

This root is found in many common words. A *script* is the **written** form of a television program, movie, or play. When small children make **written** marks, they often *scribble.*

Words to Learn

Part 2

-gram, -graph, -graphy, graph

13. **demographic** (adjective) dĕm′ə-grăf′ĭk

From Greek: *demos* (people) + *-graph* (write)

referring to population characteristics

Demographic studies showed that by 2002 Hispanics had become the largest ethnic minority in the United States.

► *Related Words*

demography (noun) (dĭ-mŏg′rə-fē) The U.S. Census Bureau is working to update data on *demography* every year, rather than every ten years.

demographer (noun) *Demographers* analyze census data.

demographics (noun, plural) U.S. *demographics* reveal that an increasing percentage of people are choosing to remain single.

NOTE: In an informal usage, the word **demographic** is now used as a noun, as in "The Star Trek series is hoping to attract a younger *demographic*."

14. **epigram** (noun) ĕp′ĭ-grăm′

From Greek: *epi-* (on) + *-gram* (write)

a short, clever saying, often in rhyme

"He that goes a-borrowing, goes a-sorrowing" is an **epigram** that warns against debt.

"A second marriage is the triumph of hope over experience" is an **epigram** attributed to Samuel Johnson.

15. **graphic** (adjective, noun) grăf′ĭk

From Greek: *graph* (write) (*Graphe* meant "drawing, writing.")

a. referring to drawings or artistic writing (adjective)

The website gives a map that describes the route in **graphic** form.

b. described vividly or clearly (adjective)

Graphic scenes of sex or violence usually earn a film an "R" or "X" rating.

The witness's **graphic** description of the crime shocked the jury.

c. artistic design or drawing (noun)

The "swoosh" **graphic** has come to symbolize the Nike brand.

scrib, script

16. **ascribe** (verb) ə-skrīb′

From Latin: *a-* (toward) + *scrib* (write)

a. to attribute to; to credit

A quote commonly **ascribed** to Shakespeare, "all that glitters is not gold," should actually read "all that glisters is not gold."

Physicians **ascribed** the sudden increase in allergy symptoms to increased pollen in the air.

b. to assign as a quality or characteristic

In the plays he wrote, Tennessee Williams **ascribed** tension, poverty, and passion to the city of New Orleans.

▶ *Common Phrase*
ascribe to

17. **inscription** (noun) ĭn-skrĭp′shən

From Latin: *in-* (in) + *script* (write)

a. carving or engraving into a surface

Visitors to the Vietnam War memorial in Washington, D.C. can run their fingers over the **inscription** of each fallen soldier's name in the stone.

b. a signed message on a picture or in a book

At the book signing, the author wrote short **inscriptions** such as "Hope you enjoy this book," inside the cover of her new novel.

▶ *Related Word*
inscribe (verb) (ĭn-skrīb′) Darby found his great grandparents' marriage *inscribed* in the town records. (*Inscribe* can mean to enter formally.)
Atif, an excellent student who died in a car accident, has *inscribed* himself in Professor Judy MacDonald's memory.

Mannie Garcia/Stringer/Getty Images

This *inscription*, found at the 9/11 memorial site at the Pentagon, commemorates the victims of the terrorist attack.

18. **manuscript** (noun, adjective) măn′yə-skrĭpt′

From Latin: *manu* (by hand) + *script* (write)

a. the original text of a book or article before publication (noun)

Army officials read the book **manuscript** to assess whether publication would reveal any defense secrets.

The Karpeles museum of **manuscripts** holds such important documents as the original Bill of Rights and Webster's dictionary. (Here, *manuscript* means the original, handwritten copy.)

b. referring to writing done by hand, or printing (adjective)

Beautiful medieval **manuscript** lettering took years to master.

Children use **manuscript** writing until they learn cursive in the third grade.

An Unusual Manuscript

In 1951, Jack Kerouac produced a manuscript for his book *On the Road* that consisted of a single, continuous 120-foot long scroll of paper. This item recently sold for $2,200,000 at an auction.

Confusable Words

19. **affect** (verb) ə-fĕkt′

to have an influence on; to change

The moon **affects** ocean tides.

20. **effect** (noun) ĭ-fĕkt′

a result

The moon has an **effect** on ocean tides.

NOTE: Try to remember that *affect* is usually a verb and *effect* is usually a noun, as in the following.

The great teacher *affected* my life.

The great teacher had an *effect* on my life.

▶ *Common Phrase*
effect on

Edible Special Effects

Food can be used to produce special effects in movies. Mixing milk with water made the rain more noticeable in the 1952 movie *Singin' in the Rain*. The blood in the movie *Psycho* (1960) looks thick because the mixture contained Hershey's chocolate. And that awful sound we hear of bashing in heads in horror movies? It's a watermelon being hit by a hammer!

21. **conscience** (noun) kŏn′shəns

sense of right and wrong; moral sense

The child's guilty **conscience** made her return the candy bar she had taken from a friend's lunch box.

▶ *Related Word*
conscientious (adjective) (kŏn′shē-ĕn′shəs) Anna's good grades could largely be due to her *conscientious* class attendance. (*Conscientious* can mean thorough and careful.)

22. **conscious** (adjective) kŏn′shəs

aware; awake

The teenager was **conscious** of the fact that shoplifting was wrong.

Marsha was **conscious** of the tension in the room.

We are not **conscious** when we sleep.

▶ *Common Phrase*
conscious of

▶ *Related Word*
consciousness (noun) The man in the coma regained **consciousness** after three months.
unconscious (adjective) The man was knocked **unconscious** after he fell from the ladder.) (*Unconscious* is the opposite of *conscious*.)

NOTE: Remember that *conscience* is a noun and *conscious* is an adjective, as in the following sentence.

My *conscience* bothers me when I am *conscious* that I have done wrong.

23. **imply** (verb) ĭm-plī′

to suggest; to say something indirectly

The man's tilted head and shy smile **implied** that he was attracted to the woman.

Grandma's statement that we needed to speak louder **implied** that she wasn't wearing her hearing aid.

▶ *Related Word*
implication (noun) (ĭm′plĭ-kā′shən) Professor Lois Daly feels that the *Star Trek* series has many religious *implications*.

NOTE: The *y* of *imply* changes to *i* in the third-person singular (He *implies*), past tense (I *implied*), and noun form (*implication*).

24. **infer** (verb) ĭn-fûr′

to conclude; to guess

People **inferred** from the man's tilted head and shy smile that he was attracted to the woman.

▶ *Related Words*
inference (noun) (ĭn′fər-əns) The chemistry student drew an *inference* from the results of her experiment.
inferential (adjective) (ĭn′fə-rĕn′shəl) This difficult problem requires *inferential* thinking.

NOTE: A speaker or writer *implies*; a listener or reader *infers*.

▶ *Common Phrases*
draw an inference; infer from

An Implication *and an* Inference *About a Famous Book*

James Joyce's *Ulysses* was voted the most important book of the twentieth century by the prestigious Modern Library. About the same time, it was reported that many original copies of the book, given by Joyce to publishers and friends, had uncut pages. These pages, joined at the edges, have to be separated in order to be read. This strongly *implies* that, indeed, the great masterpiece was not read by many people. From the location of the uncut pages, we can *infer* that some people started the book but read fewer than one hundred pages.

Exercises

Part 2

■ *Definitions*

Match the word and definition. Use each choice only once.

1. conscious ______
2. inscription ______
3. manuscript ______
4. infer ______
5. affect ______
6. graphic ______
7. epigram ______
8. ascribe ______
9. demographic ______
10. conscience ______

a. short, witty saying
b. a sense of right and wrong
c. to attribute to; to credit
d. to draw a conclusion
e. to hint
f. referring to drawings or charts
g. carving on a surface
h. text of a book before publication
i. to influence
j. a result
k. referring to population statistics
l. aware

■ *Words in Context*

Fill each sentence with the best word. Use each choice only once.

a. demographic
b. epigram
c. graphic
d. ascribe
e. inscription
f. manuscript
g. affect
h. effect
i. conscience
j. conscious
k. imply
l. infer

1. Rita had a guilty ____________________ after she ate all of Steve's birthday cake.

2. "Rita, were you ____________________ of the fact that that birthday cake was for your brother Steve?"

3. When you use a quotation in your paper, be careful to ____________ it to the original author.

4. We ____________________ from the annoyed tone in your voice that you are angry with us.

5. An annoyed tone in somebody's voice will often ________________ that he is angry.

6. Benjamin Franklin's ____________________ on hard work is "Little strokes fell great oaks."

7. The ____________________ description of the dirt and crime in the slum helped the organization raise money to aid people who lived there.

8. I try not to let distractions ____________________ my ability to study.

9. I don't think the distractions will have a(n) ____________________ on my ability to study.

10. This Dead Sea Scroll is a(n) ____________________ of the Bible made over two thousand years ago.

■ *Using Related Words*

Complete each sentence with the correct form. Use each choice only once. Capitalize letters where necessary.

1. inscription, inscribed

The first U.S. coin bearing a Spanish ________________ was coined in 2009. This quarter, which honors Puerto Rico, is

________________ with the words "Isla del Encanto," or "Island of Enchantment."

2. demographics, demographic, demography, demographers

   The Pew Researcher Center has a group of ________________ who analyze census statistics. Among their findings are that if current ________________ trends continue, the population of the United States will be 438 million in 2050. Further, 82 percent of the increase will consist of immigrants and their descendants, according to new projections. These ________________ suggest the large role immigrants play in the ________________ of the U.S. population.

3. infer, imply

   When a plane crashes, the Federal Aviation Administration tries to ________________ the cause. An accident may be due to human or mechanical failure, and loss of life can be great. However, statistics ________________ that passengers are still safer riding in a plane than driving a car.

4. consciences, conscientious

   Early Protestant settlers in America were said to have had a "Protestant work ethic." According to this, their ________________ would bother them if they did not work hard enough. Thus, these people were generally ________________ workers.

5. affect, effect

   Which has a greater ________________ on a person, heredity or environment? In the 1800s and early 1900s, scientists believed that heredity had a far greater influence. Since then, environment has been shown to ________________ people strongly. For example, a study done by Skeels in the 1930s showed that when children placed in an orphanage were given loving attention, their IQs increased dramatically.

■ *Find the Example*

Choose the example that best describes the action or situation.

1. An epigram that implies danger _______
   a. "That toy is harmful to children" b. "That toy's good for a boy!"
   c. "That toy may destroy."

2. A graphic manuscript _______
   a. an action novel b. copy of proposed law on land use
   c. romance novel submitted to publisher for approval

3. What people would be most likely to infer if an author ascribed his insights to others _______
   a. ideas don't work b. author is original c. author is honest

4. Inscription that implies love _______
   a. "To my one and only" carved on a watch
   b. "My wife is the best," said on a TV show
   c. "I love you," carved on a picture frame

5. Demographic effect of a huge earthquake _______
   a. water and food are not available
   b. plates under the Earth hit each other
   c. population of area goes down

Chapter Exercises

■ *Practicing Strategies: New Words from Word Elements*

Use your knowledge of word elements to determine the meanings of these words and complete each sentence. Use each choice only once.

a. climatology	e. graphology	i. scribe
b. dialogue	f. malediction	j. travelogue
c. diction	g. pictograph	k. vocalist
d. graphite	h. revocalized	l. *vox populi*

1. People who do not know how to write may dictate their letters to a(n) _________________.

2. The material _________________ is used for writing in lead pencils.

3. When people talk about their trips, they give a(n) _________________.

4. In the science of ____________________ people study weather conditions.

5. A ____________________ sings lyrics, or gives "voice" to them.

6. Ancient human beings used ____________________ writing based on drawings.

7. The ____________________ musical background was sung again.

8. Some people believe that ____________________, the study of handwriting, can reveal things about people's character and future.

9. A(n) ____________________, or "bad speech," is a curse.

10. The ____________________ refers to the popular sentiment, or "voice" of the people.

■ *Practicing Strategies: Context Clues and Word Elements*

In each sentence, one word is italicized. Use the meaning of the word element and the context to make an intelligent guess about its meaning.

1. Delivering a *eulogy* at his grandfather's funeral, Winston said many wonderful things about him.

   Eulogy means ____

   ____.

2. Three people discussed their opinions in the *interlocution*.

   Interlocution means ____.

3. The bride hired a *calligrapher* to address the invitations so that they would look beautiful when they arrived in the mail.

   Calligrapher means ____.

   The next two items are from newspaper sources.

4. The New Zealand *entomologist* known as "The Bug Man" stars in his own program premiering Wednesday at 7 p.m. on Animal Planet.

   Entomologist means ____.

5. "We do this *colloquium* two or three times a year, a combination of a course and public lecture series," said program moderator Kate Kane.

   Colloquium means ______________________________

   ______________________________.

■ *Companion Words*

Complete each sentence with the best word. You may use choices more than once, and some items may have more than one correct answer. Choices: of, on, to, draw, for.

1. Parents are often conscious ________ their baby's every movement.
2. I can vouch ________ the fact that sleeping on a floor is uncomfortable.
3. After the revocation ________ civil liberties, people fled the country.
4. He ascribes his success ________ hard work.
5. Criticism can have a harmful effect ________ children.
6. Lightning is a prologue ________ thunder.
7. I am an advocate ________ women's equality.
8. What inference can you ________ from the evidence?

■ *Writing with Your Words*

To practice effective writing, complete each sentence with an interesting phrase that indicates the meaning of the italicized word.

1. People often *ascribe* their failure to get work done to ______________

   ______________________________.

2. Her *monologue* was interrupted when ______________________________

   ______________________________.

3. My favorite *colloquial* expression is ______________________________

   ____.

4. One thing I am *conscious* of that bothers my *conscience* is __________

   ____.

5. I found the rare *manuscript* among ______________________________

   ____.

6. People *imply* that others are not worthy of respect when __________

   ____.

7. The *dictator's edict* ______________________________________

   ____.

8. I knew she was *loquacious* when ______________________________

   ____.

9. The ancient *inscription* read ________________________________

   ____.

10. The *ecologist advocated* ____________________________________

    ____.

■ *Making Connections*

To connect new vocabulary to your life, write extended responses to these questions.

1. Describe a cause or position you advocate. Why do you feel it is important?
2. Do you feel that graphic scenes of violence in video games are harmful? Why or why not?
3. Under what circumstances would you contradict an elder, such as a grandparent, to whom you wanted to show respect?

Passage

Planting the Green Belt

Wangari Maathai is helping to save the environment of Kenya, one tree at a time. Her efforts have won her a Nobel Prize—and a life of danger.

As a child, Wangari Maathai admired the natural beauty of her native village in Kenya. But, twenty years later, widespread destruction of trees had dramatically **affected** the landscape. Forests had been replaced by dry, hard dirt; broad rivers had become narrow, dirt-filled streams. Matthai thought of a simple plan: plant trees to hold the water and soil. Forty-five million trees later, Maathai has become a world-renowned figure, and trees are helping to improve the **ecology** throughout Africa.

Born into a humble family in Nyeri, Kenya, Maathai spent her childhood gathering water and wood to help grow crops and cook food. Her academic skills, however, brought her notice, and she was sent on a scholarship to the United States. At that time, in the 1960s, **(1)** the environmental movement was just entering public **consciousness.** Maathai listened, learned, and thought of her homeland. Returning to Kenya, she became the first woman from east Africa to earn a Ph.D. **(2)** This was the **prologue** to many other firsts.

Wangari Maathai's efforts on behalf of human rights and the environment have made her a world-renowned figure.

AP Photo/John McConnico

Maathai became a professor and began to work in community groups. She noticed that the needs of poor and humble women in Kenya were being ignored, so she started to **advocate** for them. **(3)** Her efforts gave voice to a **demographic** group that is often ignored. In 1977, seeking to aid their lives by improving the environment, she began a campaign by planting seven trees. **(4)** She **invoked** the aid of women throughout Kenya to follow her lead.

Why did she choose trees? Trees play a crucial part in **ecological** systems. Their roots break up rocks into soil and help to hold this soil. In turn, the soil stores water and minerals for plants. Fruit trees provide food, and forests shelter birds and animals that can be used as food. The wood of tree branches is also a critical source of fuel. Finally, trees are beautiful. **(5)** The poet Joyce Kilmer wrote the **epigram:**

I think that I shall never see
A poem as lovely as a tree.

But in Kenya, widespread cutting down of trees was done to sell lumber and to build commercial property. As a result, soil washed away into rivers, and these rivers narrowed as they filled with silt. In addition, with fewer trees nearby, women often had to walk several miles a day to gather firewood. Trees were critical to life in Kenya, and they needed to be replaced.

Planting a tree can be done by anyone, woman or man, rich or poor. Because of her own background **(6)** Maathai could speak **colloquially** to poor women. They listened—and began to plant. With new trees came improvements in their lives and those of their families. Maathai insisted that her organization, "Green Belt," be controlled by the local women who planted the trees. Women were paid for trees that survived, and the recordkeeping, payment system, and distribution of trees provided jobs.

Her efforts to protect the environment soon forced Maathai into politics. In 1989, Daniel Arap Moi, the **dictator** who ruled Kenya, decided to destroy Nhuru Park, Kenya's largest green space, to build an industrial area. The new area was supposed to feature a four-story statue of himself! Maathai protested so effectively **(7)** that foreign investors **revoked** their promises of funding for the new buildings and the park remained.

As Maathai can **vouch**, Kenya at this time was a dangerous place. Her courage can be **inferred** from many brave actions. In 1992, Moi plotted to assassinate opposition leaders, including Maathai. She, along with others, revealed the plot in a public press conference. Moi then had some of them arrested, so Maathi barricaded herself in her house. Police surrounded her home and, after three days, broke through and arrested her. She was released only after an international outcry.

Despite the danger, Maathai continued to follow her **conscience**. Later that year, Moi arrested men who were trying to establish democracy. To attract attention, Maathai led a group of their mothers in a protest and hunger strike. Some actually showed their bare breasts to police,

implying that the government's actions were as shameful to grown men as sons being disrespectful to the women who breastfed them as infants. This time, Maathai was beaten **unconscious**. To publicize the brutaility, she held a press conference from her hospital bed. **(8)** The photographs of her bandaged head were a **graphic** display of violence in Kenya. The strategy worked: the arrested men were released in 1993. **(9)** In large part, this must be **ascribed** to Maathai's efforts.

The planting of millions of new trees has helped poor women and their families to eat well and farm successfully. People in over thirty other countries have participated in the "Green Belt" campaign and experienced its positive **effects**. In 2004, Wangari Maathai was the first African woman to be awarded the Nobel Peace Prize. **(10) Inscribed** above the entrance to the Nobel Center in Norway are the words "Broadmindedness. Hope. Commitment." Wangari Maathai has demonstrated all of these.

And, of course, to celebrate winning the prize, she planted a tree!

■ *Exercise*

Each numbered sentence corresponds to a sentence in the passage. Fill in the letter of the choice that makes the sentence mean the same thing as its corresponding sentence in the passage.

1. The environmental movement was just entering public _______.
   a. argument b. pressure c. sense of right and wrong
   d. awareness

2. This was the _______ many other firsts.
   a. introduction to b. talk about c. assurance of d. hint of

3. Her efforts gave voice to a _______ group.
   a. environmental b. population c. moral d. talkative

4. She _______ the aid of women throughout Kenya.
   a. argued for b. gave credit for c. took back d. called upon

5. The poet Joyce Kilmer wrote the _______.
   a. clever rhyme b. stone carving c. unfinished book d. speech

6. Maathai could speak _______ to poor women.
   a. orders b. against evidence c. informally d. vividly

7. Foreign investors _______ their promises of funding.
   a. supported b. took back c. credited d. urged

8. The photographs of her bandaged head were a _______ display of violence.
   a. visual b. loud c. believable d. hinted

9. In large part, this must be _______ Maathai's efforts.
   a. credited to b. written about c. ordered by d. made aware of by

10. _______ above the entrance to the Nobel Center in Norway are words.
   a. Carved b. Ordered c. Placed d. Drawn

■ *Discussion Questions*

1. Maathai is a simple person and yet a complex one. Illustrate this with one example that shows each trait.
2. Why do you think Maathai would be more interested in empowering women than men?
3. Maathai has compared herself to a hummingbird that makes several trips, each time bringing back one drop of water to put out a forest fire. What do you think she means by this comparison?

INSIGHT INTO IDIOMS

Communication

There are hundreds of idioms about speech and writing that use language in creative ways. To *talk turkey* means to speak the truth about a difficult subject in a matter-of-fact manner. At one time, though, it meant to make friendly conversation. The idiom *talk turkey* has also given its name to a blog devoted to news about the country Turkey.

a. To *talk up* something means to advertise it positively, making it appear to be excellent.

b. When we *talk over* a problem, we discuss it for quite a while.

c. When we *talk him out of* something, we persuade him not to do it.

d. When a person is *talking through his hat* he doesn't know the facts, but makes unsupported or untrue statements anyway.

e. A person who *talks turkey* speaks the truth frankly.

f. When we say it's *nothing to write home about* we mean that we do not think something is very good.

g. To say *the handwriting is on the wall* means that it can be predicted.

Practice chapter words one more time by filling in the letter of the correct idiom into the blank before each sentence.

_____ 1. She is so loquacious that I predict she will want to __________ the matter for several days.

_____ 2. As the student's advocate, the professor will probably __________ her thesis, even though it isn't very original.

_____ 3. He may sound well informed, but I can vouch for the fact that he is just __________

_____ 4. Since the manuscript is __________, the publisher will probably reject it.

_____ 5. I can vouch for the fact that it is wise to finish college, so I will try to __________ quitting.

Links to more lists of English idioms and their meanings can be found at the Student Companion Website for this book: **www.cengage.com/devenglish/richek8e.**

REVIEW

Chapters 9–12

■ *Passage for Word Review*

Complete each blank in the passage with the word or phrase that makes the best sense. Use each choice only once.

WHY MY STEPFATHER WAS COURT-MARTIALED

a. affect	e. conspicuous	i. effect
b. audit	f. destitute	j. given carte blanche
c. beneficial	g. deviating	k. malicious
d. centigrade	h. dictated	l. verify

Background: This is a memorial tribute to the author's stepfather, Milton Markman. A few hours after this story was told to the author's vocabulary class, the elderly Mr. Markman collapsed unexpectedly and died.

In 1941, when my stepfather was drafted into the U.S. Army, he had no interest or experience in cooking. Therefore, he was surprised when told that his results on a written aptitude test **(1)** ____________________ that he become a chef. Army officials offered him a six-week course in cooking. My stepfather accepted because he was sure he would be able to eat lots of leftovers.

As things turned out, he received good grades in cooking school. He became head chef of an army kitchen and was **(2)** ____________________ to run things as he wanted. All went well until he had to deal with spinach. Because spinach contains many vitamins that are **(3)** ________________ to human health, the army supplied it several times per week. Unfortunately, the soldiers refused to eat it.

After many hours spent cooking spinach, my stepfather realized that he was throwing all of it away. To save time and effort, he decided simply to dispose of the hated vegetable before it was cooked.

Unfortunately, one day a visiting army officer, passing through the camp, noticed a large, **(4)** ____________________ pile of raw spinach in the garbage. Another officer was sent out to **(5)** ____________________ that the first officer had seen everything correctly. Then an army accountant made an official **(6)** ____________________ of the amount that was missing from the raw spinach supply. At the end of this investigation, the army accused my stepfather of destroying government property!

At his court-martial my stepfather told the army officers that his intentions had not been **(7)** ____________________. Instead, he was simply trying to save the army the trouble of cooking unwanted food. Nevertheless, the army officers found him guilty and deducted five dollars from his pay for the next three months. Because he did not have much money, this loss of pay was enough to have a considerable (8) ____________ on his finances.

After the trial, however, one officer talked to my stepfather privately and told him that cooking spinach would **(9)** ____________________the way that the army thought about the vegetable. Raw spinach was government property, but cooked spinach was considered garbage. In other words, if the spinach was cooked, it could be thrown out.

From then on, my stepfather cooked all the spinach and then immediately put it into a garbage can. By following this procedure without **(10)** ____________________, he kept everyone happy. The government did not have its property thrown out, and the soldiers did not have spinach on their plates.

■ *Reviewing Words in Context*

Complete each sentence with the word or term that fits best. Use each answer choice only once.

AN ETHIOPIAN'S JOURNEY TO THE UNITED STATES

a. ambivalent	e. colloquial	i. defied	m. expedite
b. benefactors	f. conscious	j. destitute	n. fidelity
c. beneficial	g. creed	k. edict	o. malady
d. bilingual	h. decades	l. empathy	p. nonchalant

Background: Semir, a student in the author's class, tells the story of his family's journey from Ethiopia to Saudi Arabia and the United States.

1. Ethiopia, my home, is not like the United States. It is an underdeveloped country with many ____________________ people who live in poverty.

2. For three ____________________, almost thirty years, there was civil war in my homeland.

3. A(n) ____________________ issued by the ruler ordered all young men into the army; to avoid this, my father escaped to Saudi Arabia.

4. As a teenager, my mother must have ____________________ authority, for she spent time in prison.

5. My aunt was ____________________ of the fact that my mother would be in danger when she left prison, so she worked to get her out of Ethiopia.

6. My aunt tried hard to ____________________ her departure.

7. My mother went to Saudi Arabia and married my father. I was raised in Saudi Arabia and so I was ____________________, since I spoke Tigrinya and Arabic.

8. Originally, my mother was a Christian, but she now follows the Muslim ____________________.

9. When we came to the United States, I was surprised and delighted by the ________________ that other Ethiopian immigrants felt for us.

10. We had many ________________ who gave us things to make our lives easier.

11. Watching TV shows like *Sesame Street* was ________________ to my English.

12. In school, I learned formal English; and as I listened to people talking informally, I learned ________________ English.

13. Although I am certain that my family made the right decision to come to the United States, I feel ________________ about the lifestyles here. These ways of living allow much freedom but can also lead to problems.

14. I feel that people should show ________________ and remain loyal to their families.

15. At times, people in the United States seem ________________ about family life; but in Ethiopia people care deeply about family ties.

■ *Reviewing Learning Strategies*

The words listed below are formed from ancient Greek and Latin word elements. Use your knowledge of these elements to write in the word that best completes each sentence. Use each answer choice only once.

a. audiologist	e. logophobia	i. postscript
b. biometrics	f. malediction	j. tripod
c. credo	g. nilometer	k. uniped
d. graphemes	h. osteopath	l. verdict

1. The branch of science that takes statistical data, or measurements, on living things is called ____________________.
2. A jury is said to "speak the truth" when it gives a(n) ______________.
3. A(n) ____________________ is a physician who specializes in illnesses due to imbalances in the "osteo," or bone, structure.
4. A(n) ____________________ was used to measure the rise of water during the Nile riverflooding season.
5. The term ____________________ refers to a fear of words or talking.
6. The written word f-a-n has three ____________________.
7. A(n) ____________________ is "bad speech," or a curse.
8. A(n) ____________________ is an animal that walks on one foot.
9. A(n) ____________________ is a specialist in the study of measuring hearing.
10. A(n) ____________________ is a set of beliefs.

Answers to Quizzes

CHAPTER 1

page 14 1. Latin 2. transitive verb, 2 and 3 3. pay

CHAPTER 2

page 40 1. The Bruins were losing, 3 to 1, but, to the Rangers' surprise, the Bruins ended up winning the ice hockey game, 4 to 3. 2. Ohio, not Penn, was expected to win. The game was tied at the end, so it went into overtime. Penn won. 3. The Bulls had been playing away from their home town and had been losing games. They won this game, which was also away from home, by quite a bit. **page 41** 1. b 2. a 3. c **page 41** 1. b 2. a **page 42** 1. face 2. person who speaks many languages **page 42** 1. agreement 2. interfere

CHAPTER 3

page 71 1. a sacred place in Greece 2. having indented curves 3. severe, harsh **page 71** 1. embarrassed 2. thinking about 3. short **page 81** 1. b 2. c 3. f 4. a 5. d 6. e

CHAPTER 4

page 99 1. b 2. a 3. e 4. c 5. d **page 100** 1. not believable; absurd; silly 2. hatred 3. made less clear; confused **pages 100–101** 1. huge; very large 2. mysterious; not understandable 3. increase **page 111** 1. lost his mind; gone insane 2. died 3. took; stole 4. painful 5. lied

PART 2 INTRODUCTION

page 133 reaction—prefix "re-"; root "act"; suffix "-ion" or "-tion"
unlikely—prefix "un-"; root "like"; suffix "-ly"
exchanges—prefix "ex-"; root "change"; suffix "s"
reviewing—prefix "re-"; root "view"; suffix "-ing"
invisibly—prefix "in"; root "visible"; suffix "-ly"

CHAPTER 5

page 137 1. c 2. d 3. c **page 138** reiterate—possess again; inessential—not essential; equipotential—equal in potential **page 139** reiterate—to say (or do) again; incredulous—not believing **page 151** 1. b. 2. f 3. d 4. c 5. e 6. a

CHAPTER 6

page 172 1. d 2. c 3. b 4. e 5. a **page 178** 1. a 2. b 3. e 4. c 5. f 6. d

CHAPTER 7

page 220 1. d 2. e 3. f. 4. b 5. g 6. c 7. a

CHAPTER 8

page 240 1. e 2. d 3. b 4. f 5. c 6. a **page 253** 1. e 2. f 3. d 4. a 5. c 6. b

CHAPTER 9

page 273 a. two b. three c. four d. five e. six f. seven

CHAPTER 10

page 306 in the dog house—in trouble with someone; can of worms—having lots of problems; lion's share—the largest part of something; dinosaur—large and out of date; lame duck—someone who has lost power, usually because his or her term of office is about to end; puppy love—childish, youthful love **page 312** 1. c 2. d 3. a 4. b

CHAPTER 11

page 335 1. b 2. a 3. d 4. c

Credits

CHAPTER 1

pages 5, 12, 31 From Margaret Richek, *The World of Words*, Seventh Edition. © 2008 Heinle/Arts & Sciences, a part of Cengage Learning, Inc. Reproduced by permission. www.cengage.com/permissions. **pages 10, 30** Adapted from *American Heritage Dictionary of the English Language* [Online version], Fourth Edition. **pages 14, 30** Adapted from the *Merriam-Webster Online Dictionary.* ©2009 by Merriam-Webster, Incorporated (www.Merriam-Webster.com). Used by permission.

CHAPTER 3

page 90 From Margaret Richek, *The World of Words*, Seventh Edition. © 2008 Heinle/Arts & Sciences, a part of Cengage Learning, Inc. Reproduced by permission. www.cengage.com/permissions.

CHAPTER 5

page 162 Adapted from *Webster's New World College Dictionary*, Fourth Edition, 2009 [Online version]. Copyright © 2009 John Wiley & Sons, Inc. Reproduced with permission of John Wiley & Sons, Inc.

CHAPTER 7

page 229 From Margaret Richek, *The World of Words*, Seventh Edition. © 2008 Heinle/Arts & Sciences, a part of Cengage Learning, Inc. Reproduced by permission. www.cengage.com/permissions.

CHAPTER 9

page 296 Adapted from *Webster's New World College Dictionary*, Fourth Edition, 2009 [Online version]. Copyright © 2009 John Wiley & Sons, Inc. Reproduced with permission of John Wiley & Sons, Inc.

CHAPTER 11

page 358 From Margaret Richek, *The World of Words*, Seventh Edition. © 2008 Heinle/Arts & Sciences, a part of Cengage Learning, Inc. Reproduced by permission. www.cengage.com/permissions.

Student photos were taken at Joliet Junior College, in Joliet Illinois. The author thanks the college; instructor Susanne Picchi; and students Aloush Abdulrahman, Aileen Barnhart, Robert Battle, George Demaree, Kyung-Ran Feigel, Megan Follis, Brian Harris, Rashad Jackson, Adam Johnson, Carlee Koerner, Marcus Lee, Martez Moore, Karrie Ponko, Gertrudis Rodrigues, Ashley Russell, Amber Smith, Alexandra Violette, Myron Washington, and Dionte Yarborough.

Index of Words, Word Elements, and Idioms

Word elements are printed in *italics*.